W9-BCU-768

Presented to Purchase College
by
Gary Waller, PhD Cambridge

State University of New York
Distinguished Professor

Professor
of Literature & Cultural
Studies, and Theatre &
Performance, 1995-2019
Provost 1995-2004

SHAKESPEARE
WITHOUT TEARS

*A Modern Guide for
Directors, Actors
and Playgoers*

MARGARET WEBSTER

DOVER PUBLICATIONS, INC.
Mineola, New York

Copyright

Copyright © 1955 by The World Publishing Company
All rights reserved under Pan American and International Copyright Conventions.

Bibliographical Note

This Dover edition, first published in 2000, is an unabridged republication of *Shakespeare Without Tears* as published in 1955 by World Publishing Company, Cleveland and New York.

Library of Congress Cataloging-in-Publication Data

Webster, Margaret, 1905–1972.
    Shakespeare without tears : a modern guide for directors, actors and playgoers / Margaret Webster.
        p. cm.
    Previously published: Rev. ed. Cleveland : World Pub. Co., 1955.
    ISBN 0-486-41097-8 (pbk.)
    1. Shakespeare, William, 1564–1616—Dramatic production. I. Title.
PR3091 .W4 2000
792.9'5—dc21

99-057147

Manufactured in the United States of America
Dover Publications, Inc., 31 East 2nd Street, Mineola, N.Y. 11501

Contents

     Titus Andronicus, The Comedy of Errors, The
     Taming of the Shrew, The Two Gentlemen of
     Verona, Love's Labour's Lost, Romeo and Juliet, A
     Midsummer Night's Dream.

Conclusion

Introduction

BEAUMONT AND FLETCHER, and Massinger and Ford, are names that march into the classrooms as if they were boarding the Ark. In the American theater Shakespeare and Webster (Margaret, not John) are just now becoming almost as inseparably linked. Any playgoer who has sat before the productions Miss Webster has made with Maurice Evans of RICHARD II, the uncut HAMLET, HENRY IV, PART I, MACBETH, and—to a lesser extent—TWELFTH NIGHT, can advance at least four and a half excellent reasons why this should be so. To these, this book, known so appropriately as *Shakespeare Without Tears,* adds a fifth, which is one of the most cogent of the lot.

"When I began to write," boasted Mr. George Bernard Shaw in his famous valedictory to dramatic criticism, "William was a divinity and a bore. Now he is a fellow-creature; and his plays have reached an unprecedented pitch of popularity." Miss Webster is a director who must be thanked for having performed much the same services for Shakespeare on the contemporary American stage that Mr. Shaw rendered him as a critic in the London theater of the nineties.

She, too, has approached Shakespeare knowing that he is

neither a divinity nor a bore. But, instead of exposing his weaknesses as Mr. Shaw rejoiced in doing with all his critical brilliance in order to have Shakespeare's virtues properly appreciated, Miss Webster has applied herself as a director to protecting his scripts from these weaknesses in order to project their virtues.

The critic and the director have at least this much in common. The good critic may not be able to direct but the good director must be an able critic. For the good director is a critic in action; a critic turned creator; a reviewer whose responses and perceptions are stated before, not after, a production is made; in short, a midwife with opinions. It is not surprising, therefore, to find that the same Miss Webster, who as a director has again and again delivered Shakespearean scripts into the land of the living, has written in the following pages some of the most acute and quickening Shakespearean criticism to have been produced in our time.

She knows Shakespeare as few scholars do, and writes of him in a way to make professional critics at once humble and envious. The source of her strength in directing or discussing his plays is that, much as she admires him and sensitive as she is to his wonders, she sees Shakespeare as a "fellow-creature" whose first interest was the profession they both happen to have followed.

Miss Webster is not frightened by Shakespeare. She reads his texts sympathetically, permitting his imagination to set her own imagination free. Although she responds to the magic of his verse, she never forgets (as so many have been tempted to do) that by his own choice Shakespeare was primarily a playwright; a man of the theater who wrote for actors, not for pedants; for groundlings, not for students; and who had a professional's pride in his medium.

When Arthur Hopkins and Robert Edmond Jones failed bravely many years back with an experimental production of

MACBETH, they announced their aim as having been "to release the radium of Shakespeare from the vessel of tradition." Miss Webster is not interested in breaking away from the vessel of tradition. The radium of Shakespeare is her sole concern. It is this radium which she, more than any other director of our day, has been able to reveal again and again in the theater, and which she now shares and discloses in the pages that follow.

Miss Webster approaches Shakespeare without artyness, without stunts, and with a palpable love for, and understanding of, both his poetry and his plays. Moreover, she approaches him with her eyes open and her mind quickened, rather than deadened, by exceptional knowledge. She knows there is no such thing as a final interpretation of any of his plays. But her eyes and ears are vigilantly alert for all those characterizing and dramatic values which lurk in, and between, his lines, and which lesser directors have permitted to slip by unnoticed. If she has a genius for redeeming his plays from the College Board Examiners and making audiences forget that his works were ever compulsory reading in the classrooms, it is because she can hear the heart beat in these dramas which the bedside manner of countless teachers has persuaded many to accept as dead.

Although Miss Webster is a scholar and a critic, what keeps her knowledge alive and her perceptions creative is that she is a theater person. She has learned her Shakespeare on a stage rather than near a blackboard. She comes from a long line of distinguished English actors. Her great-grandfather was Benjamin N. Webster, a leading actor-manager in his day. Her mother was Dame May Whitty and her father Ben Webster, whose activities occupied more than two and a half pages in *Who's Who in the Theatre*. Her professional debut in London was made as Gentlewoman in John Barrymore's HAMLET. And she is herself an accomplished actress, as all American playgoers can testify who saw her Mary of Magdala in FAMILY PORTRAIT, her Andromache in THE TROJAN WOMEN, and, most memorably, her Masha in the Lunt-Fontanne production of THE SEA GULL.

Miss Webster was born in New York in 1905 when her father and mother were acting in this country. As a matter of cold fact, she was born in what is now a parking lot on 58th Street but what was then an apartment house owned by Finley Peter Dunne, better known as Mr. Dooley. As a girl Miss Webster twice appeared in England with Ellen Terry, studied in Paris, and was still under twenty when at a dramatic school in London she first met Maurice Evans.

Thereafter came fruitful years of apprenticeship, touring the provinces with Sir Philip Ben Greet's company, and several seasons at that best of Shakespearean universities, London's Old Vic. Meanwhile she had appeared in and directed several West End productions. It was not until 1937–1938 that, with Mr. Evans, she rediscovered RICHARD II for theatergoers in this country. Thereafter followed the uncut HAMLET, HENRY IV, TWELFTH NIGHT, and 1941's exciting MACBETH, productions which have deserved the widespread praise and popularity they have won.

It is reported that the occasion of one of Miss Webster's girlhood appearances with Ellen Terry was a Nativity play. According to the story, Miss Webster had to walk down a long aisle and then climb up on to a stage and up some steps before speaking the prologue. All this she is rumored to have done with so much success that when her piece was delivered and she was preparing to make her exit, Miss Terry's golden voice was heard to ring out from the wings, "Very good, Peggy, very good."

The chroniclers insist this unexpected praise, from so high a source, so unnerved Miss Webster that she thereupon proceeded to trip on her robes and tumble headlong into the audience. What is more important from the point of view of both Shakespeare and his admirers is that she has not tripped often since. Considering what she has done for Shakespeare in the theater, and is now doing for him in this volume, only a person possessed of an Englishman's gift for understatement would think of thanking her in such restrained terms as "Very good, Peggy, very good."

JOHN MASON BROWN

New York City

Part One

1. First Person Singular

IN THE FORTY-SECOND STREET LIBRARY of New York City there is a room whose walls are lined solid with trays of filed index cards. The labels on these trays indicate, as a rule, such orderly progressions as "Guinea to Guitry" or "Providence to Prune." But among them are fourteen on which no progress whatever is noted; they are marked, quite simply, "Shakespeare." It would seem that the addition of even one small card to this massive array of scholarship would require an explanation and an apology.

Let us assume, to begin with, that Shakespeare was Shakespeare. This new card will have no place under "Bacon, Sir Francis," nor under "Oxford, 17th Earl of." Fashions in Shakespearean pretenders change, and, at the time when all playwrights and historical novelists favored Lord Leicester as the hero of Queen Elizabeth's secret love life, Shakespearean mystics pinned their faith to the dry and mighty Lord Bacon. Nowadays the Earl of Essex has won the allegiance of the historical romanticists, and the Earl of Oxford has secured an ardent and formidable following of literary disciples. In the meantime, however, painstaking scholarship has unearthed and codified a numberless array of tiny records which taken together form an impressive, one would almost say an impregnable, case for the despised player from Stratford-on-Avon. But there is no arguing with a Baconian or an Oxford devotee. You cannot dispute logically with an act of faith nor tear down a religion with puny extracts from the tangled records of minor litigation around the year 1600. Nevertheless, people of the theatrical profession find it next to impossible to believe that the writer of the thirty-seven plays was an amateur to whom the drama was a side line only; and the majority of mankind is content with the assumption that Shakespeare was Shakespeare. Let us proceed on the basis that he was.

My second assumption, one upon which alone this book may be justified, is that the plays can be kept alive, in the fullest and most vivid sense, only through the medium of the living theater, of whose inheritance they constitute so rich a part. They were written to be acted, to be seen and heard. "The onely grace and setting of a tragedy," wrote one of Shakespeare's contemporary playwrights, "is a full and understanding Auditory." The living theater, too, has an obligation to keep before its public the work of the greatest dramatist who ever wrote in English, not as an academic chore, but as vital entertainment which will enrich the theater-going lives of many thousands of people. Any theater with blood in its veins will produce its own playwrights, deal with the problems of its day, provide a commentary, and weave a pattern around the events of its own time. But as long as the English language is loved and freely spoken, as long as the imaginations of men can be caught up and glorified by great dramatic power, Shakespeare will remain a living playwright.

I can make no pretension to deep Shakespearean scholarship. I first made his acquaintance many years ago, just about the time when I first learned to master in print such a sentence as "The cat sat on the mat." My mother was then moved to observe that "To be or not to be" should lie equally within my power and indignantly repudiated on my behalf any such intermediaries as Lamb's *Tales*. Nevertheless, I did acquire a volume of stories from the plays, illustrated in color with pictures of vaguely medieval beings, all highly affable and apparently boneless. I remember particularly Rosalind, with a Robin Hood cap and a boar spear that would certainly have snapped if it had struck any antagonist more formidable than a chicken; Beatrice, emerging from behind a hedge like a large pink pincushion, and Lear, with a slightly depressed expression and the longest and whitest of beards blown in every direction at once. The fascination these stories held for me has since caused me to wonder whether Shakespeare's plots are really quite as silly as critical sophistication suggests.

At school I fell in love with RICHARD II and MACBETH. I do not remember that this was due to particularly imaginative teaching. Perhaps the soil of my mind had been thoroughly prepared by four generations of theatrical ancestors, most of whom had had a bout with Shakespeare at one time or another. But it is a matter of the gravest regret that most children learn to regard Shakespeare as an undesired task to be mastered as superficially as is consistent with the necessity of pleasing a given body of examiners. Few of them are led to know and understand the people in the Shakespeare plays or to appreciate the music of his spoken verse. Little is done to feed the eagerness of their imaginative curiosity or to quicken their sense of the power and beauty of their own language; and their minds are crammed with a mass of basically irrelevant detail, which they thankfully reject as soon as possible. If, in later years, they are lured into a theater where Shakespeare is being played, they are astonished to find that there is really nothing difficult about him and that he can even supply very reasonable entertainment.

My own Shakespearean education, after the inevitable collegiate appearances as Portia and Puck, was greatly advanced by Sir Philip Ben Greet, in whose company I played many plays in many places, usually in the open air and under the oddest conditions, apt to be productive of more hilarity than art. The Ben Greet productions were not of the highest standard, but his companies were filled with eager young people, none of them awed by the works of the master and all of them ready to tackle anything. You had to learn to make a running exit of anything from twenty to a hundred yards, tossing blank verse blithely but audibly over your left shoulder as you went; to play Lady Macbeth up and down a fire escape and convince an audience of irreverent school children that you really were sleepwalking at the same time; to climb stone walls in an Elizabethan farthingale, crawl behind a hedge or two, and emerge in view of the audience unruffled in dress or speech; and to be heard in great open spaces above the sound of the wind and the tossing branches of the trees above your head. You had to sink or swim. There wasn't much finesse about it, but it gave you a sense of freedom and of power. You had the feeling that Shakespeare himself would have felt at home there and enjoyed the sensation of driving the play clear through against the odds, as you hold a boat against a high wind.

After various interludes, I had the good fortune to play a season at the Old Vic in London and to meet there a tradition of Shakespearean production which in its essentials was probably as sound as any now practiced in the English-speaking theater. Playing parts which ranged from Audrey in AS YOU LIKE IT to Lady Macbeth, watching the work of distinguished actors and directors through many seasons, and feeling the collaboration between actors and audiences continuously but quite unself-consciously devoted to the Shakespeare plays, I learned many things. Here Shakespeare was both exciting and familiar; the atmosphere was full of challenge, not of awe. I realized the enormous value of this sense of comradeship among actors, audience, and author. Here, too, Shakespeare was played almost uncut. The Old Vic public would have resented blue-pencil evasions of difficult passages on the part of the director or the actors; we could not take refuge in the escapism of the old-fashioned cut versions; and this led, necessarily, to a much closer study of Shakespeare's dramatic intention in its less facile aspects. It resulted in a greater appreciation of his theater reasoning and also in a healthier respect for the full texts which recent scholarship has unearthed from beneath a mass of wanton "editing." Nevertheless, the audiences expected entertainment, "theater," in its best sense. Entertainment, it appeared, was not incompatible with scholarship.

My first directorial task was a curious one. Eight hundred women of the county of Kent in England combined together, through their village institutes, to give an outdoor performance of HENRY VIII. Each village contributed the crowd and small parts for one of the big scenes, and only a dozen principal characters remained constant throughout the play. The experience I gained in handling this massive problem taught me, principally, two things: firstly, that anybody, man or woman, young or old, fat or thin, tall or short, can, with the aid of the famous Holbein stance and make-up, look the living image of Henry VIII; secondly, that every member of any Shakespearean crowd is as important as the principal speakers in the scene. These village women, some of them unable to read the text itself, were lost at first, listening sheepishly and uncomprehendingly to the flood of speeches. But when I gave to each of them an identity, a character, an individuality of her own, they played with an impassioned conviction that made the crowd scenes genuinely thrilling.

I realized, too, that the problems of Shakespearean production are not basically different in the amateur and professional theater. In these days, when so many of his plays are left to the devoted labors of student societies, collegiate bodies, and amateur groups, it is valuable to remind oneself that the problems, and the rewards, of producing Shakespeare are not by any means confined to the professional stage.

In February, 1937, I directed RICHARD II for Maurice Evans in New York. It was my first wholly professional Shakespearean production and my first glimpse of the opportunities and challenges which confronted a producer of Shakespeare in the United States. This play was virtually unknown to American audiences. The most that was hoped of it was an "artistic" success; yet it enjoyed a record-breaking run in New York, as well as two extensive road tours. The uncut HAMLET, which followed, was also produced for the first time in the American commercial theater; and HENRY IV, PART I, though it had been done by the Players' Club in 1926, had never been considered as having potential value for the theatrical manager with a living to earn. Both of them found eager audiences all over the country. So did the better known TWELFTH NIGHT, presented with Evans and Helen Hayes by the Theatre Guild in 1940, and the Evans MACBETH, with Judith Anderson, in 1941. The reputation and personal quality of the stars were undoubtedly a great factor in this result; but it seemed that Shakespeare was still one of America's most popular dramatists.

The aim of the Evans productions was a collaboration with both author and audience. We tried honestly to interpret the author's intention, as nearly as we could divine it, to the audiences for whom the productions were intended. We never supposed that we were providing any definitive answer to the problems of the plays, especially those of the inexhaustible HAMLET.

We had to face a number of difficulties of which we only

gradually became aware. There was, for instance, the minor one of accent. Several actors went so far as to refuse parts in the productions on the grounds that they either could not "speak English" or were afraid that by so doing they would endanger their chances of future employment as gangsters. We tried to obtain some homogeneity of speech that was neither dude English nor localized American, pertaining neither to Oxford University nor Akron, Ohio. We found that actors were plainly frightened of Shakespeare, particularly of the verse. Modern habits of speech, both English and American, incline us to careless enunciation, flattened inflections, and brief, spasmodic phrasing. It is virtually certain that our Elizabethan forebears had a liveliness of utterance which we have lost. Nor were Shakespeare's colleagues abashed by speaking in verse; they must have seized upon it with zest and understanding.

We found, also, that our actors were disinclined, at first, to tackle the characters as real people, flesh-and-blood human beings close to themselves. Audiences, too, approached Shakespeare in the theater with caution. On both sides of the footlights we were faced with these inhibitions, the result of regarding Shakespeare as high-brow and remote. One of our most difficult tasks was to overcome this unwholesome reverence for the Bard. At a performance of HAMLET in a Middle Western city, the balconies were crowded with school children, noisy, skeptical, restless. Owing to a shortage of ushers, a couple of policemen were called in to keep a watchful eye on the children. The policemen were very conscious of their responsibilities; and when the children, as quick as they were critical, began to laugh at Polonius, they were cowed by a fiercely respectful "shush" from the police force. Poor Polonius played frantically to solemn faces throughout the afternoon.

Left to themselves, however, children and adults alike

proved eager, swift, perceptive, and delightfully ready either to laugh or cry; they were the kind of audience Shakespeare himself might have wished for. This was my first impression of the American theater-going public, and subsequent experience has done nothing to change it. I have staged and produced and played Shakespeare in all sorts of places since then and to all sorts of people: in "streamlined" form at the New York World's Fair of 1939; to a superbly responsive public in New York and right across the United States with the Robeson-Ferrer OTHELLO; on Broadway and in the Eastern cities with THE TEMPEST and HENRY VIII; and at the New York City Center with RICHARD II, RICHARD III, and THE TAMING OF THE SHREW. The faithful patrons of the City Center, who come regularly to the drama seasons as they do to opera and ballet, are the finest audiences I have ever encountered since the days of the Old Vic. It is worth remarking that they pay considerably less than Broadway prices for their seats and that many of them are not regular attendants at the playhouses of Times Square. They are not super-sophisticated; they come to enjoy themselves. So did the citizens of London, circa 1600.

But the most instructive and rewarding experience I have ever had came during the seasons of 1948 to 1950, when I took four Shakespearean productions over the length and breadth of the United States. I had a talented young company, without stars, which traveled by road, playing mostly what came to be known as "the gymnasium circuit." We covered over thirty thousand miles during each season, and some eighty per cent of our dates were in places where Shakespeare had not been professionally played in a generation. Quite often the audience would be composed of young people who had never even seen live actors—known in Vermont as "meat actors"— before. The response to these performances demonstrated beyond the shadow of a doubt that Shakespeare well played has lost nothing of his power and enchantment. When living actors play living characters to living audiences, the words put on flesh and become incandescent. Then, and I think only then, we understand his true magic and find ourselves miraculously transfigured in the mirror of his genius.

It is a question of the highest importance, and one to which I shall return at the end of this book, as to how we can preserve Shakespeare in the twentieth-century American theater, how we are to keep his plays alive throughout the forty-eight States. The old actor-managers and their companies, who used to play Shakespearean repertory from coast to coast, have long since been forced out of business. I myself was forced to abandon my "Shakespeare on Wheels" enterprise for economic reasons, and no fully professional company has since been able to make a similar attempt. There has been a steadily decreasing number of Broadway productions and almost no first-class tours during recent years. Shakespeare is rapidly disappearing from the professional theater.

One of the results of this process of attrition is that there is no longer any tradition of Shakespearean acting or staging in the United States, especially in the matter of speech and style. The absence of tradition is not entirely without advantages, in that young actors and directors are not bound by convention or hampered by a rigid orthodoxy. But there is no longer any established standard against which they can measure themselves, no yardstick of excellence, little informed or firsthand knowledge of the plays as they come alive in the theater. Tradition need not be merely a collection of fusty and outworn shreds from the dramatic wardrobe of an earlier time. The truth and validity of newly divined interpretation should be reinforced by proved and practiced skill in the crafts of the theater. The art of acting has been handed down from one generation to another in the flesh, through the actor himself and through the eyes and ears of those who watch him. It cannot be preserved in books: the lifeblood escapes, the skeleton alone remains. Production methods can, however, be described and analyzed. Stage designs are preserved in photographs and drawings. There is plenty of valuable material available for us to study.

We neglect it as a rule. We are apt to approach a classic play in considerable confusion of mind. Lacking the old skills, we try to compensate for them by a determination to be "timely" and novel at all costs. Not infrequently this results in a distortion of the author's intention and a loss of the essential and the universal qualities in his plays. Shakespeare must be used to this by now; it has been happening to him through three and a half centuries of stage history. But during the past sixty or seventy years some major revolutions have taken place in the field of Shakespearean theater. They have tended to bring us round to the beginning again; we are now probably closer to the Elizabethans than to the Victorians. But for our own future guidance it is perhaps worth examining the artistic aims of our predecessors; their mistakes as well as their achievements may have some bearing on our own.

In America and England the nineteenth century wore itself out in a blaze of star actors, playing Shakespeare very much as he had been played for the preceding hundred and fifty years, using the plays as vehicles for the principal players, blissfully unaware of the power of their craftsmanship as the uncut texts have since revealed it. Edwin Booth in America was the last of the giants, the latest glory of a long period which had been distinguished by superlative actors and ridiculous plays. In England the succession devolved upon Sir Henry Irving, whose particular twist of genius was complemented and graced by the radiant humanity of his leading lady, Ellen Terry. Like Booth, he was a single-minded man of the theater. His productions at the Lyceum Theatre, which he also played extensively in America, followed the long-established precedent. They interpreted Irving rather than Shakespeare.

Settings of cumbrous magnificence served as a background for his genius. There were long intermissions or musical interludes while the next stage picture was prepared. Everything was done with lavish care. Nothing was cut, except Shakespeare.

All of this was the splendid culmination of a theatrical epoch and was almost universally admired. But at the end of the Eighties a rebellious voice began to make itself heard. It was that of William Poel, a single-minded and utterly intransigent enthusiast who maintained that to play Shakespeare at all you must play him on the kind of stage for which he wrote and with a company dedicated to serving the author rather than to supporting the star. He studied carefully the work of W. J. Lawrence and other scholars who were beginning to reveal the true nature of the Elizabethan playhouses, and he studied the evidence afforded by the early Shakespearean texts. He built apron stages over the orchestra seats of respectable London theaters. He staged the First, or "Bad," Quarto of HAMLET, perhaps for the first time since it originally appeared in print. His companies were often inept and amateurish and his own direction marred by some extremely peculiar idiosyncrasies. But his innovations were too startling to be ignored.

Poel and his friends soon found a powerful ally who was only too delighted to tilt at the established giants and especially at Irving. "In a true republic of art," wrote the critic of the *Saturday Review,* "Sir Henry Irving would ere this have expiated his acting versions of Shakespeare on the scaffold. He does not merely cut the plays, he disembowels them." The prophet of the new scholarship and the new stagecraft was George Bernard Shaw.

Mr. Shaw was no Bardolater. "Oh, what a *damned* fool Shakespeare was!" he wrote, in a moment of exasperation. And repeatedly he inveighs against Shakespeare's "monstrous rhetorical fustian, his unbearable platitudes, his sententious combination of ready reflections with complete intellectual sterility." But he never ceased trying to goad producers, Irving, Tree, Augustin Daly, and the rest, into doing the plays as "the wily William planned them." The interchange of letters between Shaw and Ellen Terry prior to her first appearance as Imogen with Irving in 1896 provides an invaluable object lesson in lucid critical thinking, supplemented and humanized by the truth and simplicity of an actress's feeling.

The apostle of the new Shakespeare did not have long to wait for the results of his campaign. In October, 1897, Forbes-Robertson produced HAMLET, also at the Lyceum, and the *Saturday Review* greeted him thus:

> The Forbes-Robertson HAMLET at the Lyceum is, very unexpectedly at that address, really not at all unlike Shakespeare's play of the same name. I am quite certain I saw Reynaldo in it for a moment; and possibly I may have seen Voltimand and Cornelius; but just as the time for their scene arrived, my eye fell on the word "Fortinbras" in the programme, which so amazed me that I hardly know what I saw for the next ten minutes.

The movement toward textual fidelity never lost momentum. People began to discover that Shakespeare really did know what he was doing when he wrote a play and that you really could put it on the stage the way he wrote it. Poel's theories bore fruit through a brilliant man of the theater, Granville Barker, who evolved from them a fresh and different approach of his own. His TWELFTH NIGHT in 1912 inaugurated a new era in Shakespearean production, with clean texts and a stage stripped for action.

These theatrical developments were the reflection of a new school of scholarship and criticism, especially in the field of textual research. In the forefront of this movement were Dr.

A. W. Pollard, with his emphasis on the value of the neglected Shakespearean Quartos as against the hitherto canonized Folio; Dr. W. W. Greg, whose bibliographical discoveries are of the greatest importance and interest to every theater student; and Sir E. K. Chambers, whose monumental works commend themselves to the plain man by virtue of their pithy and even testy refusal to give way to the fancier theories of the new scholars.

Of recent years there has been a renewed impetus toward "dramatic" rather than "literary" criticism of the plays, exemplified by Professor E. E. Stoll, Mr. Frayne Williams, and others. Dr. Dover Wilson has gone so far as to express the view that no criticism is "safe" which is divorced from theatrical experience. There is much in contemporary Shakespearean scholarship that is of interest to theater people. For instance, Dr. Flatter, writing on the Folio punctuation, gives an actor many valuable hints. Professor Kökeritz, at Yale, has done some most interesting research into the pronunciation of English in Shakespeare's day. It is to be feared that this would prove a two-edged weapon in the theater. It is hard enough to make modern audiences understand a vocabulary now largely fallen out of use, without adopting a strange and archaic accent into the bargain. Nevertheless, such studies provide interesting side lights as to the meaning of obscure passages. In the field of stagecraft, Dr. Leslie Hotson continues to disturb existing theories and stimulate the imagination of Shakespeare enthusiasts with newly discovered documents and controversial conclusions.

Despite all this, scholars and theater people continue to show signs of considerable maladjustment. Some of the bibliographers deny that the theater has any contribution to make towards solving the problems of Shakespearean interpretation; and most theater people, fearful of choking in library dust, believe that literary commentaries and bookish research have nothing whatever to do with the practical business of putting on a play.

It seems to me to be of the highest importance that the theater and the scholars should learn to appreciate each other. I myself have obtained valuable help and collaboration from such men as Dr. Matthew Black of the University of Pennsylvania, who, during his labors on the preparation of RICHARD II for the Variorum edition of Shakespeare, was deeply interested in the staging of Mr. Evans's production of the play. But as yet there have been few liaison officers between the stage and the library. Granville Barker, in his series of *Prefaces to Shakespeare,* has proved the most valuable among them. His work is full of imaginative penetration into Shakespeare's thinking, of considerable scholarship, and of vivid theater sense. Yet in his later writings one may detect a tendency toward the bookshelves and away, not from the stage itself, but from the auditorium. The Quarto texts loom larger and larger, and the faces looking down from the second balcony recede into a dim and darkened background.

For the factor which, I think, even Barker is inclined to underrate is the audience. The modern producer has to be, in some sort, a translator; and he may not translate, as Shakespearean commentators do, for individual readers, one by one. He may not count with the single mind, slowly absorbing the power and beauty of the written word, with the aid of a fire, a lamp, and a comfortable armchair. He has to produce an integrated piece of theater, carrying as nearly as possible the full intention of the author and projecting it instantaneously to several hundred people of the most variously assorted character and receptivity.

Given half a chance, Shakespeare will still bind an audience with the old irresistible spell. There is much in him that you simply cannot destroy however hard you try. But there is also much which was familiar to an Elizabethan audience but which is strange country to us. The whole background of the listener has changed, even though his emotions answer to the same stimuli. His ears, unfortunately, are nothing like so good as they were. Today movies and television have trained our eyes to a high degree of critical expectation. But our ears they have coarsened and made lazy by the continuous ministration of amplifiers. The theater is practically the only place left where we may hear the unadulterated beauty of speech in the full flood of the English language. And we have, to a great extent, lost our language by neglect and habitually use no more than a poverty-stricken remnant of its resources.

The whole convention of our theater has changed. The tacit covenant between actor, author, and audience is on a wholly different basis. How can we preserve Shakespeare's intention in our modern terms? We may, we must, try honestly and devotedly to divine his meaning. We must know, for that purpose, the instruments of staging that he used, for they shaped his craftsmanship; and without a knowledge of them we shall often divine his intention wrongly. But it is not, I think, enough to study the exact way in which he swung his action from inner stage to outer stage, to upper stage and back again; to assess the extent to which the use of boy players influenced his characterization of women's parts; to scan the Quarto texts for signs of his theater thinking expressed in cuts, additions to, and revisions of his script; least of all to follow the scholars in their passionate disintegration of the texts into "early Shakespeare," "another hand," "a late addition," "a playhouse omission," and so on. Our business is not disintegration, but integrity. For the scholars' "true texts" we are grateful indeed; but it is still our business to transmute them into terms of the living theater today.

If, however, we were to consider only "audience effect" in its most superficial sense, we should be likely to go as far astray as the great actors of the eighteenth and nineteenth centuries did and to lose as much of the essential Shakespeare. We have yet to produce a dramatist who is more skilled in audience psychology than "the wily William." We shall be foolish to underrate his methods or to disregard his conclusions.

We must know our author and our audience and see to it that the actors interpret justly between them. The resources of the library, the skill of the theater technicians, the influence of individual creative talent among actors and directors, designers and musicians—all these must be fused into the "two hours' traffic of our stage." It will be the business of this book to suggest some bases from which this fusion may be effected, dealing firstly with the author himself, secondly with the general problems of Shakespearean acting and production as they confront us today, and lastly surveying in broad outline the dramatic values of the plays themselves as we see them more than three hundred years after their author died, from a country of whose existence he never even knew.

2. Introducing an Englishman

THE SOIL which produced Shakespeare and the living and working conditions which molded him are of high importance to us who try to interpret him. We have much more in common than is generally realized; and there is much, a background of the spirit, which it is not beyond our power to recapture. In particular, the study of the Elizabethan stage yields, cleared from a mass of statistical jungle, plain and heart-warming evidence that we of the theater today may claim with Shakespeare a close and genuine "fellowship in a cry of Players." As an author he was not, as many authors are now, tied by a mere "silken thread" to theater life and practice. He was soaked in it; it was part of his life, warp and woof; and though theater conventions have changed very radically in three hundred and fifty years, theater people seem to have changed remarkably little. An actor's instinct will many times guide him through tangled paths that have caused the literary scholars volumes of perturbation.

When Shakespeare came to London, about the year 1587, from the bosom of the Stratford middle class, the Elizabethan stage, as well as the English way of living, was in an extremely fluid and formative condition. He and his fellows were the most powerful influence of their time in creating a mold for the theater; what we do on Broadway today derives in lineal descent from the Elizabethan theaters of the Bankside. As good descendants, we should take the trouble to find out a little about our forefathers.

The theater which Shakespeare found when he threw up his job as a schoolmaster's assistant in a country grammar school, left his wife flat, and went off to London with Lord Leicester's Men had already evolved a form of drama as yet fairly rudimentary. It still carried traces of the medieval mystery and morality plays from which, on the paternal side at least, it traced its ancestry. The players themselves were imperfectly disentangled from their own earlier selves. They had started, long before, as small groups of professional entertainers supported by great lords and noblemen as members of their households.

Elizabethan actors inherited, among other things, the variety of skill which their fathers' patrons had required. They could still sing, dance a jig, and give exhibitions of superlative swordsmanship in an age when every gentleman was an accomplished swordsman. They were, indeed, the finest exponents of these arts and drew the kind of public which, today, would go to the Met to hear fine singing or to Madison Square Garden to see a boxing match. There were no fumbling, dangerous duels, with heavily blunted points; there was no faking of singers off-stage. If the dramatist could introduce a song, a dance, or a fight, he had a troupe full of experts, panting for the chance to exhibit their skill and assured of an audience passionately eager to applaud them. There is a record of payment in Richmond, Surrey, to the Admiral's Men for "shewing certaine feats of activitie." Will Kemp, the leading comedian of Shakespeare's early days, danced his famous morris dance all the way to Norwich and toured it through Germany and over the Alps into Italy. It was a more lucrative accomplishment than his ability to play Dogberry and Bottom and Justice Shallow.

But with the fuller way of living inaugurated under Elizabeth, the horizon of the old actor-retainers had expanded. They had begun to travel, under the protection of a kind of passport from their masters; and they were available for hire at other private houses of the great, or even at the court itself. They ceased, finally, to be mere retainers and maintained themselves, though they still needed the protection of a master and were at his service when he so required. But they were beginning to apprehend another market and another audience. They turned their eyes to London City, growing, prospering, teeming with a new life; London the boom town; a little town, as we look back at it from the top of the Empire State, snuggled along the banks of the Thames River; a little wooden town, never wholly free of the fields and marshes that encircled it and closed in around its straggling outposts; but the heart of a new life, beginning to pump its blood far across the seas, sending its citizens in tiny wooden cockleshells westward to Virginia, northward toward Hudson Bay, and southward through the Strait of Magellan, to a New World.

But Shakespeare's predecessors, Shakespeare himself, found in London the capital of a nation at war, engaged in a protracted life-and-death struggle against the mighty Spanish Empire, which ruled by conquest, by fear, or by alliance almost the whole continent of Europe. The Lowlands of Holland and Flanders were the cockpit of the contest between the great armies of Spain and the little companies of men from countries which had not yet learned to call themselves democracies, Dutch and Flemings and French, and troops of Englishmen. Channel ports were in enemy hands; the danger of invasion was constant and imminent. The crisis came with the assault and destruction of the Invincible Armada in

1588. Shakespeare was already in London, already, perhaps, trying his hand at some tentative play tinkering; and looking back years later he could write, through the mouth of the Queen in CYMBELINE:

> . . . Remember, sir, my liege,
> The kings your ancestors, together with
> The natural bravery of your isle, which stands
> As Neptune's park, ribbed and paled in
> With rocks unscaleable, and roaring waters,
> With sands that will not bear your enemies' boats,
> But suck them up to the topmast. A kind of conquest
> Caesar made here, but made not here his brag
> Of "Came, and saw, and overcame:" with shame
> (The first that ever touched him) he was carried
> From off our coast, twice beaten; and his shipping
> (Poor ignorant baubles!) on our terrible seas,
> Like egg-shells mov'd upon their surges, crack'd
> As easily 'gainst our rocks: for joy whereof
> The famed Cassibelan, who was once at point
> (O giglet fortune!) to master Caesar's sword,
> Made Lud's town with rejoicing fires bright,
> And Britons strut with courage.

But the war dragged on with varying fortunes for many years. In 1596, Calais was besieged by the Spaniards and fell. For many days the sound of cannon was clearly heard in London, and men were afraid. But the fleet struck back at the enemy in a brilliantly successful expedition to Cadiz, which was taken and sacked. In 1598, the French, contrary to their treaty with England, made a secret peace with Spain. There were other expeditions and flaming exploits, and there were muddled, languishing campaigns, both in the Low Countries and in rebellious Ireland, dark with wasted opportunity. Men saw only too clearly the consequence of war:

The imminent death of twenty thousand men,
That for a fantasy and trick of fame
Go to their graves like beds, fight for a plot
Which is not tomb enough and continent
To hide the slain.

There were rumors and counter-rumors, "Alarums and Excursions," faint hearts and Fifth Columnists, uneasy crowds of citizens who lived in an unanchored world, and swaggering soldiers of fortune who delighted in:

Matter deep and dangerous,
As full of peril and adventurous spirit
As to o'er walk a current roaring loud,
On the unsteadfast footing of a spear.

Shakespeare wrote of a nation at war, or clinging precariously to an uneasy peace, watchful always against the danger of attack. The modern world should find no difficulty in understanding him.

At home, there were further causes for unrest. The uncertainty and turbulence of our world are not without parallel in Shakespeare's. There was bitter religious strife; the Catholics perceived a perilous "divided duty" between the Queen and the Pope; the Puritans were growing in power and were prime enemies of the players; the new Established Church had not as yet grown firm roots. There was an unemployment problem, as the structure of the medieval guilds began to crack under the strain of an expanding economy. There were plots and treason in the highest places; and the great Lord Essex himself, "idol of idiot worshippers" and closest to Elizabeth of all her noblemen, died on the scaffold as a traitor. There was, above all, the great Queen, old, childless, whose throne must shortly stand dangerously, unimaginably empty.

But in spite of all this, the Englishman was becoming conscious of England, of its past and of its future. He wanted to hear about and to see on the stage the glorious wars his ancestors had made in France. The fact that these wars were mostly bullying forays of greed and aggression was unimportant and unremembered. The chronicles of British triumph enabled him to feel reassuringly the throbbing pulse of his nation, so that he, the plain man, could stand up and say: "Britain is a world by itself, and we will nothing pay For wearing our own noses." We shall miss something of primary importance in Shakespeare's plays if we neglect this surging of the blood behind them.

For him, too, when he came at last to his great business of playwrighting, a world of the mind was opening. The stage derived its maternal ancestry from the university wits and scholars. For source material, there was not only Holinshed's *Chronicles of English History* but North's translation of Plutarch's *Lives*. Florio was translating Montaigne; and numberless Italian and French romances began to find their way into English, bearing the seeds of ROMEO AND JULIET, MEASURE FOR MEASURE, and OTHELLO. Englishmen were trying their hands at embryo novels, naturally unaware of the service they would render posterity through the medium of AS YOU LIKE IT or THE WINTER'S TALE. "Little Latin and less Greek," said Ben Jonson of Shakespeare, with a University man's scorn. But there were plenty of translations.

It was little more than a hundred years since Caxton had set up his first printing press at Westminster and written in his Epilogue to the *Recuyell of Troy* that "in the writing of the same my pen is worn, mine hand weary and not steadfast, mine eyen dimmed with overmuch looking on the white paper, and my courage not so prone and ready to labour as it hath been." But he prayed his readers "not to disdain the simple and rude work" and finished the first printed book from his English press with the sigh of relief, "and say we all Amen for Charity." In that intervening hundred years the riches of the Renaissance culture came pouring from the new English printing presses, and the language itself began to take full and glorious form. Shakespeare found the instruments of immortality ready to his hand.

The first bands of players who came to London were not concerned with such flights as these. They unpacked their wardrobe and props in the inn yards of the Saracen's Head, the Red Lion, the Bull, the Boar's Head, the Cross Keys, and the Bel Savage and set to work first to attract and then to entertain their rowdy, fickle audiences. They began a long struggle for their livelihood, which seesawed between the opposition of the city authorities and the favor of the court and the nobility.

The city aldermen disapproved of players on principle and feared that the places where they played would become meeting grounds for riotous and disaffected elements in the community, as well as dangerous centers for infection in time of plague. Such outbreaks were frequent, and the plague statutes perpetually forced players to close down and take to the road. The court, however, demanded its players; and an exasperated Privy Council, tired of the tug of war, finally evolved a licensing system primarily controlled by the Master of Revels. This system, long outgrown in utility, persists in England to this day. The Lord Chamberlain, an official functionary of the court, is still censor and licensor of plays.

But even before this, ten years before Shakespeare came to London, the players had taken a most decisive step. Badgered by his reluctant hosts, the landlords of the inns, and harried by the city authorities, one James Burbage, actor and manager of Lord Leicester's Men, had taken himself off to Shoreditch outside the city limits, leased a plot of ground, and erected on it a building which he called, with simple grandiloquence, The Theatre. His example was soon followed, though the center of activity shifted to the south bank of the river. The Theatre became merely a theater.

The early period of Shakespeare's stage experience in theatrical companies, which had not yet crystallized into permanent units with an unchanging personnel, must have been immensely valuable to him. It brought him into contact with the Burbages, with Edward Alleyn, considered the greatest actor of his time, and with all the leading playwrights of the day—Marlowe, Kyd, Peele, Greene, and others. They taught him the craft which is so nearly related to their own in his early plays and which he gradually developed into a dramatic technique infinitely beyond anything they had ever achieved. Most of their plays make very dull reading nowadays; in the very rare stage revivals they acquire some color, but their characters remain maddeningly wooden. Occasional lines find startling echoes in our minds: Pedro's "We burn daylight" in THE SPANISH TRAGEDY; Edward II's "Gallop apace, bright Phoebus through the sky" (indeed this whole play leads us inexorably up toward Shakespeare's deposed Richard); and a line in the disputed SIR THOMAS MORE, which may indeed be Shakespeare's own, and he twice uses it later, "I do owe God a death."

But even Marlowe, to whose name we automatically tack the addition "mighty line," thunders on the ear like a dynamo of decasyllables. Kyd's SPANISH TRAGEDY, the greatest hit of its day, has still the flash of power and theater effect; but for us it is too full of darkness and murder and madness and ghosts and the whole dreary bag of Elizabethan tricks which Shakespeare alone was able to galvanize into lasting life. Peele and Greene manipulate their comic interludes like puppeteers. The scholars rightly tell us that here are to be found all the embryonic ingredients of Shakespeare's plays, but we can no longer make them into a theater whole.

We do not know for certain what Shakespeare's first job was; his first coming to London is a matter for speculation based on doubtful tradition. He is supposed to have held horses at the theater door; it seems more than likely that he was some kind of assistant to the stage manager, or "Prompter" as he was then called. At all events he acted and began the journeyman play tinkering, revising, and odd-job collaboration from which he spasmodically emerged as an independent author in his own right.

By 1592, he was well-known as an actor. There are several contemporary references to him in that capacity, as well as a large number of small personal records, engagingly human. In St. Helen's Ward in Bishopsgate "the petty collectors . . . neither might nor could by any means" get hold of him for the payment of back taxes. It is good to know that a few years later, in a more prosperous time, he offered to lend money to a fellow townsman from Stratford, "which," writes the borrower's brother warily, "I will like of, as I shall hear when, where and how." By 1594, not bad progress for some seven years, Shakespeare is certainly one of the foremost members of the newly formed company of Lord Chamberlain's Men, for there is a court record of a payment to them made in the names of Richard Burbage, Will Kemp, and William Shakespeare.

A study of the history and working habits of this company provides us with a very entertaining chronicle. We realize with surprise that we of the theater today come extraordinarily close to our predecessors in the pattern of our work and lives in the theater. The evidence which the scholars have accumulated for us, freed from a dusty mass of deductive addenda, reveals to us people whom we might hail as friends and comrades, whose prototypes are to be found today in every drugstore around Times Square. We can no longer be oppressed by any odor of sanctity, once we have entered this very recognizable workshop where Shakespeare learned and developed his craft.

The basis for Shakespearean study which we may thus establish is sufficiently humdrum. It is no part of the imaginative reach which we shall finally need, but it is possibly a better point of departure than the feeling of remote respect with which many actors approach Shakespeare. We shall at least begin by planting our feet on solid, sawdust-covered ground.

3. Backstage in 1600

THE LORD CHAMBERLAIN'S MEN, promoted to King's Men in 1603 when James I succeeded to the throne, remained together as a closely co-operative working unit all through Shakespeare's lifetime and for many years after his death in 1616. In 1598, they decided to leave The Theatre, which had fallen into a bad state of disrepair, and, after much embittered argument with the ground landlord, finally took matters literally into their own hands. The young Burbages and their fellow actors arrived one morning with picks and axes, pulled the entire building apart, and transported it, lock, stock, and barrel, across to the south bank of the Thames, where they "built the Globe," as the Burbages later testified, "with more sums of money taken up at interest, which lay heavy on us many yeeres, and to ourselves wee joined those deserving men, Shakespeare, Hemings, Condall, Philips and other partners in the profittes of what they call the House."

It was this theater which saw the production of Shakespeare's greatest plays. In 1613, during a performance of HENRY VIII, some wadding from one of the stage cannon caught the thatched roof, and the whole theater was "casually burnt downe and consumed with fier." Sir Henry Wotton describes the incipient fire as being "thought at first an idle smoke, and their eyes more attentive to the show, it kindled inwardly, and ran round like a train, consuming within less than an hour the whole house to the very grounds. This was the fatal period of that virtuous fabric, wherein yet nothing did perish but wood and straw, and a few forsaken cloaks; only one man had his breeches set on fire, that would perhaps have broiled him, if he had not by the benefit of a provident wit, put it out with a bottle of ale."

Shortly afterward, however, the "partners in the said playhowse resolved to reedifie the same," which they did. In 1608, they had already acquired the Blackfriars, an inheritance from James Burbage which had been leased to one of the boys' companies, the children of the Queen's Chapel. It was an indoor theater, and the new method of staging which it inaugurated had a noticeable effect on the elaborated stagecraft of Shakespeare's later plays, such as CYMBELINE, THE WINTER'S TALE, and THE TEMPEST.

The company also played many command performances at court or in private houses, not always under the most ideal circumstances. At a performance of PERICLES in honor of the French ambassadors, it is reported that "after two actes the players ceased till the French all refreshed them with sweetmeates and . . . wine and ale in bottells, after the players began anewe." However, the constant court performances provided not only glory but a useful income.

The members of the company are well-known to us. Burbage was the leading man from the time of RICHARD III until his death at the age of forty-five. He is described as "wholly transforming himself into his part and putting off himself with his clothes . . . animating his words with speaking, and speed with action . . . an excellent actor still, never falling in his part when he done speaking, but with his looks and gesture maintaining it to the heighth." Will Kemp was a famous comedian, much beloved by contemporary audiences. Hamlet's rueful admonition to the clowns may perhaps have been aimed at him: "And let those that play your clowns speak no more than is set down for them; for there be of them that will themselves laugh, to set on some quantity of barren spectators to laugh too, though in the meantime some necessary question of the play be then to be considered." Kemp left the company at about the time this play was produced. Perhaps he did not relish the public rebuke. He was succeeded by Robert Armin, for whom Shakespeare wrote the more oblique and delicate fooling of Feste, Touchstone, and the exquisite Fool in KING LEAR.

The kindly Philips is clear to us; Condell and "old stuttering Hemings," who rendered us the inestimable service of publishing the 1st Folio edition of the collected plays; Lowin, creator of Henry VIII; and his predecessor, Thomas Pope, whose method as Falstaff and Toby is satirized by Ben Jonson in an embittered reference to his "barren, bold jests with a tremendous laughter between drunk and dry."

The leading boy-ladies are less richly documented. Most of them graduated to the status of hired men or even sharers. Among them is a mysterious "Ned," who may have been Shakespeare's young brother Edmund. The dashing Will Sly, who, as Laertes, Hotspur, and Macduff, crossed many swords with Burbage, is conjectured to have started his career as Rosaline; and Richard Robinson graduated so successfully from his apprenticeship that he ended by marrying Burbage's widow.

We have accidental records of the small-part actors in the company from stage directions and speech headings in the texts, where the marginal notation of the actor's name made in the theater script has inadvertently leaked into the published edition. One John Sinklo, a hired man, is especially persistent. His name crops up over a speech in THE TAMING OF

THE SHREW Induction, for a Keeper in HENRY VI, PART III, in company with "Humphrey" for the other Keeper, and as the Officer who comes to arrest Falstaff at the end of HENRY IV, PART II. Jack Wilson is marked as the singer of the lovely "Sigh no more, ladies," in MUCH ADO ABOUT NOTHING; and we know that he afterward became a Doctor of Music and bequeathed a very dignified portrait of himself to the Music School at Oxford University. Kemp and Cowley are used for the speeches of Dogberry and Verges through an entire scene in MUCH ADO, and Kemp appears again for Peter in the Quarto ROMEO AND JULIET. "Harvey," "Rossill," "Will," and others are similarly, by a chance inefficiency, assured of a lasting link with Shakespeare's fame.

The small-part actors were hard worked owing to the universal practice of doubling parts, and not merely doubling, but tripling and quadrupling them. Up until the 1560's, four had been the standard complement of actors to a troupe. The Players in HAMLET do faithfully represent a theatrical company of the period immediately preceding Shakespeare's own. In SIR THOMAS MORE, there is a dialogue between the visiting Actor-manager and More, his patron for the night. More asks the Player, "How many are ye?" "Four men and a boy, sir," answers the Player.

MORE: But one boy? then I see
There's but few women in the play.
PLAYER: Three, my lord: Dame Science, Lady Vanity,
And Wisdom, she herself.
MORE: And one boy play them all? By'r Lady, he's loden.

Henslowe records that Dick Juby played seven parts in TAMAR CAM; and on a tour, which carried a reduced personnel, Burbage not only played the lead in THE BATTLE OF ALCAZAR but threw in the First Spanish Ambassador and a Moorish Soldier, for good measure.

Even Shakespeare was sometimes compelled to adapt himself to limitations of manpower. It is probable that the unaccountable replacement of Poins by the insignificant Peto in HENRY IV, PART I, at the end of Act II, scene 4, enabled Poins to change himself rapidly into Young Mortimer; and that the unfortunate Antigonus in THE WINTER'S TALE made his abruptly ignominious final exit "pursued by a bear" (it used to be a real bear) in order to reappear shortly afterward as a different character, conceivably the Clown.

Even though we no longer accept a hasty beard and a cloak as adequate disguise, as did the zestful Elizabethans, modern actors can achieve some doubling too. In fact, Sybil Thorndike's wartime touring company of MACBETH, visiting the villages of South Wales, carried one actress who played Donalbain, the Third Witch, Young Macduff, the Gentlewoman, and an army or two. Why should the modern actress be outfaced by a lot of Elizabethan children?

The Globe Company was in many respects, and important ones from the dramatists' point of view, radically different from the haphazard collection of actors from whom we, today, expect the same results in three or four weeks of work on the isolated problems of a single production. It approximated more nearly to an institution; not to the highly formalized and richly encrusted traditionalism of the old Comédie Française, but more closely to the recent transformation of that great theater under the invigorating impact of the producers of the Cartel. A closer parallel might well be found in Stanislavsky's Moscow Art Theatre Company. The methods of the two companies are as widely apart as the poles, but it is probable that Chekhov and Shakespeare would have found a common ground of experience in the simultaneous and inseparable evolution of a dramatist and a company of actors.

The hierarchy at the Globe was intricate and exact. Certain members, including Shakespeare, were "Housekeepers," or joint owners of the lease and property, and as such received among them a half share of the takings. They were also, with the other principal actors, actor-sharers and in this capacity divided among them the other half of the gross. The proportion of expenses borne by each category of sharers corresponds roughly to the front-stage and back-stage division still prevalent today between theater owners and the current producing company. The rest of the Lord Chamberlain's Men were made up of "hired men," paid on a salary basis, and boy apprentices for the female parts, who were often ex-members of the children's companies.

When there was a landlord, like Henslowe of the Rose and the Fortune, matters became more complicated. Henslowe, the first of the commercial managers, is an Awful Warning. He received at first half the gallery receipts from his tenant company; then, as they grew more and more deeply indebted to him, he took three-quarters, and finally the whole gallery receipts, part of which went to pay off the debts the company had contracted. Sometimes these were as high as £658 6s. 4d. in Elizabethan money, which has been very roughly computed as worth about five times the same amount in sterling today, fairly close to $10,000. When his company, the Lord Admiral's Men, were elevated to the position of Prince Henry's Men, also at the accession of the new king, they apparently made a Herculean effort to extricate themselves from the toils of the commercial manager and reduced the debt to £24, "casting all the accounts," Henslowe notes in his diary, "from the beginninge of the world until this daye," March 14, 1604.

Henslowe is undoubtedly a portent. But posterity may be grateful to him, because, ironically enough, it is from his meticulous accounts that we draw much of our present knowledge of the Elizabethan theater. One of his hack authors writes of him:

Most of the Timber that his state repairs
He hews out of the bones of foundered Players.

But he himself notes wistfully at the end of a murky computation of unpaid loans, "When I lent I wasse a frend, when I asked I was a foe." Many of the loans were evidently made to the Company for production expenses, such as:

"For hose for Nick to tumble before the Queen . . ."

"For the mending of Hugh Davies tawney coat that was eaten with the rats . . ." [£2, this.]

"Pd for the poleyes and worckmanshipp for to hange Absalom . . . xiiii pence."

Such entries as "lane aperne wraght eaged with gowlde lace and creamson strings" and a black velvet cloak which cost as much as £20, so richly was it decorated, were presumably for theater wear. But on the other hand, Dowton borrows £12 10s. to redeem two cloaks—and Henslowe keeps the cloaks as security! He has to lend Dekker, the playwright, £2 to "discharge him out of the Counter." Another author borrows for his reckoning at the Sun. Richard Jones gets a loan of £5, "to be payed me agayne," notes the cagey Henslowe, "by ten shillings a weake." We may be sure that ten shillings were stopped from Richard's salary until the debt was discharged. Even the sum of five shillings for the heartening purpose of "good cheer at the Tavern in Fish street" is noted as a loan. We can almost hear a young actor's protesting "Look, Mr. Henslowe, my salary's sixpence short this week." "Your share of the party, dear boy, your share of my party."

Several of the hired men who were not sharers were doubly in Henslowe's grip, for, contrary to common practice, he put them under personal contract to himself. One was engaged to play for two years at 5s. a week the first year and 6s. 8d. the second; another signed for 10s. a week and 5s. on the road;

others were bound to him for three years under penalty of forfeit. Such practices as these were probably not current in Shakespeare's company, which was a co-operative joint-stock actor-managerial affair; but the bases of its financing may be deduced from Henslowe's accounts.

The authors attached to his companies were paid something like £4 to £6 for an entire play, which would seem little enough, judging from the comparative munificence of the sums expended on props for their plays—£5 13s. for instance, for BEROWNE. The initial payment bought the play outright, and it became the property of the company. As prices rose, the author's fee rose also to an average of £7 or £8. In 1613, Daborn actually extorted £20 from Henslowe, £6 on signing, £4 on the completion of three acts, and the balance on delivery of the finished play.

When, as was very frequently the case, a play was written by several authors in collaboration, they divided the fee among them. Chettle, Dekker, Heywood, Smith, and Webster must have done some unsatisfactory arithmetic over the £8 they jointly received for THE FIRST PART OF LADY JANE.

Very often, too, an author earned a few shillings by revising an old play for revival, or adding a scene or two to someone else's script. The method is startlingly paralleled today in any Hollywood studio. It has caused commentators endless headaches in their diligent efforts to disentangle the early Shakespearean hand from that of his fellows, particularly in the HENRY VI's. Several of the late ones are unmistakably the product of collaboration, such as HENRY VIII and PERICLES; and most of his work bears the mark of addition, revision, or hasty cutting, either by himself or one of his fellows.

There was no system of continuing royalties. But Shakespeare was not dependent on them, nor on such down payments as Henslowe's hack authors received. He owned his share in the Burbage theaters and properties and his further share as an active member of the company. He was, in a sense, employer and employee; and his income was a steady one. The shares were salable and could be left to the owner's heirs. In addition there were rewards for court performances and other miscellaneous remuneration. Shakespeare and his fellows were, by the standards of their day, pretty prosperous men.

The plays in all the companies were, of course, played in repertory. They were seldom performed even twice consecutively. HENRY VI, PART I, which was a hit on its first production at the Rose in the season of 1592–1593, received only sixteen performances. Marlowe's popular JEW OF MALTA was played thirty-six times, but over a period of four seasons. His FAUSTUS was done twenty-five times, according to Henslowe's playhouse records. But these do not include the additional performances given by special command at court or in private houses. RICHARD II was played "over forty times in public streets and houses," according to Queen Elizabeth's furious comment, and presumably this was typical of a successful play. Few of them seem to have held their place in the theater repertory for more than three or four consecutive seasons.

Some unsuccessful ones may literally have been given "not above once." But despite the extensive and rapid changes of bill the players had to be prepared to play practically anything at practically any moment. Hamlet's request to have THE MURDER OF GONZAGO played "tomorrow night" reflects current practice. The court authorities or private patrons might make similar demands at any time, as Essex's friends did for the performance of the already obsolete RICHARD II, which had been produced five years earlier and had completely dropped out of the repertoire. Sir Walter Cope writes to Robert Cecil on one occasion:

I have sent and bene all thys morning huntyng for players Juglers and Such kinde of Creaturs, but fynde them harde to finde, wherefore Leavinge notes for them to seeke me, Burbage ys come, and Sayes ther ys no new playe that the quene hath not seene, but they have Revyved an olde one, Cawled LOVES LABORE LOST, which for wytt and myrth he sayes will please her excedingly. And Thys ys appointed to be playd to Morowe night . . . Burbage ys my messenger Ready attendyng your pleasure.

All this "attendyng" must have pleased Burbage, with two shows, several rehearsals, and a revival to get ready for the following night.

A stock revival, which would always fill a gap, was vividly known as a "get-penny." But the repertory changed very rapidly, and authors were consequently called upon to turn out new plays like sausages from a machine. There was no sitting in a vacuum clasping his domed brow and waiting for the Muse to descend, in Shakespeare's busy life. Two hundred and eighty-two plays are mentioned by Henslowe in the records of his company, during their years at the Rose and the Fortune. The modern impresario may well stand aghast at such a feat of continuous production.

The living people in the Elizabethan theater have left us traces of experience amusingly, and sometimes touchingly, analogous to our own. Burbage and Kemp interview potential apprentices, in the play RETURN FROM PARNASSUS, and Burbage starts off with some familiar phrases: "I pray you take some part in this book and act it, that I may see what will fit you best. I think your voice would serve for Hieronimo." To another, Kemp says: "Your face methinks would be good for a foolish Mayor or a foolish justice of the peace." And Burbage winds up one audition with the old-new vagueness of "you may do well, after a while." Ben Jonson gives us a nervous author on an opening night undergoing an experience with which members of the Dramatists' Guild are familiar and describes the strain on the actors "to have his presence in the tiring-house, to prompt us aloud, stamp at the bookholder, swear for our properties, curse the poor tireman, rail the music

out of tune, and sweat for every venal trespass we commit."
The author was something of a director, too, and seems to
have acquired some directorial habits.

And we have, of course, accounts of Shakespeare and his
friends at the Mermaid Tavern, or Lambs Club, which are endearing, even if some of them are apocryphal. "Many were
the wit-combats between him [Shakespeare] and Ben Jonson, which two I behold like a Spanish great Gallion and an
English man of War; Master Jonson was built far higher in
Learning; Solid, but Slow in his performances. Shakespeare
. . . lesser in bulk, but lighter in sailing, could tack about and
take advantage of all winds, by the quickness of his wit and
invention." If this is fancy, it has the ring of truth, and we do
know that Jonson argued Shakespeare into cutting some lines
out of JULIUS CAESAR, that he called PERICLES "a mouldy
tale," which in parts it is, and assured the author of MACBETH
that some of the bombast speeches were simply "horrour."

Although these people are so familiar to us in their ways of
thinking and the details of their theater lives that we can almost stand in the wings and hear them talk, it is hard in some
respects to get the "feel" of an Elizabethan performance. We
have to think in terms of a stage which used no scenery whatever but simply shifted the action from the curtained alcove
of the inner stage to the balcony of the upper stage and out
onto the projecting forestage, on three sides of which the audience stood or sat. The size of the playing area was considerably greater than ours. The forestage alone was as deep as
our deepest sets today; and its width, nearly half as great again
as our average proscenium opening.

We might feel a little lost without our familiar scenic background to indicate locality, though of recent years producers
have begun to prove the complete fluidity of action which
such freedom affords. An Elizabethan play was free of inter-
ruptions too, in the sense of scene changes or act waits, and

gained thereby a flowing unchecked rhythm. Props were used: furniture, usually set up on the inner stage while the curtains of it were closed for the preceding scene, and such things as a caldron, a gibbet, or even "a cloth of the Sun and Moon."

This radical difference in physical production caused Shakespeare to obtain, by methods different from ours, effects at which we too aim, with our picture stage and act curtains. It is essential that we should remember the craft by which he was governed.

Sometimes the scholars, in their invaluable efforts to reconstruct for us the minutiae of Elizabethan performances, come to conclusions which make curious reading to anyone engaged in practical theater work today. The details of staging—what was placed where, and who did this or that backstage task—have caused much "throwing about of brains." The available data leave a wide margin for guesswork as to practicalities. Professor W. J. Lawrence, for example, is much exercised as to whether or not the side doors to the stage were fitted with practical locks; he comes to the conclusion that they must have been and instances such scenes as the York family party in RICHARD II, where the Yorks, each in turn, arrive and thunder vigorously on the locked door. I am irresistibly reminded of a production in which I myself played the Duchess of York and held the door closed with a foot and one hand, while I shook it with the other and the stage manager pounded on the floor with a padded stick.

Professor Lawrence is further engaged in a valiant attempt to find out what exactly represented such things as the "City Gates," before and through which so much action passes in Shakespeare's plays. He arrives at a complicated conclusion. The back center could not, it seems, be the gates; but "the leaves of the gate formed the permanent background of the rear stage, and in one of them there was a door through which, when the scene represented something otherwise than outside the City Walls, the characters came in and went out." One cannot believe that the vaunted Elizabethan aptitude for joining wholeheartedly in a game of make-believe really required such intricacy as this.

Authors' stage directions as reproduced in the printed texts and even in extant manuscripts are not especially informative in helping us to arrive at what the author himself really had in his mind's eye in matters of staging. The brief indication "Alarums and Excursions" serves for an entire sequence of marchings and countermarchings, trumpets and drums, victories and defeats. "Alarums and Excursions," says Shakespeare, and we are left with our imaginations and a rather frightening margin for opportunity or error.

His early plays are especially sparse in their directions, despite a few which have slipped into print unintentionally from the playhouse manuscripts. Some of these tiny but vivid touches from the first printed texts are seldom reproduced today in popular editions. In ROMEO AND JULIET, Sampson and Gregory should make their first entrance "with swords and bucklers," and later the citizens arrive "with clubs." This should be helpful to a harried director trying desperately to evolve some variety of action in the street fights. In the same play, the impossible lamentation scene over Juliet's dead body is at least slightly ameliorated by the Quarto direction: "All *at once* cry out and wring their hands." In the Folio MIDSUMMER NIGHT'S DREAM, a careless corrector has left in the text "Enter Tawyer with a Trumpet" preceding the Clown-actors when they enter to the Duke. Tawyer, of course, was an actor's name; but it is possible that he made quite a funny and usable noise with his trumpet.

Some similar entrance directions, generally left over from an earlier version of the play, give us mysterious characters who never speak at all nor seem to have any purpose in the text as we have it. Such a one is "Innogen" to whom the

Quarto of MUCH ADO gives two entrances as Leonato's wife. As Sir E. K. Chambers justly observes: "A lady whose daughter is successively betrothed, defamed, repudiated before the altar, taken for dead and restored to life, ought not to be a mute. It is not motherly."

Wearing apparel is fairly frequently described in printed Elizabethan plays, placing of characters more rarely. In Shakespeare's later plays, besides full descriptions of processions and shows, we have a few such indications. Following a general entrance in CORIOLANUS, Act III, scene 1, "Sicinius and Brutus take their places by themselves"; (Act IV, scene 1) "they all bustle about Coriolanus"; and (Act V, scene 3) "he holds her hand." THE TEMPEST has "Enter Prospero on the top, invisible"—*i.e.*, on the upper stage. TIMON OF ATHENS contains an even rarer type of direction in Act I, scene 2: "Hautboys playing loud music. A great banquet is served in; Flavius and others attending; then enter Lord Timon, Alcibiades, Lords, Senators, and Ventidius. Then comes, dropping after all, Apemantus, discontentedly, like himself."

But these stage directions which seem to scholars "extremely full" and "showing the hand of a master" do not enlighten the modern director much. A modern author would not appreciate the perhaps salutary process of having his beautiful dissertations confined to such notations as "Enter James in a striped lounge-suit" or "The butler comes on carrying a tray with a bottle of Dewar's, some White Rock, and three glasses." We have to do a lot of careful deduction in order to get a picture of Shakespeare's plays. The characters, even their age and appearance, are conveyed by what they say and what others say of them and not by pages of Shavian prefatory comment.

Two sets of contemporary documents yield us more data as to Elizabethan staging than the printed texts afford. The first is the dozen or so prompt copies existing in manuscript and bearing notations by the "prompter" or "book-holder." Unfortunately, none of these is a play of Shakespeare's, though it is strongly held that 147 lines in the composite manuscript of SIR THOMAS MORE are by him and in his handwriting. The prompter's stage directions in these manuscripts are mostly written in the left-hand margin and comprise sound cues, underscorings of actors' entrances, many names of the smaller part actors, full descriptions of props, and occasional illuminating actors' business, such as "shewinge his tongue"! In FRIAR BACON AND FRIAR BUNGAY, opposite a speech of Miles, the soldier, is the direction "You knocke your head." This is of some interest, in view of the fact that the use of the pronoun "you" has entirely died out in English prompt copies today, where such a direction would run "knocks his head." But in America it is still preserved, particularly in actors' parts. The English actor, new to the American stage and habitually self-conscious, is generally a little embarrassed when he first reads such an admonition as: "You pause in the doorway; after a struggle with yourself you overcome your emotion and advance rapidly to your mother."

The prompters' directions, like the authors', get fuller as they get later in date. In MORE and JOHN A KENT, the authors' directions are fairly full, but the prompter has made only insignificant marginal notations. The SECOND MAID'S TRAGEDY, in 1611, carries brief specifications for props and music, a couple of actors' names, the signature of the licensor, Sir George Buc, and a good deal of doodling. A few years later the prompter of SIR JOHN BARNEVELT indicates that he is economizing on the author's optimistic "attendants" and "others" by firmly allotting two actors to do the job. The careful fellow also telescopes two supernumerary characters. Props are noted in the margin.

In later scripts the notes for props, furniture, and actors to be "ready" begin to anticipate the actual cue. "Stet" is used to restore a cut, as it would be today. By 1631, with Massinger's BELIEVE AS YOU LIST, we are in the full stream of the modern prompt-copy tradition. "Table ready and 6 chairs sett out" comes a page ahead of time; "all the swords ready," several pages ahead. It was probably quite a job collecting all the scattered swords. "Harry Wilson and boy ready for song at ye arras" comes thirteen speeches ahead. The "stars" are pampered, too, witness: "Gascoine; and Hubert below: ready to open the Trap Doore for Mr. Taylor." Actors are getting soft. The stage-managerial dog's life is on the way.

Our second set of data comes from the seven extant backstage "plots," some merely fragmentary, preserved among the papers of the invaluable Messrs. Alleyn and Henslowe. These are sheets of cardboard with a hole at the top for the nail on which they hung, pasted over on both sides with a list of successive entrances naming both actors and characters, notes for props, and music cues in the left-hand margin. In up-to-date Hollywood idiom, the musical flourishes are marked simply "Sound." They come pat simultaneously with the entrances and accompany nearly all the important ones.

Sometimes the prop plot is a callous descent from the sublime to the ridiculous. "A fatal murdering brand" referred to in the text of THE BATTLE OF ALCAZAR becomes succinctly "chopping knife." There are notations of impersonal brevity calling for "3 violls of blood and a sheep's gather" (*i.e.*, liver, heart, and lungs) for "Dead mens heads and bones banquett blood." The principal actors, presumably the "sharers," are respectfully noted as Mr. So-and-so; the others, in a variety of abbreviations.

The plots afford exact evidence as to the doubling business, in which the apparent problems are sometimes capable of quite simple solutions. Dr. Greg, who has edited an admirable facsimile edition of THE BATTLE OF ALCAZAR, is greatly puzzled as to why Richard Alleyn should have had to do a very quick double as the Governor of Lisbon when another actor was doing nothing in that scene. It is possible that Richard was just a better Governor of Lisbon. We gather, however, from Greg's analysis that the small-part actors dashed from one "army" to another, presumably changing helmets as they went, and that page-boys to anyone were page-boys to everyone, occasionally pairing off differently just to make it more difficult.

The use of the plots is not altogether clear. I cannot see, myself, what possible service they could have rendered the prompter, for his own prompt copy gave him all the cues he needed; and the plot sound cues, not being marked ahead of time and having no dialogue beside them, afforded him no guidance for signaling the musicians and "effects" men.

It seems to me more probable that the "plot" hung in the tiring house as a "call board," in a sense more literal than ours. The "Sound" notations should also have been a guide to the actors, who could compare them with whatever "sound" they heard from the stage and so judge how far the play had progressed. I should, however, be amazed if so optimistic a system really resulted in everybody getting on-stage as the right character at the right moment. Of course they did not. A contemporary description of a man in a high fury runs: "He would swear like an elephant, and stamp and stare (God blesse us) like a play-house book-keeper when the actors missed their entrance."

This personage, "book-keeper," "book-holder," or "prompter" as he is interchangeably described, is, to me, one of the greatest puzzles of the scholars' reconstructed Elizabethan theater. He is a superman, an Atlas, an everywhere-at-once multiple genius. He is, in fact, our stage manager. But the functions credited to him could not possibly be fulfilled by less than three people, all working twenty-four hours a day.

He is supposed to have been the literal "book-keeper,"

whose duty it was to take charge of scripts, copy them if and as necessary, take them to the office of the Master of Revels to be licensed, and make any alterations required by that official. One, Knight, did this job for the King's Men in 1633. Before that time Thomas Vincent is described as "book-keeper or prompter" at the Globe; it was probably he to whom Shakespeare was once an assistant. Incidentally, both Knight and Vincent are listed in other documents as having been musicians as well. But even this does not complete the list. John Rhodes, whom we know as the compiler of the BELIEVE AS YOU LIST script, is described in his later years as "former wardrobe-keeper to the King's Men." Wardrobe-keeper, too.

We now have a librarian-secretary-copyist-musician-wardrobe-keeper. But he is credited with many other "feats of activity." He fitted the play to the capacity of the small-part actors, casting the small parts himself and probably teaching them their lines if they were unable to read themselves. He was head property man and bought both props and wardrobe for the productions.

This hypothetical "prompter" is also accredited with keeping his eye on the actors and getting them on at the right place and moment in the midst of all the scuffling, wig changing, and lost-cloak trouble occasioned by the prevalent doubling. He is further responsible for giving "effects" cues (very complicated effects at that) and all music cues, without any warning signals marked ahead of time in his book or plot. The musicians, moreover, are in an inaccessible gallery where he cannot possibly signal to them with a mere flick of the hand. Sir E. K. Chambers does in fact surmise mildly that someone may have been needed to transmit the prompter's orders. But who? Everybody was apparently fully occupied changing hats and getting ready behind the arras and climbing up and down stairs to the upper stage.

The "prompter," however, is not through yet. In a contemporary play he is exhorted thus:

You might have writ in the margent of your play-book, Let there be a few rushes laid in the place where Backwinter shall tumble, for fear of raying his clothes; or set down: Enter Backwinter, with his boy bringing a brush after him, to take off the dust if need require. But you will ne'er have any wardrobe wit while you live. I pray you hold the book well, we be not non plus in the latter end of the play.

For, of course, as an afterthought in occasional lucid intervals, the "prompter" prompts.

Even in this capacity he manages to get himself tinged with the miraculous; for he stands, says one, behind the arras curtains, which, we need hardly be told, he also manipulates. But he is also recorded as standing at one or both sides of the stage, for the stage area is wide, and the actors are not "pen-feathered" and must get the prompt when they need it from near at hand. We may assume that, with a daily change of bill, they need it. The "prompter" must have learned the art of being in at least three places at once.

Contemporary literature does, as a matter of fact, speak of various individuals loosely described as "stage keepers." In the Induction to BARTHOLOMEW FAIR, there is a conversation between the "stage keeper" and the "prompter." In this play, too, a "tire-man" brings on stools and lights. Perhaps aid is in sight for our overburdened hero. But no. The Stage Keeper depicted in RETURN FROM PARNASSUS obviously performs a prompter's office. And so Professor Baldwin, our authority for much invaluable research, decides to brush aside such minions as being no more than terminological inexactitudes and lumps their combined duties back onto the shoulders of our Pooh-Bah "prompter." It is not, Professor Baldwin summarizes judicially, an unimportant position.

We are forced to assume that Shakespeare's picture of a prompting-stage-manager as poor Quince in A MIDSUMMER NIGHT'S DREAM was a most ungrateful piece of caricature. Poor stage managers! The theater has always treated them with ingratitude. They have no share in the applause of the public; no critic salutes their achievements; no chronicler hands on their fame to posterity; they remain faithful, hardworking, generally anonymous—and absolutely indispensable. There can be no performance without them. If the Elizabethan "prompters" did in fact accomplish all the feats of activity attributed to them by the scholars, they must have been indeed "the choice and master spirits" of the age. Let us accord them, at least, a belated vote of thanks.

4. Old Tools and Modern Usage

SUCH, THEN, was Shakespeare's workshop; such were the conditions under which he lived, the people with whom he worked, the conventions and the theater habits which formed the background of his writing. It is unwise to underestimate their importance. But we must further ask ourselves: what qualities did he draw from his human and physical material? How far did he succeed in reshaping the tools he found to his hand, how far did he transform and how far transcend them? How much, in the plays, may we ascribe to an unwilling submission to conditions imposed upon him, and how much must we respect as dramatic achievement upon which we are extremely unlikely to improve? In other words, what should we, in our staging today, emulate, what can we adapt, and what may we discard?

Our regard for his theater knowledge must take into account the fact that besides being an actor, a stage manager, and a business partner in his own theater he was also to a great extent the director of his own plays. A contemporary traveler from Germany relates that in the English theater "even the actors have to allow themselves to be instructed by the dramatist." One of the characters in BARTHOLOMEW FAIR remarks bitterly: "The Poet . . . has kicked me three or four times about the Tiring-house for but offering to put in, with my experience." Here is a familiar accent, indeed! Ben Jonson also writes, from experiences which Shakespeare must have shared, as every director that has ever been in any theater has also shared them: The actor "does over-act, and having got the habit of it, will be monstrous still in spite of counsel."

Some of the things which Shakespeare asked of his fellows must have seemed strange and doubtful novelties to them. But at least he "knew his stuff"; and, if he comes more and more to rely on the actor, to the exclusion of all adventitious aids, it is a tribute to the comprehending and full-hearted co-opera-tion of his fellows, as well as to his utterly sound theater in-stinct. For we shall find, I think, that this will prove for us also the only practical solution of our problems.

The physical resources on which he was able to draw were meager in the extreme; he used their paucity to stimulate his own dramatic imagination to an overwhelming richness. The simplicity of his stage conventions, their formlessness as to the elements of space and time, did not lead him back to the classical restrictions of time and place unity but to a delicately suggested dramatic dimension of his own, subservient to, and reflected in, the projection of the characters, the people, by whom alone he was inspired.

He wrote, supremely, with his eyes and ears in the theater; what he saw was not what a modern designer would envisage, but the barest of pictorial elements: ragged banners for the English at Agincourt, flaring colors and burnished golden armor for the French; withered and wild attire, not like the inhabitants of the earth but yet on it, for the incarnate power of evil; white hairs for age, a "smooth and rubious" lip for un-fledged youth. What he heard was merely trumpets for a bat-tle, leaden weights rolled about on the tiring-house floor (with water poured down through a sieve) for a storm, some rather sparse flourishes for a state occasion, or music "under the stage" for a ghostly visitation. But he made his audience see and hear much more than that. He dazzled them with the force and splendor, the tenderness and haunting echoes of the English language. He conjured up his visions with the dramatic potency of words; and he relied, for the rest, on the imagination of the spectators, on their ability and willingness to take part in the process of creation.

It was the contention of William Poel and his followers that we could not make the same demands upon our audiences unless we made them in Shakespeare's own terms; that only by returning to the physical conditions of the Globe and the other Elizabethan playhouses could we recapture the freedom of action and the intimacy of contact which are essential to success. There are many who agree with him, and passionately, too. The age of the Bardolators, to whom every syllable that Shakespeare wrote was Holy Writ, seems to have been succeeded by an age of Globolators who contend that every stick and stone of the building in which his plays were performed should be equally sacred to us in producing them today.

To me, however, there is very little value to be derived from the actual reconstruction of an Elizabethan playhouse. My own experiences, both of playing on such a stage and of directing in what was allegedly a miniature replica of the Globe, have taught me more about its drawbacks than about its advantages. To begin with, the line of sight is extremely bad from a large proportion of the house. The use of the inner and upper stages is reduced to a minimum in consequence; only a small triangle of space, sharply angled to vanishing point, is visible to any but a spectator sitting on a line with the dead center of the stage. I am led to believe that the inner stage must have been used largely as a jumping-off place for a scene in which standing furniture or props had to be "discovered," and that the main action must have been brought forward as soon as possible to the main stage itself. No intimate scenes can have been played on it with any degree of effect; they would have been invisible to the spectators sitting at the sides of the theater and between twenty and thirty feet away from the front row of the audience in the center of the "yard," or "pit," owing to the projecting forestage. It is, of course, true that a modern director thinks principally in terms of the orchestra seats, whereas in Elizabethan times the "carriage trade" sat in the galleries or on the stage itself, where they were not troubled by the perpetual "masking" which must often have hidden important actors when the whole cast was ranged around a flat stage.

There is another important factor to be considered in relating the Elizabethan stage to modern audiences, and that is that the pictorial background provided by a facsimile of the Globe or the Fortune or the Swan is very specific indeed. The imagination of a twentieth-century audience may well be fettered rather than freed by it. In Shakespeare's day the spectators took one look at the stage surroundings and instantly forgot them. The physical features of the structure were completely familiar to every playgoer; they were reminiscent of the inn yards or halls or galleries which he saw every day. They made him feel at home. Whatever went on against such a background gained in intimacy, came closer to himself. But for us, the reverse is true. We examine with curiosity the strange arrangement of galleries and platforms and pillars and doors. We are diverted from the play just because we pay so much attention to them. They do not help us to imagine an English forest or a Roman temple; neither are they our own natural habitat. Given time, we shall ignore them and concentrate upon the play; but they are sufficiently obtrusive to delay us. The advantage which the Elizabethan stage setting had for Shakespeare was that it was at once familiar and anonymous. For us it is neither.

Moreover, Shakespeare's stagecraft cannot possibly have been devised to fit the precise specifications of the Globe or the Blackfriars. He must have planned it to be adaptable to widely differing physical conditions; for it is clear that his acting company played practically everywhere. They left their own theaters to go on tour or to give special command performances. They appeared in Guildhalls, manor houses, inn yards, probably in the open air as well. At court, according to Leslie Hotson, they played "in the round," as it is now called. Even Poel admitted, indeed insisted, that there were no rules to be laid down about Elizabethan staging, other than its limitless flexibility.

One thing, however, must have been common to all these performances: the players were brought into much closer contact with the audience than is possible from behind the frame of a proscenium stage. An actor could almost always touch the nearest of the spectators, whether from the projecting "apron" platform at the Globe or from the cleared space of the inn yard or from the floor of the Great Hall at Whitehall Palace. He played with, almost from, the audience, not merely at it. He could really speak the "To be or not to be" soliloquy as if it were his thought made audible; the emotional contact he was able effortlessly to establish is at the very root of Shakespeare's writing. His comedian-commentators, like Faulconbridge in KING JOHN, and nearly all his Fools could get on hailfellow-well-met terms with his audience so that they voiced, almost as a member of it, what Shakespeare hoped it was itself thinking. The Fool's successful joke was a personal triumph for the audience, each of whose members would have said just that, if only he had thought of it. Thornton Wilder's Stage Manager in OUR TOWN is no distant relative of Faulconbridge and his fellows.

We should be suicidally unwise to neglect the value of this intimacy. The modern penchant for arena or platform stages is sound in this respect. In a proscenium theater it is often helpful to build out some form of apron stage. The actors do not then need to "project," as they must from across an orchestra pit; and this is a technical skill in which many microphone-trained modern actors are sadly deficient. But if they are playing in the round, they must be meticulously truthful. They cannot cheat or hide behind the flashier tricks of make-up or theatrical "effect." The spectators are too close to be deceived, whether by a false reaction or a clumsy wig-join; they must be included in the illusion; they must be made to feel "we were there."

But it is an exaggeration to maintain that a platform stage is the only one from which intimacy can be achieved. If an actor cannot reach the hearts of his audience from behind a proscenium frame, it is generally due to his own shortcomings and certainly not to any limitations in the material Shakespeare provides. Years ago, at the Old Vic, when Sybil Thorndike was playing Imogen, a man in the gallery became so excited that he leaned over and called out to her during her scene with Iachimo: "Don't you trust 'im, Mrs. Casson! 'e's up to no good!" During the last scene of OTHELLO in New York, I once heard a girl in an orchestra seat saying over and over again to herself: "Please, God, don't let him kill her. . . . don't let him kill her. . . ." Helen Hayes as Viola, left alone on the stage for the "I left no ring with her" soliloquy, confided her troubles to the audience so that her problems immediately became their own; Ralph Richardson as Falstaff made everyone in the theater share his views on "honour." These instances are all drawn from proscenium productions; they could, of course, be multiplied indefinitely. You do not need an apron stage to make contact between Shakespeare and his audiences. But your actors must have voices and spiritual stature. The technique of mumbling and nudging will not do.

Our "peep-show" stages frequently get the blame for a lack of acting craft and also for the lazy incapacity for listening which afflicts modern audiences. It has now become positively daring to suggest that, in fact, they have certain advantages over their Elizabethan prototypes. To group actors in the round, like a sculptor, without blurring or masking the crucial action is a difficult technique. The flexible use of rostra, steps, and levels will afford the director just as good a pictorial opportunity and frequently a better dramatic one than he can get by working on a flat platform stage. The endings of Shakespeare's plays can often be heightened because we can drop a curtain in front of the final picture. There was, of course, no "act drop" at the Globe. At the end of a tragedy, it was eternally a case of "Take up the bodies" and everybody march off. There is no sense in pretending that this is not, as a rule, an ineffective and clumsy necessity with which Shakespeare did the best he could. But we can leave in an audience's eye and mind an indelible picture which should represent the sum and resolution of our story. Such plays as ROMEO AND JULIET and HAMLET offer us magnificent opportunities in this respect. In the same way, the charming Epilogue farewell of AS YOU LIKE IT is much more graceful if the actors do not subsequently have to turn their backs on the audience and troop sturdily off.

Some of the most successful modern Shakespearean settings have been devised for the Stratford, Ontario, Festivals through the use of a permanent structure made with different levels, highly adaptable to variations of placement, grouping, entrances, and exits, and set in a tentlike auditorium with no proscenium. The same designer, Tania Moisewitch, apparently achieved equally successful results with her permanent set for the Histories cycle on the proscenium stage at Stratford-on-Avon. In this case a kind of skeletal Elizabethan framework was erected on the main stage. Brooks Atkinson, the critic of the New York *Times,* who has become an impassioned advocate of arena staging, claims that it is impossible nowadays to play Shakespeare properly in any other way. Fortunately he has contradicted himself wholeheartedly by his complete capitulation to the magic of such proscenium-stage productions as the Stratford-on-Avon ANTONY AND CLEOPATRA in 1953. It would be a sad blow to Shakespeare and the professional theater if we could never again play him in a proscenium playhouse, since there are practically no others available for our use. The plain truth, of course, is that you can play Shakespeare anywhere—in a gymnasium or a cathedral, on a baseball diamond or at the Comédie Française—if the director respects the author and the actors have passion and truth.

But whatever the nature of our playing area, we must make very sure that we do not allow it to be cluttered with unnecessary objects. We must not impede Shakespeare's spatial freedom nor interfere with his fluid manipulation of the element of time. Speed is vital; for he himself used the flexibility of his unrestricted stage to establish conventions of place and time subtly and meticulously fitted to his dramatic purpose. His time rhythm is badly jarred by our scene waits, which in his theater did not exist. The scenes flowed into each other, often marked by a musical "flourish" or "sennet" to introduce fresh sets of characters, just as the Chinese theater still uses a gong to punctuate but not separate its changing scenes.

We sometimes, though not always, dislocate his convention further by our act intermissions, for, during the major part of Shakespeare's career, there were no act waits either. After the indoor playhouses began to be used, the practice of having brief pauses filled with music gradually came into being. The five-act division is marked by the Folio for some, though not all, of the plays; it is probably Heminges's salute to the pseudo-

classical scheme of play division which Ben Jonson was bringing into fashion, but it certainly does not represent Shakespeare's common practice.

The scene divisions indicated in almost all modern editions
are the entirely gratuitous invention of an eighteenth-century
editor, Nicholas Rowe. They are the favorite object for the
almost emotional invective of modern scholars and critics and,
indeed, are now retained in printed texts mainly for purposes
of reference. It is important that we should clear our minds
of anything which obstructs the unbroken flow of Shakespeare's writing and that in staging we should eliminate as far
as humanly possible the breaks and checks which scene
changes impose on it.

We are not likely to be seduced into four act-intermissions,
though we are forced to allow our audiences at least one. This
is often a contrived affair, and in such a play as ROMEO AND
JULIET it is impossible to find any point whatever where the
controlled swiftness of its momentum will not be disturbed by
an intermission. RICHARD II, by contrast, seems to me to invite
two entirely legitimate act pauses: one after the scene of
Gaunt's death and another after Richard is taken at Flint
Castle. In the first instance, Shakespeare's time emphasis,
which is always a matter of the most delicate dramatic suggestion, is actually helped by the break in playing; and there
are many similar cases where we gain rather than lose by an
act pause.

We need not feel any difficulty with Shakespeare's manipulation of time in the theater, unless we create it for ourselves
by the unskillful placing of intermissions or by unnecessary
scene waits. Even in RICHARD III, when he had not yet evolved
his later technique of time reflected by psychological progression, we do not find it hard to accept the more rudimentary
formula which he uses to indicate the passing of the night
before the battle. First comes Richmond's line "The weary

sun hath made a golden set" followed soon after by Catesby's "It's supper time, my lord, it's nine o'clock"; then come the alternating ghost scenes which demonstrate, using the timeless dimension of a dream world, the passing of the night itself; and finally the announcement to Richmond that it is almost dawn, climaxed by Richard's "Who saw the sun today? . . . He should have braved the East an hour ago." We have lights too, if we need them, to help us emphasize the clock.

Shakespeare's later method is a more abstract but no less effective treatment of time's passing. Reading OTHELLO, it is easy to detect the fact that Cassio and Desdemona would simply have had no opportunity to commit the "act of shame" with which they are charged and to feel one's credulity challenged by the circumstance that Lodovico arrives from Venice with the news of Othello's recall on the very heels of Othello's own arrival. But in the theater we are swept away, as we are intended to be, by the torrent of Othello's mounting agony, an avalanche of passion too powerful to be checked by chop-logic considerations. The play needs momentum and gets it; emotional pressure successfully defies the calendar.

In MACBETH, the action moves remorselessly from the murder of Duncan through a steadily unfolding cycle of blood, of thickening and haunted darkness, to Macbeth's

> . . . my way of life
> Is fall'n into the sear, the yellow leaf,
> And that which should accompany old age,
> As honour, love, obedience, troops of friends,
> I must not look to have; . . .

Macbeth has been established at the play's opening as a man in the full vigor and prime of manhood; there has been no indication of any lengthy passage of time; on the contrary, the play is filled with an increasing sense of pressure. On the very morning following the murder, we are told that Macbeth is "already named, and gone to Scone to be invested." Banquo's "Thou hast it now, king, Cawdor, Glamis, all," follows immediately, and in the same scene Macbeth tells his hired gangsters that Banquo must be murdered "tonight." After the banquet at which the ghost of the newly murdered Banquo appears to him, he says "I will tomorrow, and betimes I will, to the weird sisters," and, at the end of his scene with the "sisters," he resolves upon the immediate murder of Macduff's wife and children:

> Time, thou anticipat'st my dread exploits:
> The flighty purpose never is o'ertook
> Unless the deed go with it: from this moment
> The very firstlings of my heart shall be
> The firstlings of my hand. And even now,
> To crown my thoughts with acts, be it thought and done:

Ross travels immediately to England with the terrible news he must break to Macduff, and Macduff and Malcolm return with as much speed: "Our power is ready, our lack is nothing but our leave."

But it is not a sudden qualm about the fact that the historical Macbeth reigned in Scotland for twenty years which causes Shakespeare to precipitate him into "old age." He, in his single human soul, has passed through a timeless cycle of spiritual blackness whose beginnings stretch back through the centuries and down into the fathomless abyss of man's primeval heritage. If Macbeth can invoke for us even a fragmentary consciousness of a force as mighty as this, we shall not question that its concentration upon himself leaves him an "old" man.

Modern thinking is receptive to the treatment of time in terms of relativity. Theater practice renders us less amenable to a similar flexibility in the treatment of space. For here Shakespeare is equally content to use suggestion and, having no scenery to bother about, shifts the place with the actor instead of laboriously transporting the actor to the place. In the convention of the Chinese theater, we may still find a close analogy to the accepted place scheme of Shakespeare's day. An actor leaves by one door and comes in by another, thereby moving from one locale to another. He walks from the back of the stage to the front and so leaves the inside of the "house" for the street outside it. He crosses the stage and in doing so accomplishes a journey of many leagues. So it was with the Elizabethans.

Shakespeare uses his inner and upper stages to indicate a shift of locale, but he is not particular about geographic rigidity in his handling of them. Juliet says good-by to Romeo standing on the upper stage and then, according to the Quarto's specific stage direction, "descends," bringing her bedroom with her so to speak, to play the scene with her parents. Cleopatra's "monument" is placed sometimes above and sometimes below, as the necessity of the action dictates; the battlements of Elsinore swing from level to level.

Space can be telescoped also; Richmond and Richard, Hotspur and Henry IV will pitch their embattled camps within touching distance of each other. Where the actor is, there is the place, concentrated around the magnetic pole of his personality. When necessary, the place will be described in terms of dramatic atmosphere, physical features, and, much more importantly, poetic value. The moon "tips with silver all those fruit-tree tops," shedding a radiance which no arc lamp can emulate, simply for Romeo to swear by. The "morn in russet mantle clad, Walks o'er the dew of yond high Eastward hill," bringing to Horatio the sanity and strength of day.

> This castle hath a pleasant seat, the air
> Nimbly and sweetly recommends itself
> Unto our gentle senses.
>   This guest of summer,

The temple-haunting martlet, does approve,
By his loved mansionry, that the heaven's breath
Smells wooingly here: . . .

These words are not merely a picture in themselves; they fall on ears which still ring with Lady Macbeth's "Come, thick night, And pall thee in the dunnest smoke of hell"; and we know that Duncan will pass through these gates to his death.

With such scene painting as this, Shakespeare is meticulous and unerring. With local color he is more haphazard. Venice is indicated by a few casual references to gondolas and the Rialto; Cyprus has some cliffs and a harbor, which might be those of Dover but most unmistakably are not; CYMBELINE is as frankly Renaissance as a Veronese picture, for all its references to Early Britain; and around Athens grows a wood filled with Warwickshire wild flowers and Stratford artisans, all transfused with magic. But there is no doubt about the stripped savagery of Lear's world, nor about the luxury and dalliance of Cleopatra's Egypt set against the discipline of Rome, nor about the swaggering hot-blooded gallants who carry with them the sun and color of fifteenth-century Verona.

Once or twice Shakespeare apologizes for the visual shortcomings, especially in the overquoted Chorus to HENRY V:

> . . . But pardon, gentles all,
> The flat unraised spirits, that hath dared,
> On this unworthy scaffold, to bring forth
> So great an object. Can this cockpit hold
> The vasty fields of France? or may we cram
> Within this wooden O the very casques
> That did affright the air at Agincourt?

This arrogant apology from an author who knew perfectly well that there was going to be nothing flat nor unraised about his HENRY has nothing to do with the specific limitations of his particular stage. We, equally and always, have to beg our audiences to "piece out our imperfections with your thoughts." It is the artist's eternal sense of frustration when he compares his vision with his power to fulfill it. But Shakespeare knew that his audience would accept the challenge to their imagination. He does not appeal primarily to their eyes but to their hearts; and when, in a later play, he promises them that they shall "see away their shilling Richly in two short hours," he knows that the richness will have nothing to do with the play's physical mounting.

Because he achieved his effects without benefit of scenery, working with words on the "imaginary forces" of his audience, scenic productions of his plays have been continuously at odds with themselves. Long ago Charles Lamb registered his protest against wood and painted cloth: "The elaborate and anxious provision of scenery, which the luxury of the age demands . . . works a quite contrary effect to what is intended . . . In plays which appeal to the higher faculties" it "positively destroys the illusion which it is introduced to aid."

A modern echo of the same point of view comes, in 1954, from Robert Speaight, the biographer of William Poel and himself a distinguished Shakespearean actor: "I shall not go so far as to say that poetry is always destroyed by scenery . . . but what scenery does destroy is the poetic realism which was the secret of the Elizabethan achievement."

Through the nineteenth century, however, and on through the days of David Belasco and Beerbohm Tree, scenic effects were still thought to be one of the intrinsic glories of a distinguished Shakespearean production. Nobody minded the long stage waits which preceded each pictorial revelation— the meticulously painted backdrops, with their trees and towers, the mossily upholstered banks, the formidable rocky rocks. The early opponents of realistic scenery had to move some very literal mountains.

Subsequently, under the influence of Appia and Gordon Craig, stage designers became much preoccupied with line and "mood." They turned toward severely architectural arrangements, massive steps and rostra, which were shifted into different positions as the action of the play progressed, and illumined by dramatic shafts of light. Lear, Hamlet, and Macbeth were costumed impartially in what might be called the Early Bathrobe period and sometimes ended by looking as if they had got themselves unintentionally benighted on the steps of the Lincoln Memorial. Productions such as these invited the mockery of the frivolous-minded; but they did enable the Shakespearean texts to be presented in unbroken continuity, and some designers, like Robert Edmond Jones, attained a genuine harmony and beauty with the simplest of means.

The vigorous, if erratic, impulses of the rebellious Twenties encouraged unorthodox scenic experiments. Revolving stages and other newly invented mechanical devices fostered them. Since then, stage design has been flexible and various; it has moved closer to the Elizabethan spirit and practice as it grew less representational. The late nineteen-forties brought a renewed interest in the cult of arena staging and, in America, the elimination of all scenery. This has been partly due to economic pressures. The huge cost of building and painting and the high salaries of the stagehands required to handle a heavy scenic production have driven us toward an austerity which is by no means to be regretted. In England, the opposite trend, toward rich and complex stage décor, can still be indulged without bankruptcy. In both cases the touchstone of success is the same: to what extent has the stage design served to interpret the play? Our modern theater has cast a wide net in its efforts to revitalize plays which, in fact, have never lost either vitality or significance.

Modern use of stage lighting, though a dangerous weapon

in the hands of those who fall too deeply in love with it, has probably done more than any other single factor to free Shakespeare from the imprisonment of realism. Through the imaginative and dramatic use of lighting we can retain an element of visual beauty against even the simplest of backgrounds. Although Shakespeare himself knew nothing of it, there is no reason to suppose he would disapprove. By the skillful manipulation of spotlights we can change the locale of the different scenes with simplicity and speed; also we can focus the attention of the spectator where Shakespeare wanted it—on the actor. We can grade the balance of varying groups of characters in any given scene and relate them to the background against which they are playing. Light and, most vitally, shadow can be made our servants.

We shall do well not to compete too strongly with Shakespeare in such matters as the "temple-haunting martlet" and the silvered fruit-tree tops. They will do better in the audience's imagination than in our three-ply and paint. We shall do better still to let Lear raise the storm from the whirling tempest of his spirit and not drown him out with thunder sheets and "twelve-penny hirelings making artificial lightening in the heavens," to the utter distraction of all beholders.

We must remember that the Shakespearean actor needs space and generally a sense of the sky. Few, if any, of the plays are of the drawing-room variety. Sooner or later they get out and walk the surface of the world; in Shakespeare's day theaters had, until his last years, the open sky always visible overhead; we do not need to tempt the elements that far, but it will usually be helpful to have a good stretch of sky somewhere around. The plays are full of stars, of the cosmic variety. A star dances and under it Beatrice is born; Sebastian's stars shine darkly over him; Helena might love "a bright particular star"; Laertes'

. . . phrase of sorrow
Conjures the wandering stars and makes them stand
Like wonder-wounded hearers.

And Lorenzo still catches us by the throat with the matchless beauty of his "pattines of bright gold." The sun blazes from Shakespeare's heavens in an endless glory of imagery dramatically and purposefully used. The moon wields every kind of beautiful and evil magic. The west and the east bear exquisitely and ominously the burdens of the sunset and the dawn.

We need not, again, compete with Shakespeare; but we should spare him more than one corner of wrinkled blue cloth and a couple of spare spots that we happen to have left over, especially in such a play as ROMEO AND JULIET, which is drenched through and through with the imagery and influence of the heavens.

Generalizations on the subject of stage settings for Shakespeare, as on most other subjects, are apt to become dangerously misleading. Each play presents a separate problem, and every broad solution is encompassed with a hundred difficulties of detail. For, as Granville Barker very clearly puts it: "However high, with Shakespeare, the thought or emotion may soar, we shall always find the transcendental set in the familiar . . . Their [the plays'] rooted humanity blossoms in a fertile upspringing of expressive little things."

This is as true for the physical as it is for the emotional and imaginative aspects of a production, and it is in this very fact that our modern difficulties lie. For, although the transcendental qualities remain constant in value, the "familiar" has changed radically since Shakespeare wrote for an audience whose "familiar" background he shared; and here we return, once more, to our neglected partner, the audience. We do not and cannot look or listen with either the eyes or ears of our ancestors; and for the difference in an audience's capacity to look and listen the modern director, designer, and actor must carefully allow.

The Elizabethan audience was, as we have seen, taken into much closer partnership with both dramatist and actor than is its modern successor. It had, further, a hugely voracious appetite for a form of entertainment which was still novel, plastic, and capable of being molded to its will. In the theater, as in the streets, it was vigorous and uninhibited; and it had an enormous capacity for make-believe. It did not have to be coaxed, lured, teased, and cajoled into accepting the illusions of the theater; it positively rushed to embrace and further them. Yet there is evidence that when the theater attempted any visualization of things or people that were known to its audience, these things had to be tangibly and visually accurate: hence the squirts full of red liquid for the blood which a modern audience would far rather not see, Antigonus' real bear from the neighboring bear pit, and the artificial rain contrived on principles still in use today.

The public was, presumably, exacting in the matter of costume, on which the Elizabethan producer spent by far the greater proportion of his budget; but this costume was, whatever the supposed period of the play, predominantly contemporary, with the vaguest of leanings toward the classic or the pagan if the play required. Elizabethan hats and farthingales and ruffs and rapiers are abundantly referred to throughout the whole range of the plays. Food and drink and flowers and games and pastimes are all such as the audience knew, whether in Elsinore, Egypt, or ancient Britain, and must have been so represented. Surrounded by these small, familiar objects, the characters were not strange and distant beings from another world but old acquaintances who had somehow acquired another dimension.

On the other hand, the audience was more than happy to

accept Verona and Ephesus at second hand, as indeed Shakespeare himself accepted them. Bohemia was a never-never land in which magical things happened; it almost *had* to have a seacoast, like all self-respecting lands of fantasy, particularly the fantasy of the seagirt English. There were no illustrated travel brochures to familiarize every member of the audience with the exact topographical features of the Rialto; and probably the great majority of Londoners had never even seen the "high wild hills" of Gloucestershire, which consequently loomed far higher and wilder in their mind's eye than the cozy, precipitous hummocks of the Cotswolds actually are.

These values are hard for us to recapture. A much more knowledgeable public makes demands upon us equal to its knowledge. Our answer cannot be Hollywood's superrealism, obviously; and the pageant productions of thirty or forty years ago sufficiently demonstrated the futility of any such attempts, even before the cinema arrived on our horizon. But we must, in each case, consider the demand and not run flatly counter to it.

This shift of angle and of emphasis goes deeper than considerations of scenery or physical staging. The very framework of each play is affected by it, and in balancing the structure of our productions we must take it into account from every aspect. Most vitally we must realize the metamorphosis which has come about in the relation between our audience and the plot or subject matter of the plays. They have much too accurate a knowledge of what is going to happen, right through to the final curtain. Their angle of vision is distorted because it lacks the possibility of surprise.

There are cases where, as it seems to me, we shall have to exchange plot tension for tension of character in order to compensate for the missing factor. For instance, it would be wonderful if we could present THE MERCHANT OF VENICE to a theater full of people who had never heard of it before and did not know that it was the leaden casket which contained Portia's picture or that she would succeed in rescuing Antonio from Shylock's clutches by the quibble of "this bond doth give thee here no jot of blood." Obviously, they would assume that Shylock was going to be foiled somehow, but how easy our problem would be if our audience were not, to a man, waiting with smug superiority for the inevitable "Tarry a little! There is something else."

I would suggest that it is for us to reinterpret the scene by shifting its focus of tension. Suppose that Portia arrives from her interview with Bellario *not* knowing exactly what she is going to do. She has never seen the bond, and neither has he. He has told her that if she can find a flaw in it, she can rescue Antonio and also deliver Shylock over to the provisions of the Aliens Act; but if the bond is legally good, she may have a hard time proving that Shylock has "indirectly and directly too" conspired against the defendant's life.

After all, no one has even told Portia of the detailed "pound of flesh" proviso. All she knows, or all we know she knows, is Jessica's:

> . . . he would rather have Antonio's flesh
> Than twenty times the value of the sum
> That he did owe him,

and Antonio's phrase in his letter: "since in paying it [the bond] it is impossible I should live." These are pretty vague data for Bellario. It is true that the Duke's messenger had presumably acquainted Bellario with some further details; but in the theater, with our attention concentrated on the protagonists, we shall not pay very close attention to what one off-stage character may have told another.

On comes Portia to the trial. In a few seconds she has pulled herself together and measured the antagonists; Antonio confesses the bond; to Shylock she makes her famous plea for mercy, but it breaks against his implacable resolve. She asks whether Antonio is able to discharge the money, knowing of course that she herself has made it possible and hoping that a "settlement in court" may be effected. More merciful than Shylock, she does not immediately threaten him with possible penalties, nor has she, as yet, the clear power.

But Shylock refuses the settlement. She is really driven back on the hope that there may be some flaw in the bond; she asks to see it, but a hasty glance reveals no loophole. Again and again she delays, while she frantically searches the wording of the bond. Her very repetitions—"You must prepare your bosom for his knife" and "therefore lay bare your bosom" —are a desperate pretext for delay. She asks are there balances ready to weigh the flesh, is there a surgeon in attendance, hoping in each case to secure a respite. She sits down with Nerissa while Antonio makes his last farewells, praying by this time for enlightenment, panic-stricken that she may fail. Her wry little "your wife would give you little thanks for that" to Bassanio is not a heartless joke while she plays callous cat-and-mouse with Shylock and Antonio but is wrung irresistibly from her. She makes a last desperate bid for time with her double "The court awards it and the law doth give it" (her eyes still searching the fatal bond), "the law allows it and the court awards it"; and then at the very last second the solution, simple and complete, flashes over her.

"Tarry a little! There is something else."

If these words can blaze from her in an uncontrollable burst of passionate relief, she will have brought into the scene a new element of genuine and thrilling emotion. I do not claim that this can have been the scene's original interpretation; I do believe that it is legitimate interpretation, designed for a present-day audience. In almost every one of the better known plays, there are instances where such factors as these must be taken into consideration.

Many elements in the subject matter of the plays have changed in value for us. Ghosts and witches and feigned madness seem to have had a certain dramatic appeal for the Elizabethans. The closest modern equivalent is probably to be found in psychiatry and the manifestations of mental suggestion. Again, war is no longer to us an exciting pictorial tournament, filled with "pride, pomp and circumstance," in which picked representatives of opposing sides can do battle much in the manner of baseball teams, where even death is glorious and the misery of the vanquished is minimized. Nowadays war is an irredeemable planetary disaster from which not one of us is immune. It has grown hard for us to participate with eagerness or excitement in the "once-upon-a-time" issues of Shakespeare's mimic battles.

To a lesser degree, we are troubled by innumerable topical allusions, some of which elude even the scholars and all of which need a program note for their elucidation. It is possible to wonder just what an audience three hundred years hence could conceivably make of THE MAN WHO CAME TO DINNER. Parts of such plays as LOVE'S LABOUR'S LOST are equally obscure to us. We are apt to think that a blue pencil will remedy our difficulty. But sometimes the line or allusion, however unintelligible in its exact meaning, remains essential to the pattern or sequence of the scene, and we must retain it and grace it as best we can. Sometimes a topical allegory is woven into the design of the play, as the story of Essex supposedly suggests the story of Achilles in TROILUS AND CRESSIDA. But the plays are never dependent on such by-products for their main strength. Shakespeare was too good a dramatist to write a dramatized gossip column filled with allegorical nomenclature.

But there remains one very important barrier between us and the ideal actor-audience collaboration at which we aim. Our public can no longer take the great characters in Shakespeare fresh, newly blazing from the mint of his mind, bursting with an astonishing revelation of undreamed power. Our audience may feel that no Hamlet, no Lear, no Cleopatra can match the individual vision which the printed page has already created for them. This is a hard challenge for the theater to meet. Moreover, the majority of our adult hearers have actually seen the great plays performed many times. They nurse ecstatic memories of Barrymore's Hamlet, or Forbes-Robertson's, or John Gielgud's, or Maurice Evans's. They remember what So-and-so looked like when he did such-and-such a thing, how a certain scene was staged, what piece of business the "comics" did at some given moment. They yearn for all these things, grown dearer with memory.

It is the actor's task to present an interpretation that is fresh, arresting, genuine, which will not imitate or consciously strive to supersede the performances of his predecessors but claim its own new life. It is the actor alone who can bridge for us all the gulfs between us and Shakespeare. As Shakespeare relied primarily and finally on the power of his characters to hold attention and arouse emotion, to project the play's content to the exclusion of all facilities or shortcomings in its physical production, so we must rely on the actor to do precisely the same thing today.

5. "These Our Actors"

IT HAS OFTEN BEEN SAID that Lear is unactable. Antony and Cleopatra have resoundingly defeated a continuous array of glittering names—and incidentally provided an equal number of play-stealing successes for the happy portrayers of Enobarbus. Yet RICHARD III, which cannot be placed anywhere near the top of Shakespeare's greatest plays and is indeed definitely among his juvenilia, was the most constant Shakespearean vehicle for all the great actors who dominated the English-speaking theater for a period of a hundred and fifty years; and Hamlet is to an English or American actor what Phèdre is to a French actress—the final test and hallmark of his stature.

We might as well admit that Shakespeare's continued appearance on the marquees of the world's theaters is due largely to the fact that he provided an array of parts which no actor can resist. By the same token, he wrote no parts which an actor sufficiently equipped cannot encompass; nor need there ever be the tug of war between the performer and the pattern of the play which for so many years practically invalidated Shakespearean productions and even caused the clumsy butcherings of Nahum Tate and Colley Cibber to be accepted as better theater vehicles than the original dramatist had himself provided.

After all, he wrote for actors. He even wrote with specific actors in his mind. He knew their limitations; and, if his driving genius sometimes led him to stretch his human material practically to snapping point, his sound theater experience never allowed him to render his fellows ridiculous. There is no valid reason to suppose that he looked upon his work as "going through the agony" of fitting his genius to the pattern of his actors, which is how some scholars regard it. Robert E. Sherwood cannot have thought that the writing of such diverse plays as REUNION IN VIENNA, IDIOT'S DELIGHT, and THERE SHALL BE NO NIGHT for the Lunts was particularly agonizing. The results have certainly proved the reverse. It was part of the Elizabethan actor's business to be flexible and various; a modern actor seldom has such opportunities to practice the varied facets of his art as was enjoyed by Shakespeare and his company. The standard of the "original" productions seems to have been remarkably high, though it is hard to judge from contemporary criticism just how a modern audience would view them.

The standard requirements of a good actor have, however, never been more succinctly put than by Shakespeare himself in Hamlet's famous speeches to the Players. They could be learned by heart by every acting student today with profit to everybody concerned. Heywood in 1612 writes a similarly valid discourse on the art of acting, going back to Roman times for his initial authority. He then continues: "A delivery and sweet action is the gloss and beauty of any discourse that belongs to a scholar, and this is the action behoveful in any that profess this quality: not to use any impudent or forced motion in any part of the body, nor rough or other violent gesture, nor on the contrary to stand like a stiff starched man, but to qualify everything according to the nature of the person personated; for in overreaching tricks, and toying too much in the anticke habits of humours, men of the . . . best reputations may break into the most violent absurdities."

This does not sound very much like the "ham" method with which so many great actors of the past are charged. This fear of being "ham" is the bogey of the modern actor, trained to a tradition of Anglo-Saxon self-consciousness coupled with a reticent "reserve" which is too often barren of anything to reserve. When an actor rises to the greatness of his vision with the full armory of his physical powers, that, if his vision be great enough, is genius. When his physical prowess outruns the fervor and truth of his vision, ceases to be any sort of impersonation, and becomes merely the actor on parade, then we may call him a "ham."

We may accept that the Elizabethan style of acting was much fuller and physically freer than ours. It was an open-air style, deriving at only one remove from the days of the inn yard, with all its free-and-easy crudities, let alone the competition of any and every street noise or neighboring activity. Shakespeare's company, still, let us remember, playing in the open air, must have used a broad and vigorous method. In the plays themselves are strong hints for us. Regan knits her brows and bites her lips; Katherine is exhorted by Petruchio not to "look big, nor stamp nor swear nor fret," an implied stage direction with which the Shrew of today somewhat apologetically complies. In TROILUS AND CRESSIDA, there is a reference to the actor who

> _____ . . . thinks it rich
> To hear the wooden dialogue and sound
> Twixt his stretched footing and the scaffoldage;

and Hamlet, putting in his evidence as usual, directs the Players not to "saw the air too much" with their hands, and says of the Player King that, given the cue for passion,

> . . . he would drown the stage with tears,
> And cleave the general ear with horrid speech,
> Make mad the guilty and appal the free,
> Confound the ignorant, and amaze indeed
> The very faculty of eyes and ears.

Vocally, Elizabethan actors were both fuller and faster than we are; it is not simply the evidence of ROMEO AND JULIET's "two hours' traffic of our stage" or HENRY VIII's "two short hours" which leads us to suppose this. The very medium of Shakespeare's verse commands it; he uses it, constantly, for speed and force and pressure, for the shading of comedy, as swift and delicate as shot silk, for verbal thrust and parry which has no counterpart today in what has been called "typewriting dialogue."

Almost the first thing a modern actor finds about playing Shakespeare is that he hasn't enough breath; he takes refuge, at first, in end-stopping the verse and in splitting the prose clean against the mathematical involution of its phrasing. Later he develops a diaphragm which is the despair of his tailors and finally makes of his voice the flexible and resonant instrument which Shakespeare's verse and prose absolutely demand. He still cannot, unfortunately, re-create his audiences' ears, dulled and slow of hearing from neglect of theater listening. He has therefore to speak more slowly than would have been necessary with an Elizabethan public.

The evolution of Shakespeare's use of verse for the predominantly dramatic purpose to which he was forging his weapons must have involved a similar progression in his actors' power to use it. When Shakespeare first wrote, or rewrote, HENRY VI for them, there can have been no one in the company who could have made very good sense of his later verse. They were used to such good straightforward cursing as York's:

> She-wolf of France, but worse than wolves of France,
> Whose tongue more poisons than the adder's tooth!
> How ill-beseeming is it in thy sex
> To triumph like an Amazonian trull,
> Upon their woes whom fortune captivates!
> But that thy face is, vizard-like, unchanging,
> Made impudent by use of evil deeds,
> I would assay, proud Queen, to make thee blush.

which he then assays for a further thirty lines straight. But it is questionable whether Burbage could have then spoken, and certain that Shakespeare could not then have written, the self-tortured frenzy of a jealous man, such as Leontes':

> You my lords,
> Look on her, mark her well; be but about
> To say "she is a goodly lady," and
> The justice of your hearts will thereto add
> " 'Tis pity she's not honest, honourable:"
> Praise her but for this, her without-door form,
> (Which on my faith deserves high speech) and straight
> The shrug, the hum or ha (these pretty hands
> That Calumny doth use; O, I am out,
> That mercy does, for calumny will sear
> Virtue itself:) these shrugs, these hums, and ha's,
> When you have said "she's goodly," come between
> Ere you can say "she's honest:" but be't known,
> (From him that has most cause to grieve it should be,)
> She's an adultress.

Shakespeare does not despise Marlowe's thunder. Who could underrate the ringing music of Tamburlaine's lament for Zenocrate, with its recurrent diapason, or the majestic march of:

> Raise cavalieros higher than the clouds,
> Batter the shining palace of the sun,
> And shiver all the starry firmament.

Certainly not the actors, whose voices were trained and accustomed to its orchestral quality. But Shakespeare, for the first time in English, evolves the use of verse as a medium for the delineation of character.

All through the plays he gives the orator his chance; with Henry V's "Once more unto the breach, dear friends," with the earlier Antony's "Friends, Romans, countrymen," right through to Timon and Lear and Coriolanus. And, Heaven help us, the elocutionists have not failed to take advantage of their opportunities.

But what comes to be increasingly important is not so much the lungs and the larynx, as the heart and the head. Actors do not, however, need long pauses in which to do their thinking and feeling, laboriously to drag up an emotion from about knee level, or conscientiously to let us see the workings of a Machiavellian mind. There is such an infinite variety of stress, phrase, pause, and emphasis in Shakespeare's writing that they will find the framework of their thinking exactly planned and provided for. But they do need clear heads to keep the motif, the thought line, of a long speech clearly held through the lavish involution of metaphor and elaboration with which Shakespeare will surround it.

Take Titania's defiance to Oberon which begins:

> These are the forgeries of jealousy:
> And never, since the middle summer's spring,
> Met we on hill, in dale, forest or mead,
> By paved fountain, or by rushy brook,
> Or in the beached margent of the sea,
> To dance our ringlets to the whistling wind,
> But with thy brawls thou hast disturbed our sport.
> Therefore the winds, piping to us in vain,
> As in revenge, have suck'd up, from the sea,
> Contagious fogs; . . .

The whole speech, another twenty-five lines of intricate and exquisite imagery, leads to:

> And this same progeny of evils comes
> From our debate, from our dissension; . . .

The actress must in each case remember the nails of argument from which the web of elaboration hangs: "And never . . . met we . . . but with thy brawls thou hast disturbed our sport. Therefore . . ." nature has been variously uprooted, because of "our debate, our dissension." It is fatal to get so lost in poetic fantasy that the audience is conscious only of a lot of pretty words which do not seem to make much sense.

Speeches such as these will find out for the actor how much breath he needs. Take Portia's speech when Bassanio chooses the leaden casket:

> How all the other passions fleet to air,
> As doubtful thoughts, and rash-embraced despair,
> And shudd'ring fear, and green-eyed jealousy!
> O love! be moderate! allay thy ecstasy!
> In measure rein thy joy, scant this excess!
> I fear too much thy blessing! make it less
> For fear I surfeit.

To linger lovingly and colorfully over "doubtful" and "rash-embraced" and "shudd'ring" and "jealousy," or to pause for breath at every comma, is to destroy entirely the very feel, the rush and wind, of ecstasy. It is always necessary to pick out the key words and to subordinate the less important ones which connect them. One director I know gives his actors the excellent advice: "Write out the speech as if it were a Western Union telegram. Then you won't have to pay for the inessentials."

The actor will need more than technical facility when he comes to think, really think, through the King's prayer speech in HAMLET. Seldom has a "villain" been given so lucid a piece of self-revelation, so supple in expression that we are hardly aware until afterward how completely Claudius has laid bare the conflict in his soul, doubts and scruples which are not so very far removed from Hamlet's own, until their bitter resolution at the end of the scene where Claudius finally puts aside compunction and hesitation. This is not an aria; it is the revelation of a subtle mind and of a soul more deeply troubled and afraid than Claudius himself had realized. The force and clarity of an actor's thinking will alone make it clear to an audience.

There are, however, lyric passages in Shakespeare which will be destroyed if clear thinking results in commonplace speaking. Thought takes wings—just as in the Chinese theater, which provides us with yet another analogy, song is used to replace speech in order to lift the audience to a different, less realistic plane of emotion. Shakespeare's imagery, his wealth of metaphor and word fantasias, often perform a similar function. The heart and passion of the lines is often conveyed in terms of sheer musical sound and harmony. Their power to stir the emotion of the hearer lies in rhythm and music, just as the dictionary meaning of the phrase expresses its intellectual content. Take, for instance, Viola's famous reply to Olivia's "Why, what would you?"

> Make me a willow cabin at your gate,
> And call upon my soul within the house;
> Write loyal cantons of contemned love
> And sing them loud even in the dead of night;
> Halloo your name to the reverberate hills,
> And make the babbling gossip of the air
> Cry out 'Olivia!' O, you should not rest
> Between the elements of air and earth,
> But you should pity me!

It cannot be maintained, after logical analysis, that this course of action would be particularly likely to win the lady.

But as pure music it is enchanting. It casts a spell over Olivia, as it should over the several hundred eavesdroppers in the auditorium. It is one of the passages of poetic truth for which the actor needs to be, as Ellen Terry put it, "in a state of grace." Prospero's speech, "Our revels now are ended," is such another. Here a beautiful voice will not do; clear analysis will not suffice either: the actor must match his author in comprehension and vision.

It is difficult, indeed impossible, to deal with verse, the wedded element of music and feeling, in the dry analysis of print. Almost at once we are in the larger realm not only of music but of character and interpretative understanding. Generalizations about verse speaking can be challenged at every point; the method of dry dissection, pulling the lines apart and pinning them down with a laborious and largely incomprehensible system of dots and dashes and hieroglyphs for stress and pause, will get us conscientiously nowhere. The actor must read the lines with his eyes and his ears, his heart and his mind, till they have come to be a part of him, till he can express their meaning in no other possible way. He must then clear from his own consciousness all the cluttering egotisms either of arrogance or fear. He must not take pride in his own fine-sounding chest notes nor reduce the more poetic flights to a trivial level of common sense. Only then can Shakespeare fill his heart and speak the immortal music through his lips.

The art of speaking Shakespeare's comedy requires from a modern actor a lucid brilliance which, also, he is not completely trained to give. It, too, requires speed of thought and great precision of enunciation if it is to be easy to hear and understand without falling into the trap of apparent effort. Shakespeare seems to have had trouble with his clowns and, as in his serious plays, came slowly to his own mature ease of touch. He found a tradition of clowning which has been, and still is, the hallmark of all the great mime clowns from the days of Aristophanes to those of Charlie Chaplin. A German stage direction of the period says:

"John Pansser comes in, wondrously clad; not clownishly, but venerably and honorably yet so that there is something to laugh at. He takes his hat off, bows to all four corners of the stage, clears his throat, wanders around a long time, and when that raises a laugh, he laughs too and waves his hands."

Good. Mr. Wynn or Mr. Clark could follow that direction today and still "raise a laugh."

Will Kemp was the Shakespearean exponent of the tradition. He was equipped with a number of sure tricks, allied to the mime method of the Commedia dell' Arte. Like Mr. Chaplin, he wore enormous slippers and had funny feet. All through theater history there seems to have been something funny about feet. Very soon Shakespeare was to find himself falling over Will Kemp's feet, for, very early in his career, his comic characters round themselves out into a deeper and more gentle humor.

He starts, modestly enough, in HENRY VI, PART II, with the armorer and his apprentice involved in a treason trial to be decided by personal combat:

FIRST NEIGHBOUR: Here, neighbour Horner, I drink to you in a cup of sack; and fear not, neighbour, you shall do well enough.

SECOND NEIGHBOUR: And here, neighbour, here's a cup of charneco.

THIRD NEIGHBOUR: And here's a pot of good double beer, neighbour: drink, and fear not your man.

HORNER: Let it come, i' faith, and I'll pledge you all, and a fig for Peter!

FIRST 'PRENTICE: Here, Peter, I drink to thee, and be not afraid.

SECOND 'PRENTICE: Be merry, Peter, and fear not thy master: fight for the credit of the 'prentices.

PETER: I thank you all: drink, and pray for me, I pray you, for

I think I have taken my last draught in this world. Here, Robin, an if I die, I give thee my apron: and, Will, thou shalt have my hammer; and here, Tom, take all the money that I have. O Lord bless me! I pray God! for I am never able to deal with my master, he hath learnt so much fence already.

SALISBURY: Come, leave your drinking, and fall to blows. Sirrah, what's thy name?

PETER: Peter, forsooth.

SALISBURY: Peter? what more?

PETER: Thump.

SALISBURY: Thump? then see thou thump thy master well.

Elementary, but serviceable. Then comes Horner's last challenge and the direction: "They fight, and Peter strikes him down." A good time is had by all, except Horner, who confesses and dies. York comments dryly: "Take away his weapon. Fellow, thank God, and the good wine in thy master's way."

But the tradition of verbal comedy, elegant and witty phrase spinning, was also at work in the Elizabethan theater, stemming from John Lyly, the author of *Euphues*. Shakespeare, young and feeling his power, determined to be as fashionable as the brightest of the university wits, devotes a whole play to the euphuistic form in LOVE'S LABOUR'S LOST. The characters bandy repartee like tennis players; the grace and precision of it are enchanting in themselves. But he is already writing with his heart, and his "comics," as well as his court ladies and gentlemen, warm constantly into a simpler truth. In the last scene Biron, supreme phrase maker among them all, speaks, perhaps, for Shakespeare:

> Taffeta phrases, silken terms precise,
> Three-piled hyperboles, spruce affectation,
> Figures pedantical, these summer-flies
> Have blown me full of maggot ostentation:
> I do foreswear them, . . .

He confesses, however, that he has yet "a trick of the old rage
. . . I'll leave it by degrees."

Shakespeare leaves it by degrees, never entirely. He splits
the two traditions into endless fragments, until the "Clown"
line of parts, as his contemporaries understood it, is gone,
divided among a dozen human elements: folly, stupidity,
humble service, bitter jesting with a sword behind the words;
high, zestful living, and pathos and pure song. Sometimes,
in the period which includes MEASURE FOR MEASURE, TROILUS
AND CRESSIDA, TIMON OF ATHENS, and ALL'S WELL THAT ENDS
WELL, there is satire and contempt and a savage disgust behind
Shakespeare's fooling. He loses, for a time, the sanity and
proportion of healthy laughter. But he comes back to it, and
with the light-feathered arrows of Autolycus brings us to the
unmalicious laughter of Stephano and Ariel's gossamer farewell.

Always the actor must first ask himself what kind of man
this "comic" is. The jokes may, some of them, have grown
"pittiful drie, pittiful drie" to us who cannot appreciate what
was once their young and daring novelty of technique or
apprehend the sting of their topicality. Sometimes the very
cadence of the line will still "get the laugh," as in Maria's
description of Malvolio smiling his face "into more lines than
is in the new map with the augmentation of the Indies." Sometimes the joke has obvious reference to some piece of stage
business, which we must conjecture or devise. Probably Sir
Andrew's commendation to Feste, "why, this is the best fooling when all's done," was motivated by what Feste did, rather
than by what he said.

But more often the humor is dependent on an interplay of
personality rather than on a verbal twist or a trick of "business." I have seen even the impossibly complicated "sorel"
scene from LOVE'S LABOUR'S LOST warmed into human and
understandable comedy through the humanity and lovable

quality of the actors who played Sir Nathaniel and Holo-
fernes. For the richness of comedy inherent in human beings
has not changed, and on this we must primarily rely. The
elements of great clowning have not changed much either,
and sometimes the director will be saved because a smiling
heaven delivers into his hands one of those rare actors who
can be funny by simply coming on and saying the alphabet.
But such great clowns have never been vouchsafed us on a
mass-production basis; and there may well come a time when
the blue pencil is, after all, our only weapon.

This will bring down on us the wrath of the professors,
but it may save our audiences some stretches where lack of
understanding would force them into a shuffling inattentive-
ness that is our greatest dread. We must, of course, be careful not to dislocate the delicate rhythm of a scene or even
an individual speech, not to underrate the value of "business," but above all not to overload the scene with an excessive
mass of it, which will slow us up and drive a heavy wedge
between the interlacing lines.

We shall depend very greatly on the actors themselves. We
cannot cut from theory. We must wait to hear how the lines
sound and what the actors will make of them. Some cuts
which we have considered possible may go back; others will
have to be made in order to ease matters for an actor who
simply cannot get over the hurdle in question. It is too optimistic to suppose that any production will find itself armed
with a full complement of ideal comedians; and, with respect
to the scholars, it is unwise and stubborn to insist on keeping
in a joke that the actor cannot make funny, even though
the fault be his and not Shakespeare's.

There is, for me, no question but that the "comedies" are
much harder to produce today than the "tragedies." The
balance between wit, fooling, low comedy, and poetic fantasy
is an extraordinarily delicate one. The blue pencil is a two-

edged weapon; the effort to substitute a stylized convention for the plainer human elements can be, when it's good, very, very good; but when it's bad, it's horrid, as the old rhyme says. "Simpleness and duty," however, will go a long way, and we had much better not be too self-conscious about it. Let us above all think the comedy, and the people who carry it, freshly, in terms of today, and make them recognizable human beings to our modern public.

There remains one means of dramatic expression which is generally strange to a modern actor—the soliloquy. As with all his dramatic tools, Shakespeare takes it over as a ready-to-wear device by which the plot may be advanced and characters may tell the audience things which everybody else in the play already knows, while loquaciously announcing their own further intentions. As with his development of other technical devices, he soon makes of the soliloquy a far more eloquent weapon than that. The noble figureheads of HENRY VI recite at us, much as they recite at each other. But Richard III uses the freedom of his monologues to much greater dramatic purpose; he takes us into his confidence with such assurance, such gleeful power, that we are his, villainy and all, right through the play. Even his use of the apostrophe

> Shine out, fair sun, till I have bought a glass,
> That I may see my shadow, as I pass,

emphasizes for us the self-appointed world in which Richard has his being, where no creature moves except in reflected light and nothing is absolute but his own will. We accept that this monstrous superman will recount to himself aloud his own schemes and celebrate his own triumphs for us to overhear, because none but we, in our all-knowing dimension, could possibly comprehend him. His soliloquies are a poetic extension of what Kipling reduced to the formula of every schoolboy in Stalky's "I gloat! I gloat! hear me!"

By the time Shakespeare reaches Iago, the formula has changed; but still it is the villain who most needs the device of self-revelation, not the hero, who will command our emotional response without any such assistance. And again with Iago, Shakespeare is reveling in the mastery of such a man; he cannot get himself to hate Iago, and neither must we. The man has stature, in his own right; he is no piece of mechanism, part of the impersonal machinery of malice; if we were to think that, we should belittle Othello, and the tragedy of the play would be totally diminished. Iago's fascination for us lies just in that smooth, flawless functioning of the mind, which is yet so fatally flawed because it cannot conceive of a power greater than the power of the intellect. Edmund, in KING LEAR, is the play's chief soliloquizer. The dash and daring of his first outburst, his hand against all the smug conventions of society, his analysis of them so brilliantly specious, will carry us most unmorally with him throughout the play.

In RICHARD II, Shakespeare is beginning to feel his way toward a new device: the blending of the true soliloquy with the interwoven reactions of the other characters. Richard has a long series of exquisite cadenza speeches, but only the last, in the solitary confinement of his prison, is a true soliloquy. Each time he turns to his hearers at the end of his lyric self-analyses, the thread of his self-revelation is knotted to the progression of their understanding of him. So, after his salutation to his kingdom's earth, he links the speech to the scene with "Mock not my senseless conjuration, lords"; after the virtual soliloquy of "Let's talk of graves, of worms and epitaphs," he turns again to them with "Cover your heads, and mock not flesh and blood with solemn reverence"; and, after his speech to the looking glass in the deposition scene, he draws Bolingbroke back into the current of his thought with the gravely bitter comment:

Mark, silent king, the moral of this sport,
How soon my sorrow hath destroyed my face.

The soliloquy reaches its greatest flexibility and glory in HAMLET, where it is so apparently an integral part of the character Shakespeare was creating that any dissertation on its use would be redundant. He does not subsequently pursue this method of introspection because he is not writing another Hamlet. His later heroes, the men of action, Antony and Coriolanus, are in no need of it; and he has, by now, found twenty other ways of dealing with the establishment of a motive or the advancement of the story. Caliban will need it briefly, grumbling to himself as he sullenly trudges about his work; Autolycus will belong to the long line of liaison-commentators, his "Ha! what a fool Honesty is! and Trust, his sworn brother, a very simple gentleman!" chiming with the echo of Falstaff's soliloquy: "Well, 'tis no matter, honour pricks me on. Yea, but how if honour prick me off when I come on?"

In CYMBELINE, almost all of the soliloquies partake of the new artifice and objectivity, the masquelike quality, with which Shakespeare is experimenting in his last plays. But Iachimo has a long, whispered monologue in Imogen's bedroom, which is economically revealing and put into words of intricate loveliness; and Imogen herself will take us to her heart, if she is true and tender, as few of the heroines have done since Juliet's day.

It is a curious fact that Shakespeare's women are not nearly so confiding as his men; it is tempting to generalize from their wariness to their author's opinion of womankind—tempting, but probably misleading. Julia, in THE TWO GENTLEMEN OF VERONA, tells us directly a little; Juliet, most of all. Afterward we receive occasional confidences from Viola and Helena —a few words only from Beatrice. The rest talk to their waiting maids a great deal, and Cleopatra sets up a hundred mirrors for her infinite variety. But only Lady Macbeth, most particularly herself and akin to no other woman in the plays, reveals herself by soliloquy first, and last by the broken fragments of nightmare.

The actress of today is divided from Shakespeare by a crevasse of which the scholars have been apt to make too much and theater people possibly too little; by the fact that his heroines were originally played not by women but by boys. It is easy to see what Shakespeare refrained from doing because of this limitation, if such he considered it, but not so easy to define what positive effect it had on the great women's parts.

He did not write many women of middle age or more. Early in his career he poured color and facile invective into Queen Margaret and gave some tragic music to Constance in KING JOHN. But only rarely did he attempt physical passion for any but a young woman. Cleopatra is the blazing exception, and she is a law unto herself. The passion of Lady Macbeth is translated into an obsession, an evil fanaticism which burns like white-hot metal. She has no love scenes, in the ordinary sense of the term, to embarrass the boy player. The Queen in HAMLET is the only notable example of a middle-aged woman in love.

There are, of course, some comedy women in the prime of life, such as Juliet's Nurse, Mistress Ford, and Mistress Page. There is a beautifully tender old woman in the Countess of Rossillion and one of the high, heroic mold in Volumnia. There are Hermione and Paulina in THE WINTER'S TALE and Katherine in HENRY VIII. The last four all appear in plays he wrote toward the end of his career, and they are all fine parts. None of them is beyond a boy actor's power; but if it is true, as some scholars believe, that the "character" women were played by men and not by boys, one may speculate as to whether this practice was on the increase during Shakespeare's later years, or whether he was becoming more confident of his boys' ability to portray women of maturer years. In any case, however, he never returned to a woman in the prime of life who, like Gertrude, was sexually in love. This was evidently dangerous ground.

The passionate purity of young love is Juliet's, and the boy actor could understand and portray it. Yet even here there is little physical contact between the two lovers; the balcony scene is one of the greatest love scenes ever written, and yet Romeo can do no more than touch her finger tips. When they meet at Laurence's cell to be married, their encounter is touched by a grave and wondering ecstasy, as if the miracle of their love were fragile and enshrined. Their parting, after passion, is all we see of physical contact between them. Shakespeare must have had in mind the weakness of his boy actor, but he derived from it a beauty and a poignant, ephemeral quality which nothing could have bettered.

It was harder for him to write for boys on the lines of:

> Rebellious hell,
> If thou canst mutine in a matron's bones,

and poor Gertrude is given practically no opportunity to show the sensual side of her love for Claudius. Yet what actress could better the image that we shall conjure up for ourselves from the "glass" that Hamlet sets up for her and us, the vivid, unsparing:

> Let the bloat king tempt you again to bed,
> Pinch wanton on your cheek, call you his mouse,
> And let him, for a pair of reechy kisses,
> Or paddling in your neck with his damned fingers,
> Make you to ravel all this matter out . . .

It is in Cleopatra that actresses have been most continually deceived. The very name registers sex appeal. Sex appeal is instantly sought and monotonously pursued in every modern production; and, as Cleopatras get born only once in several generations and, when they do, are, in their own right, people who make history, the actress of today usually fails to measure up to the comparison. But Shakespeare did not write Cleopatra in terms of spurious glamour and kisses close-up size. She is as elusive as mercury; she gleams like light reflected from the facets of a diamond, flashing and shifting in infinite variety. The boy actor could accomplish all this and bewilder his audience into a fascinated acceptance. They would not notice, they do not notice, that there is not one passionate love scene between Antony and Cleopatra which would be thought worthy of any B picture produced by Hollywood.

The modern actress could do it, too, and better, if she would try to play Shakespeare's Cleopatra instead of a Victorian oleograph of the same character, as flat and gaudy and unbelievable. She would also be helped if directors would remember that it is the setting which shows off the stone. Cleopatra is framed by the solid, carved mounting of the Roman wars and the Roman world. Shakespeare was not simply writing a straightforward love story; we shall wreck the powerful rhythm of the play if we so handle it and wreck the lovers into the bargain.

The memory of the boy actor and his probable achievements will help us to interpret many of Shakespeare's other heroines as he must have thought them. There are no sloppy, boneless, blonde milksops, wistfully bleating out their loves and sorrows. Perhaps this might be regarded as a malicious description of Ophelia; but, if so, she is serving a definite dramatic purpose. If she had been a woman of character and understanding, a Viola or a Portia, there would be no tragedy of Hamlet.

Desdemona is a young woman who has the strength of mind to marry a man from a different race and country, a "black" man, and to brave first her father's fury and then the possible censure of the whole Venetian Senate. Her lie about the handkerchief is not the lie of a spineless little ninny, scared out of her wits. The motive which prompts it is positive, if it is not wise or particularly admirable. She can face Othello and repeat the lie, more strongly, and a few moments later reason her love into forgiveness for his strange behavior and into strength to stand "within the blank of his displeasure" again, for Cassio's sake.

It is regrettable but, I fear, true that every woman will understand very easily just how Desdemona is trapped into denying the loss of the handkerchief in the hope of saving Othello's trust and love. The boy actor, as I guess, must have stood up very straight and young, without any whimpering or cringing, and said his "I say it is not lost" clearly to Othello's eyes.

Cordelia, of course, is plain downright obstinate, as obstinate as Lear himself; but she is drawn with a simplicity and firmness that make the tenderness of her last meeting with her father noble in its humility. The heroines of the great comedies are full and clear; the modern actress is in no difficulty, unless she is tempted to put too much sugar in the mixture.

But we have a great tendency to prettify the heroines of the last plays—Perdita and Miranda and Marina. It is true that Miranda shares with some of her predecessors the regrettable tendency to demonstrate her strength by insisting on loving a man her father professes to dislike. Shakespeare's heroines are, from a paternal point of view, most constantly perverse in their affections. But Miranda, fresh and tender as the first curled leaves of spring, is by no means a half-wit. Perdita, delicate as a snowdrop, is no less strong; Marina stands up in the brothel to which she has been sold and talks to its inmates like a mixture of St. Joan and Mrs. Grundy. She would become almost Shavian if Shakespeare gave her a chance; but he transports her swiftly to the meeting with her lost father and delivers her to a scene of music and dream. There, too, he gives to Pericles a description which may speak for all these "golden girls" of his last plays, who seem to stand forever in the dawn. He seems to see in them the heartbreaking gallantry of youth on the threshold of the world, and to draw from their grave tenderness the comfort that he needs, after the storms and tempests that he, like Pericles, has endured:

> My dearest wife was like this maid, and such a one
> My daughter might have been; my queen's square brows;
> Her stature to an inch; as wand-like straight,
> As silver-voiced, her eyes as jewel-like,
> And cas'd as richly, in pace another Juno;
> Who starves the ears she feeds, and makes them hungry,
> The more she gives them speech . . .
> Falseness cannot come from thee, for thou look'st
> Modest as Justice, and thou seem'st a palace
> For the crown'd Truth to dwell in: I will believe thee.

The frequency with which the heroines disguise themselves as boys does not help us, as it helped Shakespeare's original Violas and Rosalinds. In fact there are a few places where we are in bad trouble. Rosalind's epilogue, her "if I were a woman . . ." becomes nonsense, because she is; we are apt to think Orsino and Olivia really remarkably dull of eye and ear in not recognizing our modern Viola's very apparent womanhood; and Orlando, Proteus, Posthumus, and Bassanio become credulous to the point of absurdity, in the opinion of the literal-minded.

But if we cast the right spell, Shakespeare's spell, in AS YOU LIKE IT and TWELFTH NIGHT and CYMBELINE, we should dissipate all tendency to literal-mindedness in the world of fantasy and music which we shall create, a world in which a man may thankfully consent to "still his beating mind" and surrender to a dimension which is rich and strange. After all, we gratefully agree not to quarrel with the hypothesis that Lord Fancourt Babberly could continuously persuade an entire collection of assorted individuals into the unshaken belief that he is Charley's Aunt from Brazil where the nuts come from. Compared with this camel, Cesario and Ganymede are gnats indeed.

In one instance we are, it seems to me, in a particular difficulty with our woman heroine, and that is with Isabella in MEASURE FOR MEASURE, admittedly a difficult heroine in a difficult but fascinating play. It is hard for a woman, especially if her personal quality conveys to us a fulfilled woman, to prevent Isabella's refusal to save her brother by yielding to Angelo from seeming a piece of selfish wrong-headedness, arising from a sense of values so distorted that we lose sympathy with her. The boy actor must have had, in some sense, an easier time in conveying Isabella's whole-souled, nearly fanatical, passion of chastity.

As is most usual in Shakespeare, the emotion is positive, not negative. Isabella's outburst in the prison, when she turns on Claudio and furiously reproaches him for the suggestion that death is a worse fate for him than a night with Angelo would be for her, was not, as I think Shakespeare's boy played it, a pathological inhibition; it was the outburst of a young spirit, as passionately in love with chastity as a young knight keeping vigil before the altar before he received the accolade. There should be something forlornly splendid about it, "her face and will athirst against the light"; there must be no denial, but rather a fervent affirmation. The actress of today can play this and play it with added poignancy because of her womanhood, but only if she can give us the searing purity of flame.

It has been generally accepted that the employment of boy actors must have been a very limiting factor in the Elizabethan theater. We are perhaps too apt to think of them as coltish choirboys, lacking in style or grace. The evidence is against this view. It is even possible that, if the closing of the theaters during the Cromwellian regime had not interrupted the training of boys for the stage, the convention might have lasted much longer. In China, it has lasted down to the present day, though the great imperial training school of the Pear Orchard is no more, and women are gradually ousting the male actors of female parts.

It is interesting to observe the several respects in which the English theater at its beginning paralleled the dramatic conventions which have endured in China. We have seen that its freedom in space and time was very similar; and, from the playing of Chinese actors trained to impersonate women, we may glean something of what Shakespeare's boys, apprenticed from childhood to the same task, could accomplish. Those who were privileged to see the performances of Mr. Mei-Lan-Fang in America will remember the exquisite grace of his playing. Occidental actresses might well envy the truth of quality which he brought to his heroines, whether it was in seductiveness, ardor, simplicity, or passion.

Shakespeare's boys, of course, had no such tradition, worn smooth by centuries of observance, as lay behind Mr. Mei. They were a formative part of a theater still plastic, still feeling its way. Nor did they continue to play women after they themselves attained manhood and could therefore never have brought to their parts the mature comprehension of the Chinese actor. But, if they reflected any part of such perfected art as informed Mr. Mei's acting, they must have given performances which fully encompassed the glorious parts which Shakespeare wrote for them. They were, as he was, dedicated to the theater. We should not make the mistake of appraising them as schoolboys forced self-consciously into long skirts.

The importance of one section of the Shakespearean company is apt to be much underestimated today, and that is the silent actors, the "Lords, Officers, Gentlemen and Servants," the "Attendants and others," those who only stand and wait. Many important scenes are critically dependent upon them. The end-of-the-play revelations, the unravelings of the plot which we have seen worked out before our eyes, will fall very flat except in so far as we can see them mirrored in the emotions of the listeners. At the beginning of the plays, the lineless actors must often establish for us the atmosphere that surrounds our principals, the state of "public opinion." What elements in the community approved of Richard II, what sort of people disliked or mistrusted him, and why? Over what kind of court did Lear rule that he should have become the kind of ruler that he was?

In John Barrymore's HAMLET, the curtain rose on the court of Elsinore in blackness. Before the lights came on, the whispering of the courtiers standing grouped around the throne made itself audible; then, gradually, the light grew, picking out Gertrude and Claudius, and Hamlet, coiled in his chair, tense as a spring. The courtiers gradually hushed, and Claudius turned to them with the smooth facility of:

> Though yet of Hamlet, our dear brother's death
> The memory be green . . .

It sounds simple, but it took a lot of rehearsing, because the junior Equity members standing around in the blackout had to register by their whisperings that this was, to use Mr. Barrymore's phrase, "a very lecherous court." Now, that took some acting. It was the harder because it is extremely difficult for modern actors to extemporize in blank verse; and when they do try, an irresistible tendency to laugh overcomes everybody present. But it is equally dangerous when they express themselves in modern phraseology, which is apt to shatter some unexpected silence with a crash of anachronism. Once, while watching a performance of my production of HENRY IV,

I was appalled to hear members of Hotspur's army cheering each other on with the blood-curdling slogan "Art and Mrs. Bottle!"; to which the King's troops yelled back defiantly "Susan and God!"

It is of vital importance that the director should provide for every member of his "crowd" a consistent line of individuality, which the actor can follow out in its relation to every situation as it arises while he is on the stage. In scenes where an appreciable amount of audible comment is required from the lookers-on, I have even found it desirable to write the necessary words for each of them. Only in this way could I be sure of getting the right reaction from everyone and of securing a "sound-track" of the right length and audible value. I built the phrases and exclamations, of course, from words or lines out of the text. This frees the actors from self-consciousness and obviates the danger of excessive zeal, when some over-eager "Lord" or "Lady" is left to "cleave the general ear with horrid" and solo "speech." The Forum Scene in JULIUS CAESAR is a case in point. Some lines are actually written in the text; but the subsidiary ones cannot be left to the haphazard and variable invention of the minor crowd members. The psychology and orchestration of the scene are, alike, of much too great importance. But even in less obvious cases it is always essential to maintain the aliveness of the crowd. A blank-minded bystander, even one, may fatally destroy the temper and excitement of an entire scene.

It is hard for us to know, to conjure up a true picture of what the great actors of the past were like, because the innermost quality of acting, the emotional relation between actor and audience, defies printed analysis. When we read that to watch Edmund Kean play Lear and Richard III was "to read Shakespeare by flashes of lightning," we get a vivid picture of Kean's quality; but we do not really know to what extent he would move us, or how. The actor's instrument is himself, incommunicable by any alternate medium.

It is easy, in commenting on an actor's performance, to spin destructive phrases that will raise an easy laugh. Sometimes such comments do succeed in teaching us by contraries. When Shaw remarks of a Rosalind that "that dainty, pleading, narrow-lipped little torrent of gabble will not do for Shakespeare," or that a Mercutio "lounges, mumbles and delivers the Queen Mab speech in a raffish patter which takes . . . all beauty of tone and grace of measure out of it," he is not being solely destructive. We get some idea of what *will* do for Mercutio and Rosalind; more, perhaps, than a handful of superlatives would teach us.

We have old prompt copies and contemporary descriptions from which we can gather the traditional business and tangible framework with which productions of the past were surrounded; but the essence, which is all that matters, escapes us. A tradition sometimes has the hallmark of tested validity; more often it is deadwood. Those with which we are familiar should not be accepted or rejected wholesale in accordance with a general principle. Many times the powerful influence of time-honored theater values will lead us to follow our predecessors more closely than we ourselves have realized. Many times, I believe, they may bring us very close indeed to the Globe Theatre of three hundred years ago.

I do not mistrust actors, when their hearts and minds are engaged in their work. I do not accept as valid the commonly received idea that a star actor will automatically distort a play unless somebody stops him. Shakespeare has a way of bringing the best out of his fellows if they come to him with fresh and honest minds directly brought to bear on the task of interpreting him with integrity.

Many great scholars, men of letters, and poets have left us

the fruits of their study of his people and his plays. Mark Van Doren has recently written an appraisal of the plays which cannot but light candles in our minds. We shall be unwise to reject, as we so often do, the stimulus which Shakespeare critics can provide for us. But in the last analysis the actor must face his Hamlet, or her Juliet, alone.

There is not one "right" Hamlet, with all the others wrong. Shakespeare allows his actors a greater margin of interpretation than can possibly be pinioned by any single mind. He wrote to be interpreted, not to lay down a system of mathematics. The actor must use his own physical powers, his own mind, and his own personal quality, that essential flavor of the spirit which will insensibly pervade his performance despite miracles of make-up and physical assumption. It is recorded that Mrs. Siddons did not play the Lady Macbeth whom she ideally deduced from Shakespeare's text. She could not; but she absorbed her own physical assets in a totally different Lady Macbeth, not false to the text, but true to another facet of it and so powerful as to become a theater tradition for a hundred years after she died. There were probably members of the audience who said: "This is not *my* Lady Macbeth"; but it was Mrs. Siddons'; and as she, not they, was playing the part, it was in that instance the "right" Lady Macbeth.

The director of Shakespeare will be foolhardy to evolve in advance a hard and fast, detailed blueprint of his production before he has met and reckoned with his human element, the actors. He will be more than foolish to allow his pattern, Shakespeare's pattern as far as he can divine it, to be thrown out of focus by one actor's personal predilection. The theater is, we do not need to be told, a fusion of the arts. It is also a fusion of the spirit. There should be no boundaries to its vision, no barrier to the most revolutionary contribution nor to the oldest fragment of an inheritance worn smooth by time.

6. *"Unwillingly to School"*

IT IS ONLY OF RECENT YEARS that the theater has bothered itself at all about fidelity to Shakespeare's scheme. Garrick, professing his determination to "lose no drop of the immortal man," yet omitted, "very properly," as a contemporary critic thought, a great part of MACBETH, including the Porter and the "trifling, superfluous dialogue" between Lady Macduff and Ross. An extant description of Kean's RICHARD II shows how far textual patchwork could go without fear of reproof:

The scenes of Aumerle's conspiracy and the character of the Duchess are cut. In the farewell scene between the King and Queen, some lines are borrowed from the parting scene between Suffolk and Queen Margaret in HENRY VI, PART II. The scene changes to a palace. Bolingbroke speaks a short soliloquy from ANTONY AND CLEOPATRA, TROILUS AND CRESSIDA, TITUS ANDRONICUS and elsewhere. Bolingbroke concludes with a short soliloquy, the sentiments of which are quite unsuitable to his character. The last scene is laid at the Tower, instead of Pomfret Castle. After Richard is killed, the Queen enters and speaks a few lines from KING LEAR. She falls on the dead body, and Bolingbroke concludes the play.

From the Restoration until the present century, the Shakespeare texts have been continuously mangled to provide a bandwagon for the actor-managers. They are still, though for different reasons, being mutilated to suit the limitations of television or stretched to accommodate the splendors of Hollywood. Even in the theater there are still producers and directors who appear to think that they can easily improve on Shakespeare. Many of our critics have no compunction about encouraging this, as it seems to me, enviable but naive notion. A respected member of the New York critical fraternity recently accorded high commendation to a director who had seen fit to open his production of TWELFTH NIGHT with the shipwreck scene from THE TEMPEST.

These are the fantasies of self-indulgence. It is, surely, perfectly legitimate to take Shakespeare's librettos, most of which he himself lifted from somebody else in the first place, and translate them into another medium, whether into opera, as Verdi did in OTELLO, or into musical comedy like the highly entertaining KISS ME KATE. But if we are pretending to play Shakespeare in the medium for which he himself wrote, it appears to me neither sensible nor honest to substitute our notions for his on the assumption that we know his job better than he did or that our audiences are too stupid to know a fine play when they see one. If we are seriously concerned with the problems of interpreting Shakespeare himself, we must, however, devote some careful study to the texts themselves before we decide what deviations, if any, may properly be made from them.

In a book such as this, which can do no more than scratch the surface problems of Shakespearean production, there is no place for extensive textual criticism, nor am I equipped for so exact a science. Producers and directors, however, have been too apt to assume, with a relieved delegation of responsibility, that the study of textual problems merely "refrigerates the mind and diverts the thoughts from the principal study," to use Dr. Johnson's invaluable phrase. On the other hand, it is only too easy to get lost in the commentators' maze, which they can make as exciting as a "whodunit" and as relentlessly absorbing as a jigsaw puzzle.

But, if the theater is to prove itself worthy of the attention of Shakespearean students, as well as of the general public, it cannot afford completely to ignore the illuminating material which scholars such as Dr. Pollard, Dr. Greg, Dr. Dover Wilson and their successors have recently brought to light. Their general conclusions may help us too much to be tossed aside with the "what-does-it-matter" attitude generally adopted; and I believe that we in the theater have some contribution to make toward testing the validity of their assumptions through our knowledge of theater practice and our habit of theater thinking, both of which Shakespeare himself must have shared to a high degree.

Shakespeare's works as they have been preserved for us still retain "many of the shavings and splinters of the workshop sticking to them," as Professor Williams puts it. Some of the plays were published separately, in Quarto form, soon after their production in the theater. But it was not until seven years after the author's death that a collected edition of them appeared. This was the First Folio of 1623, published by his fellow-actors, Heminges and Condell. It contains all the plays now accepted as his, with the single exception of PERICLES, afterward admitted to the Third Folio as being largely his handiwork. The Folio is our sole authority for seventeen of the plays; but the remainder survive in other texts, none of which is in exact agreement with the Folio version and many of which differ widely from it. The plays for which we have more than one text may be briefly classified under three generally accepted heads:

1. Those which in the Folio have obviously been printed

directly from the earlier Quarto printing, with only minor deviations or printer's errors: TITUS ANDRONICUS, RICHARD II, RICHARD III, HENRY IV, PART I, LOVE'S LABOUR'S LOST, A MID-SUMMER NIGHT'S DREAM, THE MERCHANT OF VENICE, MUCH ADO ABOUT NOTHING, and KING LEAR.

2. Those in which the Folio prints evidently from another source, presumably an original manuscript, which, however, agrees substantially with the Quarto version: HENRY IV, PART II, TROILUS AND CRESSIDA, and OTHELLO.

3. Plays for which the earliest Quarto printing is radically different from the Folio and must obviously have been "pirated" and published without the authorization of either Shakespeare or the Globe Company: THE TAMING OF THE SHREW, HENRY VI, PART II and PART III, ROMEO AND JULIET, HENRY V, THE MERRY WIVES OF WINDSOR, and, of course, HAMLET.

HAMLET and ROMEO AND JULIET also exist in a "good" Quarto, presumably a printing authorized by the Players to replace the garbled version; these two texts are described on their respective title pages as "Newly imprinted and enlarged to almost as much againe as it was, according to the true and perfect Coppie," and "Newly corrected, augmented and amended."

It seems that the Players were reluctant to have plays printed which were still an important part of the current repertory. After they became the King's Men and were better able to put their prohibition into effect, very few Quarto printings appeared. They did not intend that the scripts should be used by any but their own company, but once in print they were liable to be appropriated by others, especially in the provinces and on the Continent.

There was no royalty system to protect the authors, though printers were able to register their publications, or intended publications, with the Stationers' Company and thus acquire a kind of copyright. It was natural that printers should try to get hold of Shakespeare's very popular plays; and, when the method of direct negotiation seemed unlikely to succeed, they tried to reproduce the text through notes taken during a performance by a system of shorthand which was even then in existence and also by bribing the actors to lend their individual parts or to help in a memorial reconstruction.

Each of the "bad" Quartos so obtained has been the subject of heated debate as to its degree of correspondence with the performance which the "reporter" saw and the degree to which that performance may be thought to have represented an earlier "tryout" version by Shakespeare of the as yet unfinished play. When Heminges and Condell finally published their Folio of the collected works they avowed their intention of providing, once and for all, a definitive text of the plays as Shakespeare wrote them:

It had bene a thing, we confesse, worthie to have bene wished, that the Author himself had liv'd to have set forth, and overseen his owne writings; But since it hath bin ordain'd otherwise, and he by death departed from that right, we pray you do not envie his Friends, the office of their care, and paine, to have collected and publish'd them; and so to have publish'd them, as where (before) you were abus'd with diverse stolne, and surreptitious copies, maimed, and deformed by the frauds and stealthes of injurious impostors, that expos'd them; even those, are now offer'd to your view cur'd, and perfect of their limbes; and all the rest, absolute in their numbers, as he conceived them.

Unfortunately, however, the Folio's compositors were unable to live up to the perfection aimed at by their employers; and of late years much weighty argument has been brought to bear in proving that the "good," *i.e.*, authorized, Quartos lie very often closer to Shakespeare's original manuscripts than the later Folio text.

Both sets of texts are subject to considerable confusion in

the very process of printing. The science was still young; the art of spelling was in an extremely formative state and, even among the most highly educated men of the day, was still liable to the most variously individual fluctuation. The hard-working compositors who tried so honestly to set up their type from the authors' extremely difficult scripts made valiant attempts at systematization and, indeed, are largely responsible for the peculiarities of spelling which the English language so confusingly displays today. Calligraphical confusion added to the compositors' woes, for handwriting still varied between the "English" script, deriving from the Anglo-Saxon, and the "Italian" hand, from which our own is taken.

Playhouse manuscripts were particularly difficult. There would generally be alternating hands, due to the several collaborating playwrights, the stage manager's notes, and even the licensor's comments. Cuts would have been made or restored, additional lines written in, or separately supplied by the author, original material transposed or deleted in handling the prompt copy for successive productions, and stage managers' directions incorporated with the authors' own. Sometimes plays were abridged for shorter, touring versions, not always with the author's consent; and, although it is extremely unlikely that Burbage would want to study a new Hamlet every few years, some refurbishings were probably thought necessary for revivals. We can also verify, from modern practices, that certain cuts might be reopened and other fresh ones made as new actors of greater or less ability came into the company. The unfortunate compositor was apt to get understandably confused between these various notations on the manuscripts, unless the author himself were on the spot to oversee the finished work.

Sometimes the printers were supplied not with the author's own manuscript but with transcripts made by a careless copyist to replace the tattered and dog-eared prompt copy; these were often the work of some theater underling who was familiar with the play from hearing it on the stage and trusted to his memory of what the actors habitually said, without troubling to check from the official script. This last source of error in the printed texts is possibly even more important than research scholars have realized. In every production, even to this day, actors unconsciously alter small words, substitute synonyms, or transpose the relative position of words and are not always corrected by the stage manager. Or they go to the author themselves and ask if they may not say "warm" instead of "hot," "because surely, my dear William, if it were really a hot afternoon, I'd never come in wearing a tweed jacket"; or they object that "this thin pretext" is a tongue twister, and can't they say "this fine pretext" instead. So the author gives his consent; but it never occurs to anybody to tell the stage manager, and the alteration is never embodied in the prompt copy. But our hypothetical copyist hears it said and embodies it in his transcript.

Theater practice is regrettably far less scientific or standardized than a scholar's thinking. Some hardy guessing based on a knowledge of its vagaries might often come closer to the truth than the carefully organized theories of the commentators but unfortunately would not be susceptible of bibliographical proof.

The theory that many of the "bad" Quartos were constructed with the help of actors' parts seems to me especially fallible. Only one actor's "part" has been preserved from Elizabethan times. The fact that there is only one is no surprise to anyone who has ever had to collect actors' parts at the end of a run. As soon as he has learned his "sides" the actor puts them down in any odd corner and forgets about them. Moreover, it seems that some of Shakespeare's actors could not read and learned by ear only, without a written part.

The only part extant belonged to the methodical Alleyn and is the lead in Greene's ORLANDO FURIOSO. It consists of small strips of paper pasted together to form a long roll, and its layout corresponds exactly to modern practice. The speeches are given in full, and the cue words are written on the right-hand side of the paper preceded by a long line. The brevity of the cues would drive a modern actor mad. Five successive ones run as follows: . . . my lord. . . . neither. . . . lord. . . . my lord. . . . lord. There are some very brief stage directions written in Alleyn's hand, usually a single word in Latin, such as "currunt," "decumbit," and, in a fight sequence, two directions spaced over the lines of a speech show at which exact point the losing combatants were to receive the coup de grâce. This would afford little data for a subsequent reconstruction of the script.

Nor is the further evidence any more convincing. For instance, in the 1st Quarto HAMLET, the actor who doubled Marcellus and Voltimand is supposed to have helped the pirate printer, for the lines allotted to these characters and the scenes in which they appear are exceptionally correct. Perhaps the written "parts" were used, but not, I think, the living actor; for if he himself did participate in the reconstruction process, we should have to conclude that he knew none of his own cues and was wholly unfamiliar with the speeches which immediately preceded his entrances and to which he must certainly have listened at every performance, for these are wildly different from the text of the authorized versions. Similarly, this same actor must have been on the stage during all the general scenes, such as the Play scene, the Graveyard, and the last scene of the play; we might reasonably expect some degree of accuracy in these sequences; yet they are incredibly badly reported. This particular actor's memory must have been extraordinarily unreliable. Yet, despite this evidence, Professor Dover Wilson goes so far as to argue that the

Folio texts for THE TWO GENTLEMEN OF VERONA and THE MERRY WIVES OF WINDSOR and parts of THE WINTER'S TALE were entirely reconstructed from actors' memories and from a collection of the acting parts, owing to the loss of the complete script.

At this, common sense utterly rebels. THE TWO GENTLEMEN OF VERONA had first been produced about twenty-eight years earlier; and, although there is evidence for later revision and revival, it seems to me completely incredible that anything approaching a full set of parts could conceivably have survived, and survived in a state clear enough or, judging from Alleyn's part, full enough to allow reconstruction of any scene comprising more than three people.

One wonders whether scholars are not partly deceived by the remarkable state of clarity in which Alleyn's Orlando part has come down to us. If it is true that two or more authors usually worked on a play and that the acting company also contributed to the final stage version, the actors' parts would undoubtedly be marked with corrections, alterations, and rewrites. It would therefore seem probable that the Alleyn example is fortuitous and not representative. We might guess that Alleyn finally got so exasperated with trying to disentangle the various alterations and additions which had been scratched all over the sheets of his part that he handed it over to "his boy, Pig," or to one of the assistant stage managers, with instructions to copy the whole thing out clean, for Heaven's sake, or how could he ever be expected to learn it?

Today plays are possibly less susceptible to alteration, especially in England, where the necessity of submitting the script to the censor, and of adhering in all important respects to the version for which license has been obtained, still parallels Elizabethan practice. Yet even so, we wonder whether research professors have ever seen a set of actors' parts, such as are left, in the state of disorganization which they have reached by the opening night. They might also be disagreeably enlightened by attending rehearsals for a revival, such as took place for the Maurice Evans RICHARD II after a three-month layoff. The difficulty is not that nobody remembers anything, but that everybody remembers, with wholehearted conviction, totally different and conflicting things.

And, with the Globe Company, we must bear in mind that they were playing daily changes of bill and continuous and extensive changes of repertoire. As the Folio was printed about thirty years after the earliest of its component texts was first produced in the theater, I cannot believe that the actors' suggestions, or their surviving parts, could result in anything but utter confusion.

In the case of the "good" Quartos, recent scholarship has produced convincing evidence that they were, in fact, honestly purchased from the Globe Company and in many cases were printed direct from Shakespeare's own scripts. Their readings, where they conflict with the Folio texts, have consequently found increasing favor, and no theater director can afford to neglect a study of them if the play he is handling exists in Quarto form. Even from the pirated "bad" Quartos, we may learn something, often in stage directions, where the reporter's eye was more accurate than his ear. The cuts and omissions in some instances are exactly what any director, conscious of a time limit and not too scrupulous about his author, would in fact strike out today.

We may glean one or two interesting hints from their title pages as to how the play stood in popular regard. For instance, the 1st Quarto of THE MERCHANT OF VENICE is sub-titled with "the extreame crueltie of Shylock the Jewe towards the sayd Merchant in cutting a just pound of his flesh, and the obtayning of Portia by the choyse of three chests." The Jew was evidently represented as the villain of the piece and not as its tragic hero. The running titles of HENRY V and THE

MERRY WIVES OF WINDSOR mention, respectively, "Auntient Pistoll" and "the swaggering vaine of Auncient Pistoll and Corporal Nym," which would seem to accord those worthies a higher place in Elizabethan regard than we are accustomed to afford them.

Poor Heminges and Condell and their devoted labors with the Folio have recently received much less than justice. It is, indeed, probable that many of the Folio texts were not printed from Shakespeare's own manuscripts. It is hard to see how the original prompt copy could always have survived years of theater handling and never been replaced by a transcript. We have, in a surviving script of BONDUCA, the unfortunate copyist's glum apology for certain missing passages, in his notation that "the booke whereby it was first acted from is lost: and this hath been transcribed from the fowle papers of the Authors which were founde." We may conjecture that trying to reconstruct a transcript from the "fowle" notes of Shakespeare's original draft was a pretty wearing task, also.

It is true that the transcript from which, to take a representative instance, the Folio text of MACBETH is supposedly drawn shows very evident signs of later additions by a hand other than Shakespeare's, notably in the childish Hecate scene. But when the scholars bitterly complain that the play is too short and must have been extensively cut, we are tempted to ask what could usefully be added which would enhance a theater pattern as exact and nearly perfect as anything Shakespeare ever wrote.

On two other counts, Heminges and Condell have almost certainly been unjustly maligned. In plays where Shakespeare has evidently worked in collaboration, usually very early or very late in his career, critical thinking is based on a subconscious desire to claim for Shakespeare everything that we approve of, and a determination to blame on somebody else everything which shows signs of lazy or second-rate workmanship. For instance, a sequence in PERICLES which is generally supposed to have been written by another hand contains the lines:

> The blind mole casts
> Copp'd hills towards heaven, to tell the earth is throng'd
> By man's oppression; and the poor worm doth die for 't.

These are too good to lose. We should like to keep them for Shakespeare.

On the other hand, MEASURE FOR MEASURE, a corrupt text but Shakespearean to its very fiber, has been split up into the most exact fragments of "Shakespeare's," "partly based on Shakespeare's original," "added by another hand," and so forth, because there are portions of it which the commentators would prefer Shakespeare not to have written.

But Shakespeare was far from writing always in his own best manner. He worked fast, hurriedly, sometimes quite apparently lashing himself to get the thing finished in time, often scamping the end once he was in sight of it and had got bored by the necessary machinery of tying up the loose threads. He stuffed in topical jokes to raise an easy, sometimes a dirty, laugh; he cut and altered, sometimes with the perfunctory method of a writer forced to go against his own better judgment. He passed through a period when his own emotional balance was so greatly disturbed that his workmanship shows plain signs of impatience and disgust, greatly to the detriment of its lucidity and poise. In the plays so produced he fits his people to a theatrical design with an almost savage disbelief that life could produce any such conclusion and writes shoddily through his own lack of conviction. Even in his best periods he gets led away from his line of thought into a web of verbal intricacy. He is by no means free of what Ben Jonson roundly told him was "bombast"; and, finally, as

Dr. Johnson judicially remarked: "It does not appear that he thought his works worthy of their posterity . . . or had any further prospects than of present popularity and present profit. When his plays had been acted his hope was at an end: he solicited no addition of honour from the reader."

We cannot blame all the roughnesses of the Folio texts on its editors. The severe accusations brought against them in this regard must in fact be shared by the author. It is as foolish to insist on divorcing Shakespeare from all traces of bad workmanship in the plays as it would be overreverent for us to preserve all such blemishes in our theater performances.

In one minor respect Heminges and Condell have been absolved for the differences between their texts and the earlier Quartos, for after the earlier set of publications Parliament passed an "Act to Restrain the Abuses of Players," which had involved the Globe Company in certain necessary revisions of lines and phrases which fell under its ban. One of its provisions forbade the "profane or jesting use of sacred names upon the stage," under penalty of a £10 fine. We are apt to be impatient of this, regarding it as a puritanical archaism. And yet, during the 1941 tour of the Theatre Guild's production of TWELFTH NIGHT—which is, incidentally, a purged Folio text—a member of the company received the following communication from a citizen of Cincinnati: "TWELFTH NIGHT would be so much better without the unnecessary and irreverent expressions, for example: 'By the Lord,' 'By Heaven' . . . Irreverence always spoils a play for some people, and, what is much more important, you do not want the responsibility of having the actors use it, or of accustoming people to hearing God's Name used lightly." Heminges and Condell would have felt justified in their obedience to the Puritans' way of thought.

The second important accusation, however, which has been brought against them, and upon which they have been widely condemned, is that they did, in fact, accept and print what may be called the "Globe Company Acting Versions" of the plays. These were not identical with the script Shakespeare had originally read to the assembled Company. Yet these versions had been tested over and over again before audiences and so had been subjected to cuts and alterations. No doubt some passages were lost which we would think most worthy of preservation, and no doubt some inferior material was added, especially after Shakespeare's retirement and subsequent death, when the additions were necessarily made by another playwright. The error lies, I believe, in the automatic assumption that each and every one of these alterations must have been for the worse. From the standpoint of the current theater, we cannot, I think, accept that assumption without strong reservations.

The texts of HAMLET provide as clear a test case as any. Let us leave aside the question of the "bad" 1st Quarto and the debate as to how and from what original material it was put together. Not that this corrupt and mysterious text is devoid of interest for us. William Poel said of it in a letter to Furnivall: ". . . . however misrepresented the text may be, the actor cannot help recognising that the Editor has endeavoured to reproduce the play as *he* saw it represented and therefore in the arrangement of the scenes, the stage directions, the omissions, and the alterations, there is much to guide and instruct him in the stage representation of the play as it appeared in Shakespeare's time."

There are other hints and signposts which are by no means without significance to us. For instance, in the Closet scene the Queen says to Hamlet:

> But as I have a soul, I swear by Heaven
> I never knew of this most horrid murder,

and further agrees to aid him in his plans against the King. Later there is an entire scene between her and Horatio, in which she ranges herself still more firmly on Hamlet's side against Claudius. Such must have been Shakespeare's original conception of the Queen's attitude, and, though he saw fit to modify it subsequently, I see no reason to suppose that he reversed it.

But it is behind the other two texts, the corrected and augmented 2d Quarto of 1604 and the Folio of 1623, that commentators have ranged themselves during three hundred years of doughty battle. Q2 and F1 become protagonists as vivid and personal as Hamlet himself. The Folio is the shorter text, omitting 229 lines which appear in the Quarto and yet including 85 which the Quarto lacks. The Folio is much the more carefully printed, punctuated, and spelled, despite the usual and obvious compositor's errors; but it differs from the Quarto in innumerable matters of words, phrasing, spelling, punctuation, line division, stage direction, and speech heading.

Until the researches of Dr. Pollard in 1915, most editors had viewed both texts with profound mistrust, holding the balance according to their individual preferences and brilliantly guessing their way out of the murkier tangles in either. But the Folio was definitely the favorite. On such a basis, numberless classroom and popular editions were built; and, for most of us, the Folio readings are the ones which ring so familiarly in our ears. This, in my opinion, must be taken into account in stage versions. For instance, it is the Folio which has the famous "O that this too, too solid flesh would melt. . . ." Instead of "solid" both the Quartos read "sallied," which modern editors guess as a misreading of "sullied," and this adjective they accordingly support with passion. I cannot myself see quite why they are so greatly disturbed by "solid."

When Mr. Evans played Hamlet, he felt, as I did, that the substitution of "sullied" either would lead the audience to suppose that he meant "solid" but was simply being rather Oxford English in his pronunciation of it, or would start an automatic debate in their minds as to what had become of their tried and trusted friend "solid." We accordingly kept the Folio reading.

Dr. Dover Wilson's fascinating book, *The Manuscript of Shakespeare's Hamlet,* unfolds the gripping human drama which lies behind the modern editors' Quarto preference, to which text they incline with increasing determination. His conclusions, in brief, are these: that the Folio was printed from the prompt copy in use at the Globe Theatre and therefore represents the text as actually played by Burbage and his colleagues, whereas the Quarto was printed direct from Shakespeare's original manuscript. Any modern author will confirm from his experience how divergent any two such texts are likely to be.

Dr. Wilson, however, postulates two "Villains" in each case, between us and Shakespeare. In the Folio, they are "Scribe P" and "Scribe C." Scribe P is the prompter, or stage manager, at the Globe. He is responsible for the cutting and pruning of the original text and also for several "actors' additions," such as Burbage's dying groans, which incongruously occur in the form of "O, o, o, o!" after "The rest is silence." Up to a point, Dr. Wilson respects Scribe P and even admits that he sometimes introduced "technical improvements and clarifications." He was "a business-like fellow," and where he had to shorten the play, or cut away what seemed to him—or to Burbage—extraneous matter, did so with skill and with a due regard for meter and meaning.

Some of the cuts were forced on the Players by the altered circumstances owing to the accession of James I and his Danish Queen Anne; long descriptions of the Danes' habitual drunkenness became inadvisable. There is the usual Folio crop of "Heavens" for "Gods," and other similar ameliorations. But the Folio cuts have been incorporated in almost all subsequent stage versions. The most inexcusable of them is the omission of the "How all occasions do inform against me" soliloquy. Apparently Burbage did not know when he was well off, or else had not the power to rise to its demands after the long, tiring sequence of the Play scene and the intervening scenes of unremitting strain on Hamlet.

Unfortunately, however, there are many smaller errors both of omission and commission for which Scribe P cannot be held responsible; and it is to explain these that Dr. Wilson postulates his Second Villain, Scribe C, or Scribe Copyist, for whom he has nothing but withering scorn. Scribe C is supposed to have made a transcript of the prompt copy, which naturally could not be spared from the theater, for delivery to Jaggard, the printer. "He was," says Dr. Wilson, "thoroughly familiar with the play upon the stage, but, confident of his acquaintance with the various parts, he often allowed his pen to run straight on without checking what he wrote from what he was copying." Dr. Wilson accuses him of "irresponsible self-confidence" and "slovenliness" which he was cunning enough to realize would probably escape detection.

Poor Scribe C. I prefer to see him as a stage-struck, rather illiterate youth, a fervent Burbage fan who sat, hour after hour, his tongue stuck in the corner of his mouth, laboriously copying out this inordinately long play, his master's greatest "vehicle," in the happy confidence that he knew every word of it. He wasn't, of course, any too sure of what a great deal of it meant and wrote down what he supposed he heard without bothering much as to whether it made sense. Thus he produced "His beard was grisly," for "grizzl'd," and "each in his particular sect and force" for "act and place." Often he "misremembered," as the children say, and probably at least as often he faithfully wrote down the lines the actors were, in fact, in the habit of speaking, whether or not these were "true text." It was laborious work for him, who was readier at learning words than at writing them; but, because of his idol, Burbage, and all his hopes and dreams of success in following his master's footsteps, he plodded away at the allotted task. He little knew that his future fame would rest upon just this and that three centuries later he would be dragged into anonymous notoriety to play a minor villain for Dr. Dover Wilson.

With the Quarto, supposedly printed from Shakespeare's own manuscript, it is a different story. Shakespeare himself seems to have been the First Villain, owing to his vagaries of spelling and more than usually illegible handwriting. One would judge from the variety of conjectural emendation of obviously corrupt words that he formed the letters of the alphabet in such a way that they were all practically identical. Among the "fowle papers of Authors," Shakespeare's must have held pride of place. The Quarto Villains are: first, the compositor, another plodder, but inexpert and not very good at deciphering (Dr. Wilson even deduces from some of his fancier flights of orthography that he was a Welshman); secondly, the press corrector, whose emendations of the compositor's efforts, although "not wholly wanton," were made very much at random; and, lastly, Roberts, the printer himself, who so harried and drove the compositor that the wretched man can hardly ever have had time to stop for a "stoup of ale" and was forced to skip through the interminable manuscript at a speed which led him to omit numberless small stage directions and other apparent trivia.

Given a cast like this, and the apparatus of modern bibliographical research, it is possible to ascribe almost anything to almost anybody and to "prove" almost everything, just as two French critics once argued themselves into a duel as to whether Hamlet was fat or thin. But in the Maurice Evans production of HAMLET, we dutifully set out to follow the Quarto lead in disputed readings. Dr. Wilson tells us that we ought to start with the Quarto readings, preferring the Folio only when the Quarto is obviously incorrect or unmistakably inferior. Dr. M. R. Ridley, whose admirable New Temple edition the actors used, is a declared Quarto champion. But over and over again we found ourselves driven back to the Folio text by the fact that it provided much the clearer spoken, as against written, word, arrangements of speech headings which seemed to us dramatically more cogent, and sometimes stage directions which provided valuable theater hints.

Let me give a few examples. In some cases the Quarto reading involves quite simply a clumsy duplication of sound, which the Folio avoids. It has "Therefore, for brevity is the soul of wit . . ." and "Wilt thou hear now how I did proceed . . ." In each case we chose the Folio's "Therefore since brevity is the soul of wit," and "Wilt thou hear me how I did proceed."

In other cases, the word or phrase given in the Quarto text is misleading to the ear when spoken aloud and I feel sure was altered by Burbage for that reason. A clear example is to be found in the Queen's description of Ophelia borne up by her garments in the "weeping brook," "which time she chanted snatches of old lauds," says the Quarto, followed by the modern editors. One wishes they had tried saying the line aloud to an audience. "Look," one hears the Elizabethan actor expostulating, "if you talk to an audience about old 'lauds' their ears instinctively hear 'lords,' and it's going to take them several seconds figuring that you can't mean that, and finally getting to 'lauds.' Can't you find another word?" So Shakespeare found "tunes," and the Folio keeps it, and so did we.

For reasons relating to the indefinable rhythmic counterpoise which can only be judged by speaking the lines, we kept the Folio arrangement of Hamlet's last exhortation to Horatio and Marcellus in Act 1, scene 5:

> . . . this not to do,
> So grace and mercy at your most need help you,
> Swear.

The Quarto has the, to me, theatrically ineffective:

> . . . this do swear
> So grace and mercy at your most need help you.

There are several similar passages in HAMLET, and many more are to be found in the other plays for which both Folio and Quarto are extant. Dr. Ridley's New Temple ROMEO AND JULIET prints astonishing variants on the Folio text, which it is impossible to believe he can ever have tested by the ear.

As an instance of the Folio's more theatrically valid speech-heading arrangements, let us take the exit of Polonius after he tells Hamlet that the Queen would speak with him in her closet, Act III, scene 2. The Quarto finishes the scene thus:

> HAMLET: Then I will come to my mother by and by. (*aside*)
> They fool me to the top of my bent. I will come by and by.
> Leave me, friends. I will, say so.
> > [*here, we presume, "Exeunt all but Hamlet"*]
> "By and by" is easily said,
> Tis now the very witching time of night . . .

The Folio rendering runs:

> HAMLET: Then I will come to my mother by and by. (*aside*)
> They fool me to the top of my bent. I will come by and by.
> POLONIUS: I will say so.   (*Exit*)
> HAMLET: By and by is easily said. Leave me, friends.

I think it is apparent that the breaking up of Hamlet's speech lends it point and decision, besides providing Polonius with a definite exit, instead of a mere drifting off.

In another instance, the Quarto heads the line "In that and

all things will we show our duty" (Act 1, scene 2) "Cornelius and Voltimand." The Folio has "Voltimand" only, which I thought preferable, because ambassadors do not habitually indulge in community speaking. My guess is that Shakespeare did not care which of them said it and that the point was cleared in rehearsal. On the other hand, at the climax of the Play scene, after the King rises, the Quarto gives the line "Lights, lights, lights!" to Polonius only, while the Folio has "All." It is very evident that in practice the cry for lights might well be started by Polonius but must be taken up by "All."

Because our methods of staging have changed so much, the stage directions of either text are to be regarded by the modern director more as indications of what was wanted or what was done than as specific injunctions which he must actually follow. The Folio is more detailed, I think very definitely the stage manager's reduction to actual theater terms of what Shakespeare had more vaguely asked for. Both are valuable in their respective indications. Judging from the Quarto, Shakespeare evidently wanted a "Counsaile" for the first Court scene, and I think we should give it to him, even though it appears by the Folio direction that the Globe Company's proceedings were more informal and allowed the presence of Ophelia. The Folio's "A Saylor" for the Quarto's "Saylers," in Act IV, scene 6, may very well have been due to the Globe Company's scarcity of manpower.

The Folio's readings at the very end of the play are illuminating. It has "Enter Fortinbras and English Ambassador" (again only one) "with Drumme, Colours and Attendants." Before the final two lines it gives Fortinbras the command "Take up the body:" and finishes up with "Exeunt marching: after the which, a Peale of Ordenance are shot off." The Quarto's version of the same sequence starts with "Enter Fortinbrasse with the Ambassadors," gives him "Take up the bodies:", and ends simply "Exeunt." This seems to me to reveal clearly the stage manager's usual definition of the author, which could be exactly paralleled in any manuscript and prompt copy today, and also the interesting information that the company had contrived to dispose of all the bodies but Hamlet's, either on the inner stage or in some place where they did not have to be taken up and removed. The avoidance of this plethora of corpses draped around the set seems to me an excellent idea, which I personally followed with the utmost alacrity.

These examples could be endlessly multiplied. I do not, however, pretend that in the Evans production we were entirely won over to the Folio text; the Quarto is manifestly superior in many places; and there were others where our choice between the two readings was frankly a personal one. I do feel, however, that, whatever the play, theater people today will be unwise to let the scholars deter them from careful consideration of what Mr. Heminges and Mr. Condell have made of it. Whatever their faults, or the degree of deviation from the probable original which their text shows, they were theater men; they had worked with Shakespeare; they and their colleagues had handled his scripts for almost thirty years; the evidence that may be gleaned from their edition of his works is in no case negligible.

The textual problem varies with every play, and its solution with every editor. But the main lines of textual derivation are fairly well established and are worthy of more study than we usually afford them. When it comes to the commentators' business of disintegration, with the texts that are not wholly by Shakespeare, we may well beg to be at least partially excused. If "another hand" did write certain passages, there they are now in the texts we must play. Sometimes the knowledge will fortify our wavering blue pencils, but in the main it is our business to produce a unity of impression which will diminish as far as possible any textual disparities. For, having decided upon our text, it now becomes our business to produce it.

In the following chapters I shall not attempt to offer anything approaching a detailed production scheme for the thirty-seven plays, which would be an evident impossibility. In the theater we work with highly flexible material, and it is, in my view, only the director of great mental poverty, or the temperament of the most unimaginative schoolmaster, who rings up the curtain at the opening night on precisely the same edifice as he had blueprinted in his script before rehearsals began. Shakespeare's plays offer an unequaled latitude of interpretation; the greatest of them, especially HAMLET, are inexhaustible. The standards by which a production may be adjudged good or bad are similarly subject to change. There is no book of rules. There are, as I have said, the actors, the audience, and Shakespeare; and it is the director's business to bring them into harmony, with justice to all parties. It is not his business to offer a set of showy directorial stunts based on an evasion of this issue, still less to lay down the law as to the right and wrong as applied to any production but his own.

I shall, however, review in outline the Shakespearean canon as it forms part of our modern theater inheritance and in some cases offer possible solutions for the difficulties which confront us, or the fallacies which beset us, in presenting the plays today. What can we show of the real Shakespeare under the cloud-capp'd towers of Manhattan and over the breadth of the forty-eight States so far removed in time and place from the little wooden playhouse by the river Thames? We may certainly suppose that Shakespeare was always stimulated by the prospect of a new audience; what can he offer this one?

In quotations from the plays, scene and line references, I

shall use the New Temple edition edited by Dr. Ridley, because it is complete and easy of access to the casual reader. The reader who desires to follow the labyrinth of modern comment cannot better do so than in Dr. Dover Wilson's enormously stimulating New Cambridge texts, as yet only partially complete. The Furness Variorum series is a mine of almost overpowering information on every point and will furnish the necessary ammunition for any controversy whatsoever.

Part Two

7. The Early Plays

THE "EARLY" PLAYS I have here grouped together
are those written between the years 1590 and 1595. The earliest of all are probably HENRY VI, PART II and PART III, PART I
being preponderantly due to other hands than Shakespeare's.
This trilogy, however, together with RICHARD II and RICHARD
III, which also fall within the early period, may be more con-
veniently considered in conjunction with the other histories.
The remaining plays show Shakespeare's full development
from a "'prentice" dramatist with a poet's gift for words and
a youthful zest for the beauty and passion of living, to assured
knowledge and dramatic skill. They are, in the chronological
order given by Sir E. K. Chambers, TITUS ANDRONICUS, THE
COMEDY OF ERRORS, THE TAMING OF THE SHREW, THE
TWO GENTLEMEN OF VERONA, LOVE'S LABOUR'S LOST, ROMEO
AND JULIET, and A MIDSUMMER NIGHT'S DREAM.

TITUS ANDRONICUS is seldom considered seriously by the
modern theatrical producer, for obvious reasons. It is a
barbaric, lusty, bloodthirsty piece of work, evidently by a young
man with no inhibitions and an unabashed determination to
please the least squeamish of the groundlings. There is only
the faintest foreshadowing of greatness to come. The fact that
Shakespeare wrote it is an object lesson to those who are so

ready to inform potential dramatists that they have no gift for the theater and had better stick to minor verse or else to go to Hollywood. Both these courses would surely be urged on the author of a modern TITUS. The poet in Shakespeare, who was writing "Lucrece" and "Venus and Adonis," perpetually breaks through:

> The hunt is up, the morn is bright and grey,
> The fields are fragrant and the woods are green.
>
> II, 2, 1
>
> Now, by the burning tapers of the sky . . .
>
> IV, 2, 90
>
> What fool hath added water to the sea,
> Or brought a faggot to bright-burning Troy?
>
> III, 1, 69

And Titus' funeral oration at the burial of his sons:

> Rome's readiest champions, repose you here in rest,
> Secure from worldly chances and mishaps.
> Here lurks no treason, here no envy swells,
> Here grow no damned drugs, here are no storms,
> But peace and silence and eternal rest.   I, 1, 151

At the end of his life, in CYMBELINE, the poet will bring the wheel full circle with the lovely song beginning:

> Fear no more the heat o' the sun,
>   Nor the furious winter's rages,
> Thou thy worldly work hast done,
>   Home art gone, and ta'en thy wages;
> Golden lads and girls all must,
>   Like chimney-sweepers, come to dust.

But in TITUS the characters, with the exception of Aaron the Moor, are wooden puppets only, and the plot is hopelessly melodramatic by modern standards. We really cannot do with a young woman who is careless enough to get herself quite gratuitously raped and have her hands and her tongue cut off to boot; who wanders through the rest of the play gesticulating with the stumps, and at one point is told by her father, whose hand has also been cut off: "Bear thou my hand, sweet wench, between thy teeth." Murder and mutilation run riot. The protagonists trade insults and lament injuries with wooden ferocity; and yet there is a certain Grand-Guignol fascination about the plot, and the puppets have a hint of grandeur. Those who have seen it played report that it has a certain crude, melodramatic power which largely overwhelms the temptation to laughter. Evidently the stage lends fire and color even to situations which appear ludicrous in print. The actors need adequate vocal equipment and must not be squeamish about their work. Nevertheless, TITUS remains a curiosity of Shakespeare's apprentice period.

THE COMEDY OF ERRORS is better, but not, I think, much better. Mark Van Doren classes it among the three "unfeeling" farces, the others being THE TAMING OF THE SHREW and THE MERRY WIVES OF WINDSOR. Its mistaken-identity theme has gone entirely out of fashion; we might possibly be prepared to take one set of twins, but two are really excessive, especially when one pair is so relentlessly funny as the two Dromios, with their everlasting puns. It is one of the few plays which may be stylized to the limit of a director's invention and with all the extended artifice of music, ballet, and comedy tricks. So trimmed and graced, and mercilessly cut, it may still serve as an hors d'oeuvre for the less sophisticated, especially if the actors saddled with the Dromios can contrive to bring a real, and personal, comic quality to our aid.

Shakespeare the poet is still with us, and to a slight degree a sense of character is allowed to creep in. One has the feeling that he has deliberately made up his mind not to try to graft too much humanity onto an entirely artificial slapstick situation, not that he was unable to do so had he tried. The Syracusan twins are just distinguishable from their Ephesian brethren. The actors will do well to emphasize the distinction. Dromio of Syracuse is not quite so brash as his namesake, and Antipholus seems spiritually younger and fresher than his brother of Ephesus; besides, he is given the advantage of being in love and therefore entitled to the lyric

> O train me not, sweet mermaid, with thy note,
> To drown me in thy sister's flood of tears;
> Sing, siren, for thyself, and I will dote:
> Spread o'er the silver waves thy golden hairs;
> And as a bed I'll take them, and there lie;
> And in that glorious supposition think
> He gains by death that hath such means to die.
>
> III, 2, 45

and

> It is thyself, mine own self's better part;
> Mine eye's clear eye, my dear heart's dearer heart;
> My food, my fortune, and my sweet hope's aim;
> My sole earth's heaven, and my heaven's claim.
>
> III, 2, 61

This is the early Romeo to his Rosaline; the later Romeo will soon come into view. Adriana has some vigor, aside from her foreshadowing of Katharine and even Beatrice. Dromio of Syracuse's description of his kitchen wench, his "mountain of mad flesh," exudes something of her warmth. The play is not bad vaudeville. Perhaps we are a little spoiled for it because we expect something more than vaudeville from the Shakespeare we have learned to know.

With TAMING OF THE SHREW, he bridges the gap which lies between us and THE COMEDY OF ERRORS, by virtue of the full-strength, flaunting, undimmed vitality of his two protagonists, Katharine and Petruchio. Here are people, people we can care about, and parts, moreover, in which actors may, do, and will "go to town." There is no lack of vigorous brutality in the horseplay of the plot; there is some juvenile artifice in the involutions of the subplot, with its inevitable tangle of everybody disguising themselves as somebody else and nobody having the elementary common sense to discover any of the deceptions. All of this is fair game for the high spirits of actors and director; and Shakespeare would, I am sure, be the last to object to anything they may choose to do with it, using any and every means to beguile the eye and ear. We have seen the Lunts brilliantly successful by such a method.

The Induction, however, points us to a different kind of writing, even if the basis of its plot is no less artificial than the Bianca-Lucentio-Tranio goings on. Christopher Sly is from a new and different vintage. Shakespeare will go to the taverns and the highroads many times again to meet and talk with him. He is

> Christopher Sly, old Sly's son of Burton Heath, by birth a pedlar, by education a card-maker, by transmutation a bear-herd, and now by present profession a tinker. Ask Marion Hacket, the fat ale-wife of Wincot, if she know me not.

We have never been to Burton Heath or Wincot, and Marion Hacket was before our time. But we have no difficulty in recognizing Christopher Sly.

The grafting of the Induction onto the play proper is more difficult for us than it was for Shakespeare, who worked in a theater where lords and their entourage did actually sit at the side of his stage; he therefore had no trouble in introducing the Sly party amongst them. Their presence is apt to become too obtrusive for us, because Shakespeare loses interest in them and only once remembers their presence. If they get between us and the Shrew herself we shall be enraged, and rightly; for Katharine and Petruchio are what we come to see.

In the strange Quarto THE TAMING OF A SHREW, which is variously supposed to be a pirating of Shakespeare's early THE SHREW or, alternatively, the foundation play on which he worked, there is more work for Sly and his Hellzapoppin' gang; and the director will be wise to have recourse to this if he wants to keep the Induction characters in the audience's view. But even so, once the play itself gets under way, it is hard to keep them in just proportion to it.

The "brutality" and "coarseness" of the main plot have been much criticized. Audiences do not seem to be so squeamish. Nevertheless, Katharine and Petruchio should not be played simply as an "irksome, brawling scold" and a "mad-brained rudesby, full of spleen," nor the progress of their relation interpreted solely as the taming of intolerable bad temper by equally intolerable physical violence. There is more wit inherent in it than that, and much more humanity.

Suppose that the two of them do actually fall headlong in love at their very first encounter; in his heart, each knows it of himself, but not of the other. This will take a little more ingenuity in the handling of the wooing scene than the set of variations on kicking, scuffling, raging, ramping, and all-in wrestling with which it is usually provided. But a few pauses, a few inflections will do it; the very moments of physical contact between the two of them, when Katharine is in Petruchio's arms, can be made to help.

If this is established, the whole play takes on a different tone. The contest will be one which we shall wish resolved. We shall know that Katharine, in her heart, wishes it just as deeply. It will be her pride that is broken, not her spirit. We shall enjoy watching the antagonists dealing blow and counterblow, not without zest, matching each other in a duel which is not based on a thorough mutual dislike, as it has sometimes appeared, but increasingly informed with love and finally overwhelmed in laughter.

Katharine has the harder task, for Petruchio scarcely lets her get a word in edgewise; but she is amply rewarded in the ironic wit of her final surrender. Agreeing, with deceptive docility, to call Vincentio "fair, lovely maid," and to accept the sun and the moon as interchangeable planets, she contrives triumphantly to better Petruchio's instruction. Here at last is a "marriage of true minds." It is not the destruction of one by the brutality of the other. Petruchio could never have endured a tame wife.

Katharine has not become a cipher; she has merged her brilliance and masked her strength. This is not the woman to deliver the final speech as a groveling creature, fatuously exalting the male sex in general. Her lines are filled with a delicious irony, by no means lost on Petruchio, in their delicate overpraising of a husband's virtues. Katharine has changed her technique.

> I am ashamed that women are so simple,
>   [*a wealth of meaning in this "simple"*]
> To offer war where they should kneel for peace;
> And seek for rule supremacy and sway
> Where they are bound to—
>   [*"quote" says Katharine for Petruchio's ears and ours*]
>   —serve, love and obey. [*"unquote"*]

And a few lines further on:

> But now I see our lances are but straws,
> Our strength as weak, our weakness—[*with a beatific
>   smile*]—past compare,
> That seeming to be most which we indeed least are.
>   v, 2, 173

At the finish the two come together in a beautifully negotiated, not an imposed, peace.

THE TWO GENTLEMEN OF VERONA has its own grace, some lyric beauty, the enchanting "Who is Sylvia?" song, two heroines, one of whom has wit and the other valiance, and the immortally endearing Launce, with his mangy, mongrel, adored dog. ROMEO AND JULIET is quick in the depths of Shakespeare's heart; tiny fragments of the mine from which he was to draw it, samples of the golden ore, gleam continuously in the sand. Proteus, an intolerable youth by any standards of heroic behavior, disarms us completely from time to time by such Orphean music as:

> Say that upon the altar of her beauty
> You sacrifice your tears, your sighs, your heart:
> Write till your ink be dry, and with your tears
> Moist it again; and frame some feeling line
> That may discover such integrity:
> For Orpheus' lute was strung with poets' sinews,
> Whose golden touch could soften steel and stones,
> Make tigers tame, and huge leviathans
> Forsake uncounted deeps to dance on sands.
> After your dire-lamenting elegies,
> Visit by night your lady's chamber-window
> With some sweet consort; to their instruments
> Tune a deploring dump; the night's dead silence
> Will well become such sweet complaining grievance.
>
> III, 2, 73

But he cannot melt us long with this "golden touch," for the exigencies of the plot require of him faithlessness to his lady, attempted seduction of his friend's beloved, betrayal of that friend to banishment and probable death, and the most perfunctory repentance when nothing is left of his other schemes, accompanied, moreover, by some nauseatingly banal moralizing in his own excuse. We simply cannot deal with this stuffed shirt. Valentine, who might rescue the play for us, is more amiable but not much more lively; he is burdened by perpetual conversations with his loquaciously wooden servant, Speed, a puppet full of wisecracks. On the stage we may do

something with music, costumes by Botticelli, a fine clown
for Launce, and the deceptive warmth of personality which
emerges from the stage presentation of Shakespeare's most
improbable plays. But we may as well accept the fact that but
for Shakespeare's name on the title page we should never
dream of bothering. The fireside, and the anthologists, seem
to be entitled to this piece.

We should, however, claim, or reclaim, LOVE'S LABOUR'S
LOST; for here Shakespeare wears his youth like a bright cloak,
his mastery like a plume of feathers, and his wit like a silver-
hilted sword. The play has been condemned from the classrooms as no more than a brilliant exercise in parody, outdoing
the verbal intricacies and studied efflorescence of the euphuistic school; but it becomes far more than that; for in the end,
Shakespeare falls in love with his characters.

Take Armado, the Spaniard,

> A man in all the world's new fashion planted,
> That hath a mint of phrases in his brain:
> One whom the music of his own vain tongue
> Doth ravish like enchanting harmony,

whom the King has hired to entertain his little court with tales
of "many a knight from tawny Spain." Shakespeare may have
started out to make him ridiculous. This intention barely lasts
out the first scene; for at the end of it, before we have seen
Armado, comes a letter from him. It starts with a flourish
of grandiloquence, endearing in its very absurdity, and pro-
gresses through a minuet of phrases to its accusation against
the rustic Costard, "that low-spirited Swain, that base Minnow
of thy mirth, that unlettered small-knowing soul, that shallow
vassal. . . ." We are more than half won already to a man
who can sauce accusation with such sublime disdain. At last
he comes, with Moth, his page, trailing his tattered finery,
his molting feathers, and his threadbare cloak, like the greatest

grandee among them all; "his humour is lofty, his eye ambitious, his gait majestical." He sits, we suppose, with studied hauteur. He sighs. "Boy," he at last addresses the page, as one affectionately condescending to a very small insect, "what sign is it when a man of great spirit grows melancholy?"

He is, of course, in love, most reluctantly in love, and "with a base wench" too, the very same wench with whom he had seen Costard dallying, and the unfortunate progress of this humiliating but delicious passion constitutes his part in the play. From his "mint of phrases" he scatters pearls of largess: "Warble, child; make passionate my sense of hearing." "Define, define, well-educated infant." "Now, by the salt wave of the Mediterraneum, a sweet touch, a quick venue of wit,— a snip, snap, quick and home! it rejoiceth my intellect, true wit!" and his majestic yielding to Cupid, saluting him like a vanquished but not inglorious duelist:

Adieu valour, rust rapier, be still drum, for your manager is in love; yea, he loveth. Assist me some extemporal god of rhyme, for I am sure I shall turn sonnet. Devise wit, write pen, for I am for whole volumes in folio.

In the pageant played at the end before the King and Princess, a scene, incidentally, capable of being made much more delicately funny than its famous counterpart in A MIDSUMMER NIGHT'S DREAM, his humiliation begins. He plays Hector and gets mercilessly heckled by the flippant audience; he is incensed, not for himself, but for Hector. "Sweet Lord Longaville, rein thy tongue," he protests; "The sweet warman is dead and rotten; sweet chucks, beat not the bones of the buried; when he breathed he was a man."

But worse is to come. He is accused by the base Costard; Jacquenetta, it seems, is with child by him. He is challenged to fight "in his shirt." He refuses, with passion. Pressed further, he is forced to the last humiliation: "The naked truth of it is, I have no shirt." But he redeems himself, with simplicity and honor. "For mine own part, I breathe free breath. I have seen the day of wrong through the little hole of discretion, and I will right myself like a soldier." Shakespeare rewards him for his reformation by letting him introduce the lovely song with which this intricate play so simply ends:

> When daisies pied and violets blue,
>   And lady-smocks all silver-white,
> And cuckoo-buds so fair of hue
>   Do paint the meadows with delight . . .

and gives him the final line: "The words of Mercury are harsh after the songs of Apollo. You that way, we this way"; and so the gleaming bubble of a play floats up out of our sight.

If an actor cannot warm Armado into our love and living memory, it is no fault of Shakespeare. An actor such as John Barrymore could give him greatness. Nor is Armado the only living figure in the play. Biron has been much discussed and praised. He has, probably, the glibbest honey tongue among them all and a good share of fine common sense. He thinks the vow he and his three companions have taken, "to fast, to study and to see no woman," the merest nonsense and says so. And when the four of them all fall in love, as they inevitably and symmetrically do, with the visiting Princess of France and her three Ladies, his ringing lyric on the virtues of love would win a saint from his vows:

> A lover's eye will gaze an eagle blind,
> A lover's ear will hear the lowest sound
> When the suspicious head of theft is stopp'd;
> Love's feeling is more soft and sensible
> Than are the tender horns of cockled snails;
> Love's tongue proves dainty Bacchus gross in taste:
> For valour is not Love a Hercules,

Still climbing trees in the Hesperides?
Subtle as Sphinx, as sweet and musical
As bright Apollo's lute strung with his hair;
And when love speaks, the voice of all the gods
Makes heaven drowsy with the harmony.   IV, 3, 332

His counterpart, more lightly sketched, is Rosaline, an early
Beatrice; and the two exchange some light, swift sallies, "snip,
snap, quick and home!" The Princess has dignity and a gentler
wit; the sonorous King, though more stilted, can be humanized
too. Costard is juicy and round, if a trifle heavy. A good
comedian can save him very easily for our liking, because he,
too, partakes of the human compassion which students have
so signally failed to discern in the play; witness his apology
for the shy, stammering little curate, Sir Nathaniel, who has
ignominiously gone up in his lines as Alexander the Great, in
the masque:

There, an't shall please you, a foolish mild man, an honest man,
look you, and soon dash'd. He is a marvellous good neighbour,
faith, and a very good bowler: but, for Alisander, alas, you see
how 'tis, a little o'erparted.

The whole play needs a gloss of style and brilliant speaking; unfortunately it also needs pretty quick listening. Whole
passages in it are too long, too wordy, and too pun-ridden for
our ears. If we are to redeem it, we shall have to be very
drastic with the blue pencil, even though we protest that
it hurts us as much as it hurts Shakespeare. The formalized
passages should be handled with all the richest visual and
aural trappings of formality. The setting should remain
unchanged, so that the flow and movement of the characters
can move through its spacious and decorated greenness with
the rhythm of a pageant. But, above all, if we can love these
people as their creator did and revel in their feast of language

as we do in a brilliant piece of orchestration, we should be able to provide an opulent return for any audience.

The remaining plays numbered among this early group have been so long a part of the practicing theater and have been so copiously commentated upon, their potentialities so amply translated into actuality, that there seems little to be added by theorizing. ROMEO AND JULIET, in particular, will prove a staple item in any theater repertory so long as there is an actress left in the world, for she will surely want to play Juliet. An actor does not feel the same yearning for Romeo; he usually spends days of troubled debate as to whether Mercutio is not the showier part, filled as it is with wit and poetry, with the zest of life and the tragic, wasteful irony of death.

The productions of this play have provided a continuous commentary on the progress and divagations of the theater, especially in its physical aspects. It is a play which makes us realize most clearly the crossroads at which we stand today. The scenes are precisely placed, without equivocation, and our modern editions ticket them neatly enough: A Veronese Street, A Hall in Capulet's House, A Friar's Cell, An Orchard, A Tomb. But we have at last come to realize that we must not split the pattern of the play by dividing it up into little sets of small, gaudy, Veronese bricks, with constant lowerings of the curtain in order to rearrange our self-imposed limitations.

For Shakespeare is deliberately following a schedule of the headlong pressure of events in a strictly limited space of time, so that their power is canalized into a dynamic force; and to achieve this, he is using his ungeographical stage with almost undisciplined freedom. The scenes following the Capulet Ball are marked by the older editors as Act II, scenes 1 and 2, but they are indivisible spatially. While Benvolio and Mercutio exchange their callous jests, Romeo presumably hides somewhere on the stage, smarting under this profanation of all that he deems holy until they go, at last, with the words: "For 'tis but vain To seek him here that means not to be found." He steps forward, completing the couplet with "He jests at scars that never felt a wound." Then, it is as if he did no more than turn and stop short with a catching of the heart,

> But soft! what light through yonder window breaks?
> It is the East, and Juliet is the sun!

And we are straight away in the enchanted orchard, Mercutio and Benvolio a thousand miles distant, poor beings from a lesser world.

It is easy to see how the architecture of Shakespeare's Globe made this possible, with the upper stage for the balcony and perhaps the "inner below" for Romeo to hide in. Modern designers are tempted to fuss with a lot of realistic paraphernalia including a bit of "street," a wall, visible on both sides and reasonably solid, some fruit trees and a balcony—cumbrous carpentry for a scene which is pure poetry and never touches the earth. It would be better to work toward a free setting, addressed not so much to "the outer eye which observes" but to "the inner eye which sees," as Robert Edmond Jones put it. Juliet must of necessity be placed above her Romeo, on the approximate level of a balcony. For the rest, the actors must create and shift their own surroundings, with the aid of some skillful spotlighting and the imaginative participation of the audience.

Later in the play we shall again need this method. In Act III, scene 4, we see Capulet, that lusty, gusty, unimaginative old gentleman, dismissing the tragic events of Tybalt's death with a commonsensible "well, we were born to die," and arranging for Juliet to marry Paris in three days' time. It is "very, very late" on Monday night. We know that this is to be Romeo's first, and last, night with his new-made wife. We know that even as Capulet is talking, exhorting

Lady Capulet "Go you to Juliet e'er you go to bed," Romeo must be with her; and in the same visual breath we see them.

JULIET: Wilt thou be gone? it is not yet near day:
          It was the nightingale, and not the lark,
          That pierc'd the fearful hollow of thine ear;
          Nightly she sings on yon pomegranate tree;
          Believe me, love, it was the nightingale.
ROMEO: It was the lark, the herald of the morn,
          No nightingale: look, love, what envious streaks
          Do lace the severing clouds in yonder east:
          Night's candles are burnt out, and jocund day
          Stands tip-toe on the misty mountain tops.
          I must begone and live, or stay and die.   III, 5, 1

We are again in another world, the heartbreakingly fragile world of the lovers.

The outer world breaks through, relentlessly, with the Nurse's announcement that Lady Capulet is indeed coming; Romeo climbs down from the balcony; he goes; almost before he is out of sight comes Lady Capulet, with her "Ho, daughter, are you up?" There follows the scene between the desperate Juliet and her enraged, oblivious father, working himself into a pretty passion at her refusal of the Paris match and the imminent wedding. Briefly we leave the stormy Capulet house for the scene at Laurence's cell, where he gives Juliet the sleeping potion which may save her. Then back to Capulet, fussing and fuming over the wedding preparations; Juliet returns, and makes her submission to him. He instantly seizes the opportunity to advance the wedding to "tomorrow" and starts an even gayer commotion. Juliet goes up to her closet; she bids farewell to her mother and the Nurse; she drinks the potion, daring all the nightmares of the unknown with the childlike gallantry of "Romeo, I come! this do I drink to thee," and—it is an authentic stage direction—"falls upon her bed within the curtains."

The curtains are barely stilled around her, our eyes deeply filled with them, when we are back with the frantic household preparations simultaneously going forward:

LADY CAPULET: Hold, take these keys and fetch more spices, Nurse.
NURSE: They call for dates and quinces in the pantry.
CAPULET: Come, stir, stir, stir! the second cock hath crow'd, The curfew bell hath rung, 'tis three o'clock.

A merry thirty lines of this, ending with Capulet's "Go waken Juliet, go and trim her up . . . Make haste, I say," and we are instantly back in Juliet's silent, shadowed room, with no more than a cold, pure, knifeblade of light slanting in and those still, unforgotten curtains. With the Nurse's drawing of them and discovery of Juliet apparently dead within, the outer world at last engulfs the oasis of sanctity which has hitherto been preserved for us, and the household lamentations complete the pattern; not without a wry little coda from the musicians engaged to play at the wedding, for whom there is nothing to do, but "tarry for the mourners and stay dinner."

It is only very recently that producers have realized the poignant heightening of tragedy which this counterpoint of domestic activity provides. But it is only effective if the juxtaposition between them is unbroken and visually so knit that we never lose consciousness of it. John Gielgud in London and Laurence Olivier in New York, both assisted by some ingenious and decorative sets by the firm of Motley, attempted the solution by showing a scenic cross section of the Capulet house. Gielgud's version held the Capulets below and the lovers above simultaneously in the eye, to very considerable effect. But the danger of this method lies in reducing the whole sequence to doll's house proportions and forcing the lovers to play the exquisite closeness and intimacy of the parting scene suspended somewhere between the floor and the top of the proscenium arch.

Here again a persistent realism will only entangle us. We can separate the scenes by means of lights and a reasonably consistent subdivision of the playing area. The indications of locality are clear, and audiences accept them readily enough. The sequence of the parting (Act III, scene 5, line 40 *et seq.*) is much the most difficult unless the stage is set with a permanent "balcony" level. If so, Juliet must probably move down from this level, as she presumably did from the upper stage of the Globe, into the "bedroom" area for the following scene. If there is no balcony, we shall have to imagine Romeo's departure, seeing him "below" only through Juliet's description which, indeed, is vivid enough.

There is a further quality in this play which must turn us away from the solidity of "indoor" scenery into a freer dimension of space and time. ROMEO AND JULIET is impregnated with the influence of the heavens, the sun, the moon, and the stars, dawn and high noon and night. The brief, ecstatic, tragic days turn to the rhythm of the turning globe of the world, defined with a procession of lovely metaphors and phrases. The lovers are "star-crossed" from the very opening lines; it is as if the wings of their passion lifted them too near to the tremendous candles of the planets. Romeo, in particular, is aware of them with his eyes and his soul. The director and designer will need what Robert Edmond Jones calls an "overwhelming sense of the livingness of light . . . Lucidity, penetration, awareness, discovery, inwardness, wonder . . . These are the qualities we should try to achieve in our lighting . . . a quality of lustre, a shine and a gleam that befits the exceptional occasion."

This is the quality which the theater must strive to recapture in ROMEO AND JULIET. The lovers themselves may do a great deal toward it, with a soaring of the spirit. The play is filled with flesh-and-blood smaller characters, which, if they are fully played, will amply give us the swift-moving life around them: Mercutio, of course, irresistible in almost any hands; Capulet and the Nurse, strongly, surely painted in with rich, warm color; the fiery, overbearing Tybalt; Friar Laurence, so full of wise precepts, so lamentably inadequate with worldly intrigue; Benvolio, dependable and sane in his own right; Peter, and even Sampson and Gregory, who start the play at a tempo which befits it; a gallery of portraits done with the opulence and clarity of the great painters of the Renaissance. No actor or director is in danger of underrating them. We can hardly miss the drama of Mercutio's death or the feast of theatrical opportunity at Capulet's banquet or the overwhelming music of the lovers. Indeed, our temptation is to get drunk with one or another of these elements. Let us remember what Shakespeare himself must have had as the theme nearest his heart:

> When I consider everything that grows
> Holds in perfection but a little moment,
> That this huge stage presenteth naught but shows
> Whereon the stars in secret influence comment . . .
>
> Sonnet 15

Let us try to invoke the secret influence of the stars.

A MIDSUMMER NIGHT'S DREAM is as moon-drenched as ROMEO AND JULIET is shot with stars. The moon is not in a malignant phase, but her radiance sheds a disturbing magic this midsummer night, holding all the play in an opalescent enchantment, where everything seems "translated." Only with Theseus' hunting horns at dawn and the music of his hounds does the thin, silver mist dissolve and a world emerge in which lovers are mortal men, trees are trees merely, and Bottom can scratch his ear without the inexplicable feeling that it has grown long and hairy. Not until THE TEMPEST will Shakespeare write a play with elements as delicately ethereal as these.

How are we to translate them into terms of scenery? The old traveling companies used to rise blithely above the problem, with a green drop vaguely bedecked with painted foliage and two or three wooden backboards covered with dusty grass-matting. They probably served the play as well or better than more ambitious producers have done. It is perilously easy to obliterate this fragile fairyland behind a stageful of massive scenery, elaborate, fantastical, and unnecessary. Our wood must be a mood, an atmosphere, where anything may happen, gauzes, perhaps, silhouettes and shadows, light, transparent, fluid—a wood of dreams.

If only the fairies also could be made of gossamer! I have sometimes wondered whether we could disembody all of them, except Oberon, Titania, and Puck, using the heliograph principle to produce dancing points of light, mirror-reflections flashing and darting like will-o'-the-wisps. Shakespeare presented his "fairies," as he later did his witches, according to the conventions of the day, and in following this lead we are generally forced to rely on the talents of the nearest available dancing school. But we must not ignore the drawbacks of the thumping of little feet. It is more important to keep the verse on tiptoe, quivering and agleam, than to indulge in dainty ballets by "fairies" who are vocally flat-footed. The allure of Mendelssohn, great as it is, should also be viewed with caution. Titania, Oberon, and their companions carry the musical burden of the play. The enchanted wood should tingle with music, "sounds and sweet airs that give delight and hurt not"; but they should never overwhelm the protagonists.

There is nothing very difficult for the actors in this play. We are apt to discount the lovers, with a secret fear that they are a bore, and to let the clowns loose with free, galumphing feet. The lovers need not be wearisome, though, admittedly, the women are better than the men. Both Helena and Hermia are vivid enough and tartly contrasted. If our "Helena" will play a rather silly girl in love as a rather silly girl in love, and not moan for our sympathy all the time, she will be fully rewarded by our surprised delight when the worm turns and upbraids her dearest friend with all the armory of feminine cattiness assured of male support. There is some very elegant fooling in the quarrel scene between the quartet.

Nor need Demetrius and Lysander lugubriously accept the usual fate of stooges, if they will play for the enchantment of the wood and make us realize the depths of bemused and driveling sentimentality to which its magic has reduced two ordinarily upstanding and normal young men. In the play's first and last scenes they are both drawn lightly but quite firmly; what they establish in these scenes will govern the degree of comedy to be extracted from their moonlit aberrations. Even so percipient a critic as Van Doren has condemned them as "dolls"; but any actor with imagination knows better, and the play will lose if he cannot establish their humanity.

For the lovers, more clearly even than Theseus and Hippolyta, form the link between the honest, tangible, homespun craftsman's world, peopled by the so-called clowns, and the airy dimension which Oberon and Titania inhabit. Puck knows both worlds and partakes of them. But to him the mortal world represents every reasonable idea standing idiotically on its head; whereas, to the lovers and clowns, Titania's domain dissolves all reliable and stable values in fluidity and bewilderment. Bottom, of course, is the most deeply entangled, and in him the most solid of the earthy elements is enmeshed by the most delicate fabric of the fairy world.

The clowns are straightforward stuff. They are apt to emerge a trifle encrusted with tradition, which has gathered as thick as barnacles around them. There is, for instance, one piece of business still in common use, whereby Thisbe, bent on self-destruction, falls on Pyramus' scabbard instead of on his sword. This seems to date right back to the original production, for it is described by a member of the Elizabethan audience. Since then, over the centuries, directors and comedians have wrung every shred of opportunity out of the Pyramus and Thisbe interlude; their inventions have been preserved in the memory of succeeding actors and handed on, with additions.

Many of them remain genuinely, if not very subtly, funny. The director must select judiciously and, above all, keep the fooling spontaneous and not allow it to stretch out interminably in order to include everybody's notion of a "comic" touch. A great clown's meat is a lesser clown's poison. "Simpleness and duty" are accredited to the amateur actors, and the fun will be heightened if they do remember that they are supposedly playing to the Duke and his companions and do not too freely caricature the traditions of village-hall theatricals. The scene offers limitless possibilities. We may treat it with temperance and do nobody any harm.

In other scenes than this the Clowns are dogged with tradition. Starveling is supposedly deaf. When he is told that he is to play Thisbe's mother, he has for generations interpolated: "Thisbe's brother?" *"Mother!"* replies the united troupe. Flute has immemorially protested that he has "a beard —" "Huh?" from his companions, "—coming!" But the Clowns are genuine, human, and indestructible. We fall for them today as they did in Elizabethan London. This is a lighthearted, irresponsible piece of mischief and magic; let us lend our best ears to its melodies and warm our hearts at its humanity. The moonlit Shakespearean heavens will not often be so beautifully cloudless, nor his lyric gift of song so purely melodious.

8. The Histories

THE PROBLEMS raised for a modern producer dealing with any of Shakespeare's historical plays have a general similarity, though they are by no means identical. For the purposes of this necessarily generalized discussion, I shall leave aside HENRY VIII, which is of a totally different vintage from the main cycle and was written, probably in collaboration with John Fletcher, at the end of Shakespeare's career. The rest of the series, with the exception of KING JOHN, covers in unbroken continuity the turbulent period of English history from 1398, two years before the deposition of Richard II, to 1485, when Henry VII succeeded to the throne, reconciled the dynastic quarrels which had so long torn the nation with civil war, and established the Tudor dynasty, whose last representative, Queen Elizabeth, still reigned when Shakespeare wrote the plays. These were not, however, written in order of historical chronology. The HENRY VI trilogy and RICHARD III come close together; then, after about three years, RICHARD II; after a further two years, HENRY IV, PARTS I and II; and finally HENRY V.

The plays are, in the main, faithful to Holinshed's *Chronicles*, from which they are drawn; but they cannot be taken as a history book of impeccable accuracy. From the very beginning, with his HENRY VI collaborations, Shakespeare reserved the dramatist's right of selection; and, as he wrote them, he became increasingly absorbed in the presentation of character. By the time he reached the mature writing of the HENRY IV's, he had realized that one Falstaff was worth much more than a king's ransom, and that the Boar's Head tavern in Eastcheap was a more fruitful sphere of action than any field of battle he had yet encountered. By this time, he was in the high meridian of his comedy power; he had already written THE MERCHANT OF VENICE; and MUCH ADO ABOUT NOTHING, AS YOU LIKE IT, and TWELFTH NIGHT were swelling in his heart.

After the completion of HENRY V, he laid Holinshed aside, and from henceforth his dukes are from Illyria and Messina and a Chaucerian Ruritania, which he calls the Forest of Arden, not from the courts of Westminster and Windsor. When he returns again to history, it will be with Plutarch, not Holinshed, in his pocket; and the scene will range throughout the Roman world. But he will have long outgrown his earlier pageant-plus-oratory manner. His stage will have become a frame for living men; there will be no puppets, indistinguishable from one another save by the reds and blues and golds, the lions rampant and leopards couchant of their varying escutcheons.

If the internal politics of England in the fifteenth century are apt to fill an American audience with anticipatory dismay, the English themselves are not, and certainly were not in Shakespeare's day, much clearer about the period. Despite the fact that Shakespeare firmly leaves out characters irrelevant to his purpose, whatever their historical importance, he cannot always divest himself of them. Edmund Mortimer, for instance, is dynastically unavoidable, though dramatically a red herring. The warring houses of York and Lancaster abounded in uncles and cousins, and the chronicle plays are cluttered with their amorphous progeny.

It is recorded that in a fairly recent production of HENRY V by a modern Shakespearean repertory company, every man, woman, and child available was pressed into double and triple service in order to cope with the procession of English and French nobility with which the play is thronged. During one general scene the stage-manager-prompter suddenly became aware of a horrible silence on the stage. Somebody, he realized, was "off"; he glanced wildly at the book, saw that the character due to speak was Westmoreland, and immediately rushed toward the dressing rooms, yelling vainly for the absentee nobleman, until finally the "Princess of France" stopped him in mid-career by inquiring mildly, "Hey! Peter! aren't you playing 'Westmoreland'?" "My God! I believe I am!" said he, and hurtled back to the field of Agincourt.

The mishap is understandable. It illustrates one of the director's problems, the differentiation of the smaller parts. In RICHARD II, for instance, the "haught, insulting" Northumberland and the poor, well-meaning, befuddled Duke of York are clear enough. But "Ross-and-Willoughby" can easily degenerate into a pair of cardboard twins; Bushy, Bagot, and Green, "the caterpillars of the commonwealth," become merely "The Caterpillars," a conglomerate species. A little diligent search will reveal distinguishing marks. Green seems to be the executive caterpillar. He brings up questions of finance and is the first to receive the official tidings of Bolingbroke's return; Bushy appears to be the dandy, talking to the Queen in language of precious affectation; Bagot turns king's evidence and tries to save his own skin by framing an accusation against his former confederate, Aumerle. Around such indications as these the director must build a complete scaffolding for the actor, in dress, in characterization of voice and movement, in supplementary business and coherent reaction to the events of any scene of which the character is a silent witness.

If we are troubled, throughout the early histories, with this plethora of peers, we are even more perplexed by a problem of staging which pursues us throughout the cycle. What on earth are we to do about the battles? Even Shakespeare grew at last dissatisfied with the inadequacies of his stage to reproduce a conflict of any significance, and our audiences are harder to satisfy than were his. He relied frankly on the method of his period.

> Into a thousand parts divide one man,
> And make imaginary puissance.
> Think, when we talk of horses, that you see them,
> Printing their proud hoofs i' the receiving earth.
>   HENRY V, Prologue

We, too, will be unable to succeed without the aid of our audience's imagination and good will. We have tried stylization, a ballet effect, a pattern of spears which we fondly hope may recall to the erudite the pictures of Uccello; we have tried the impressionist approach. This involves blacking out the entire stage except for a few dramatically angled shafts of light; a few menacing figures then rush from side to side, performing menacing motions and seeming "werry fierce"; strange cries come from the surrounding darkness, indicating further contingents of unseen warriors. This expedient has served pretty sturdily; but it is apt to lead the literal-minded to suppose that in the Middle Ages all conflicts were fought out at midnight.

We can make a great noise with drums and guns and significant music and muddle things nicely with a few smoke pots and a couple of gauzes; a few very large banners will replace a troop or so. But it is simply no good trying to be realistic in the Cecil B. De Mille manner; we have not the resources, nor had Shakespeare—and he did not write for them. He gave us the isolated duels and conflicts which were necessary to his plot; and he gave us in verse, which we can supplement with heraldic trappings, the sense of a chivalric tournament. If the audience will not help us out, if we have not brought them to the frame of mind in which they are willing to do so, we shall not save ourselves by shouting in the dark.

From the very beginning, Shakespeare seems more at home with the common people than with the confused politics of dynastic wars, the grand monotony of feudal barons, or the pageantry of inadequate armies. Even in the early HENRY VI, PART II, the Jack Cade scenes come to life, crudely but unmistakably. Dick Butcher, Smith the Weaver, the two anonymous "rebels," for whom we have nothing but the names of the actors, Bevis and John Holland, are much more lively than the nobility. These scenes, too, are vigorously informed with that mistrust and contempt for mob emotion and mob rule which Shakespeare reiterates throughout his life.

> The blunt monster with uncounted heads,
> The still discordant wav'ring multitude,

whom he is to show so terribly in JULIUS CAESAR and CORIOLANUS is here bitterly satirized. Nor is Jack Cade's form of communism so very archaic. "When I am king, as king I will be, . . . there shall be no more money, all shall eat and drink on my score, and I will apparel them all in one livery, that they may agree like brothers, and worship me their lord." His hearers seem unaware of the sting in the tail. But Jack Cade is no fool, and he dies with a prophetic word: "Iden, farewell, and be proud of thy victory. Tell Kent from me, she hath lost her best man, and exhort all the world to be cowards; for I, that never feared any, am vanquished by famine, not by valour."

These scenes are probably the liveliest thing in the HENRY
VI cycle, though there are, throughout, brilliant flashes of
poetry and pregnant phrase. Henry VI himself shows
originality of thought, and his creator's mind is already too
independent to write him off as a weakling and a fool among
his hot-blooded, wolfish, power-drunken subjects. He has a
mild vision to which we listen more attentively than to his
nobles.

> My crown is in my heart, not on my head;
> Not decked with diamonds, and Indian stones;
> Nor to be seen: my crown is called content.
>
> III-III, 1, 62

>   . . . the shepherd's homely curds,
> His cold, thin drink out of his leather bottle,
> His wonted sleep under a fresh tree's shade,
> All which secure and sweetly he enjoys,   III-II, 5, 47

these things are to be envied by all of Shakespeare's high
and mighty ones, his "packs and sets of great ones, that ebb
and flow by the moon."

Queen Margaret, the leading woman of the trilogy, is "a
part to tear a cat in, to make all split," though very few
actresses now carry the vocal guns for her continuous, pound-
ing pentameters. Her love scenes with Suffolk have genuine
passion and even, occasionally, simplicity. But her tirades are
filled with rage and clamor; there are too many of them and
they are too much alike; they are exhausting rather than touching. Margaret has stature and power but she is crudely drawn.
Shakespeare will very soon come to realize the shortcomings
of this, his first tragic heroine.

There are isolated passages which leap out from the rest
of the cycle: the macabre horror of Duke Humphrey's death,
and the whole scene of Suffolk's execution by the pirates,
from its opening lines:

The gaudy, blabbing and remorseful day
Is crept into the bosom of the sea.   II-IV, I, I

There are also lines which, because they still remain unexpectedly topical for us, should make us realize how often
Shakespeare must have caught his hearers' throats with allusions of studied topicality which no longer move us. The
pulse of 1590, however, was surely echoed in 1940:

HASTINGS: Why, knows not Montague that of itself
            England is safe, if true within itself?
MONTAGUE: But the safer when 'tis backed with France.
HASTINGS: 'Tis better using France than trusting France:
            Let us be back'd with God, and with the seas,
            Which he hath given for fence impregnable,
            And with their helps only defend ourselves;
            In them and in ourselves, our safety lies.

                           III-IV, I, 39

Here is another theme to which Shakespeare will triumphantly return, for the famous lines which conclude KING
JOHN, for Gaunt's "royal throne of kings" speech, and for
Henry V's speeches at Harfleur and Agincourt. To this extent
the HENRY VI trilogy shares the more vital qualities of its successors; but it is weakened by a processional quality, a lack of
concentration, which makes it hard for the director to achieve
a sharp, dramatic focus. Unlike the RICHARD plays, which will
follow, there is little intensification of vision.

As usual, however, the theater adds a third dimension to
these rather wooden chronicles. Part I is much the weakest
of the three, but the other two reveal a surprising vitality.
The reader finds it almost impossible to care about any of
these shouting, swearing gangster-nobles, or even to distinguish
among them. On the stage, enriched by the differing per-
sonalities and physical endowments of the actors, they do
come to life. The complex dynastic squabbling recedes into

the background, and the flashes of humanity are more vivid than the reader has supposed. There is tension in the story line, and the fights, well staged, have their own excitement. The admirable production of the trilogy by the Birmingham Repertory Company in the season of 1952–1953 proved that there is much in it that is still stageworthy. And the stage, of course, is where the plays were intended to be.

All the same, we are left wishing that Shakespeare would return to such company as Jack Cade and Peter Thump, to his common men, his artisans and tavern brawlers, who had neither the wind nor the wit for decasyllables. But we are to wait for several years yet before he will do more than give the man in the street a fleeting glance. For the next two plays are each centered on a single focus; they swing like a wheel around its axle. Shakespeare has already brought to birth in HENRY VI the miraculous monster who is to become Richard III, and he will dominate the next play, almost to the exclusion of lesser characters.

It may be this avid, all-absorbing quality in Richard III which has fascinated almost every Shakespearean actor of eminence since the play was written. He is brilliantly theatrical; he has courage, ferocity, sardonic humor, magnetism. He is blazing and brutal; he twists and gleams; he towers over lesser men. Richard is every sort of villain and we know it; but we cannot resist him. Shakespeare has stamped on the consciousness of all his readers an image of Richard of Gloucester which is completely false to the historical reality. But his Richard has succeeded in taking the place of history.

The play is very long, longer than OTHELLO or LEAR, and most of the cut stage versions concentrate on the scenes which are obvious theatrical plums, taking care, of course, not to omit a line of the actor-manager's role. But there are dangerous losses involved in this. It is unwise, for instance, to neglect the "little men": the three frightened and apprehensive citizens who discuss the death of King Edward, glancing fearfully over their shoulders for the Gestapo-Gloucester secret police; the pompous little snob who is Lord Mayor of London; the Scrivener with his bitter-sharp comment on Lord Hastings' death; and the two toughs who are hired to murder Clarence. From one of them comes a trenchant example of Shakespeare's early prose, the speech on conscience:

I'll not meddle with it, it is a dangerous thing, it makes a man a coward: a man cannot steal, but it accuseth him; he cannot swear, but it checks him; he cannot lie with his neighbour's wife, but it detects him: it is a blushing shamefast spirit, that mutinies in a man's bosom; it fills one full of obstacles: it made me once restore a purse of gold that I found; it beggars any man that keeps it: it is turned out of all towns and cities for a dangerous thing, and every man that means to live well endeavours to trust himself and to live without it.   I, 4, 128.

These minor members of the proletariat provide a valuable counterpoint to the Kings and Queens and Dukes and Peers who play the game of power-politics in contrasting iambics. While Richard, his allies and his adversaries, juggle with the fate of England's crown, her common people should not go unheard.

Some cutting of the women's scenes is unavoidable. The Queen Margaret of the HENRY VI cycle continues her thundering invectives into this play; she is an avenging fury, superb in her first scene, repetitive in her second. This scene (Act IV, scene 4) with its three wailing women is usually considered a purple patch. If RICHARD is treated as the logical continuation of the HENRY VI trilogy, the scene does provide a kind of Chorus from the women of bereavement, the bloody feuds of York and Lancaster united in a fellowship of grief. But if the play is produced as a separate entity, as it must generally be in the modern theater, then, I believe, the scene carries heavy liabilities; it belittles by reiteration the magnificent effect of Margaret's first prophetic denunciations and slows down the gathering march of the action. On the other hand, Richard's mother, the old Duchess of York, is frequently, and quite unjustifiably, cut out of the acting versions. The development of her relationship with her son is tersely handled and makes an ominous and significant contribution to our understanding of Richard himself. It is she, his mother, who first knows him for what he is; and it is she, not Margaret, whose final curse rings in his ears above the sounding drums of war.

Similarly, stage tradition generally cuts the dialogue between Richard and Queen Elizabeth, mother of the murdered princes, in Act IV, scene 4, because it is thought to be a paler repetition of the extraordinary and devilish wooing of Lady Anne at the beginning of the play. Yet this reiteration of the pattern is obviously intentional and the scene can be subtle and persuasive, if the actors can make it so. In it Shakespeare sounds again the motif which he never loses throughout the chronicle plays, the theme of England. Richard's final, and clinching, argument for the marriage he proposes concerns the welfare of England:

> Without her, follows to this land and me,
> To thee, herself and many a Christian soul,
> Death, desolation, ruin and decay:
> It cannot be avoided but by this;
> It will not be avoided but by this.

The theme is important; it will return to close the play, with Richmond's

> Now civil wounds are stopp'd, peace lives again:
> That she may long live here, God say amen!

Richmond is, as we all know, even more remote than Richard from the historical original. Henry VII was a mean, brilliant, shifty, and wholly unattractive politician. Pre-

sumably, Shakespeare dared not so depict the grandfather of
the reigning monarch. But in any case he needed a hero to
end his play. This hero, however, need not be a golden-haired
juvenile lead, St. George in shining armor. He is forceful,
authoritative, blunt, and to the point. He is, quite simply, the
man who says "No."

We have seen, throughout the play, the other men, the
men who made Richard's ascendancy possible, the men who
always make tyranny possible. Some are Richard's allies and
willing tools. Some, like Clarence, are deceived and, in their
weakness, destroyed. Some, like Hastings, are lighthearted,
easy-minded, ambitious, and not too scrupulous; they, too,
are destroyed. Some yield to a horrible fascination, like Lady
Anne, and die of the surrender; some, out of fear or supposed
necessity, temporize and let the storm pass over them, like
Stanley. Some, from recklessness or moral weakness, are seduced, like Tyrell, and lay waste their own lives. Some, the
most to be pitied and yet the most dangerous to society, help
the tyrant through the first steps of his ascent, join with him
in his first acts of aggression, believing that they can turn evil
actions to good ends and control the monster they have helped
to create. Of these, Buckingham is the universal prototype.
He, too, is destroyed as soon as he becomes expendable. Shakespeare has given us an amazing gallery of portraits, the men
who make dictatorship possible. We ourselves have seen all
of these people. We have seen the dictators who climbed on
their shoulders to the summits of absolute power. One of them
was called Adolf Hitler.

But Richmond is the man who will neither compromise
nor wait and hope for the best. He is the man whom Richard
has never yet had to face, the man who says "No." From the
first sound of his voice:

> Fellows in arms, and my most loving friends,
> Bruised underneath the yoke of tyranny . . .

we know that the days of the "bloody and usurping boar" are numbered and that the end will come quickly. The swiftness of the play's final scenes is not an arbitrary device of the dramatist in a hurry. As the sun rises over Bosworth Field and the nightmare dissolves with the morning mists, he proclaims the hollowness of the devil and the triumphant might of God. He will return to a similar affirmation in the last scenes of MACBETH.

The Second Richard, following closely on this violent and abundant play, is as complete a contrast as possible. Richard of Bordeaux, like Richard of Gloucester, is the dominant character round whom the wheel of events revolves. But he does not, like his predecessor, plunge immediately into action, fully armed and fully revealed. Indeed, he does not really take charge of the play, in the sense of possessing the audience and carrying it with him, until almost halfway through. After a deceptively facile first act, in which we see him glittering, reckless, arrogant, and irresponsible, he is absent from the stage for four entire scenes. Only when he comes back from Ireland, in the loss of his crown and his kingdom, does Richard II find himself. Yet during this elusive first third of the play the actor must lay down all the groundwork on which he is to build. Shakespeare has supplied the necessary material. Even while the protagonist is off the stage, he has, most subtly, continued to build and change the character of Richard by reflection and indirection; he has suggested and prepared the poet and the man who will pass, before our eyes, through all the ordeals of suffering.

But the play must be carried along for much of this time by the impetus supplied from its lesser characters. The director's problem is to tap the source of power in each of them, use them in their just proportion, blend and balance their component contributions so that they carry Richard himself lightly upon their shoulders and never seem to be doing so.

Shakespeare, by now a dramatist with nine or ten productions behind him, was not unaware of the danger and supplied the means for circumventing it.

The play has started, right from the beginning, with everybody at fever heat, except Richard himself and the entourage who mirror him. Bolingbroke and Mowbray swing immediately into the thrust and lunge of conflict; and behind them, we must feel, are ranged the whole strength of the kingdom, ready to back their differing opinions with all the force at their command. We must realize the power of these men; for, once united against Richard, they are to destroy him; and we are to watch them do it.

It is likely that we shall be unable to "put over" the intricacies of Bolingbroke's accusation that Mowbray has contrived the Duke of Gloucester's death; but we can achieve a sense that the country has, indeed, been shocked by this murder, that Mowbray, innocent or guilty, is in some way bound up with the King himself, and that, in accusing Mowbray, Bolingbroke is, in fact, accusing the King. The issues, therefore, which lie on their warring spears when they meet in the lists at Coventry must have raised every spectator to the highest point of tension.

At the critical moment, Richard forbids the fight; he banishes both the combatants, his cousin Bolingbroke and Mowbray, his partisan and possible confederate. Was he afraid of the issue? Did he fear that whoever won, he would lose? Whatever the motive, we must feel that by this single action he has converted two rival factions into a unity, mistrusting himself. Both combatants underscore the growing feeling against him; and their protests are based on the agony of banishment from England, denial of their right to breathe the English air and speak the English tongue. Their last words, each of them, are a farewell to England.

Two scenes later, the dying John of Gaunt raises high for all the play, for all time, the banner of England; and it is not Richard's flag but the standard of those who, for England's sake, must wish his downfall. We may not take very much to Bolingbroke, the coldly determined; we may feel that Mowbray is a man of fierce words and easy blows, no very reliable guide for us to follow; but old Lancaster sets the issue beyond mistaking, and, in flouting him, Richard scorns England itself.

With the little scene between Northumberland, Ross, and Willoughby, we see the lion of England rouse and stir. We know that Richard is not for England, nor we for Richard as England's king. We are left only with the question: What of Richard for himself? Shakespeare has split a very pretty issue and left us Richard the man, not Richard the King, whose doom is already certain.

Four more scenes will serve to heighten the unsolved question in our minds. In all of them we see Richard by indirection: first through his Queen, who cannot still the misgivings of her heart or her grief and longing for him; through his shallow friends, who run at the first hint of danger; through his bemused old uncle, York, who knows that Bolingbroke is morally in the right, should prevail, and will, but yet cannot bring himself to more than a reluctant and wavering acquiescence in something he is powerless to prevent; through Bolingbroke himself, purposeful where Richard was volatile, smooth where Richard was impatient, politely ruthless where Richard was suicidally highhanded; last, through one of the few loyal nobles, who sets the emotional key and sounds the very melody for Richard's return with his:

> Ah, Richard, with the eye of heavy mind
> I see thy glory like a shooting star
> Fall to the base earth from the firmament.
> Thy sun sets weeping in the lowly west,

Witnessing storms to come, woe and unrest:
Thy friends are fled to wait upon thy foes,
And crossly to thy good all fortune goes.   III, 1, 18

Without once bringing Richard on the stage, Shakespeare
has entirely shifted the weight of our sympathy; his friends
are ours, his enemies we cannot warm to; it is now for Richard
alone to capture our hearts and the play; and he does so, with
the armory of weakness, the gentleness of defeat, and the pure
gold of the poetry in which he speaks. The hardest part of
the director's job is over; from now on the solo instrument
will lead, and he will do no more than regulate the tempo
of the orchestral accompaniment.

Shakespeare, then, has written a concerto for the villain-
king, in RICHARD III, and enriched it with all the brass and
percussion of theater melodrama; in RICHARD II, he has written
a concerto for the poet who happens to be a king and sweet-
ened it with exquisite melodies for his solo violin. He is to
write one more historical concerto, for the hero-king, in
HENRY V; and, though this would seem the simplest of the
three problems, both for him and us, we cannot feel that his
heart was ever quite so fully engaged with it.

HENRY V is psychologically and emotionally plain sailing,
or it should be. Henry himself satisfies all the standard requirements. He is given some of the most magnificent passages
of rhetoric ever written for anybody, a wooing scene which is
delicious comedy, and, probably the most moving thing about
him, a scene where he talks anonymously with his soldiers on
the night before the battle and knows the humility and infinite
responsibility of the man who must throw a thousand lives
within the imminent reach of death.

This is the human value which we must stress, as Henry V
goes his glamorous, not very deeply explored, progress through
the play. Before the walls of Harfleur, he has inspired his

men to victory with a magnificent fanfare of words but little reckoning of the cost in human lives.

> Once more unto the breach, dear friends, once more,
> Or close the wall up with our English dead. III, I, I

Facing the terrible odds of Agincourt, he will move us much more deeply, more gently, with a new and more poignant awareness of the heroism of man against death:

> . . . he which hath no stomach to this feast,
> Let him depart, his passport shall be drawn,
> And crowns for convoy put into his purse:
> We would not die in that man's company
> That fears his fellowship, to die with us.
> This day is call'd the feast of Crispian:
> He that outlives this day, and comes safe home,
> Will stand a tip-toe when this day is named.
>
> . . . .
>
> And Crispin Crispian shall ne'er go by,
> From this day to the ending of the world,
> But we in it shall be remembered;
> We few, we happy few, we band of brothers;
> For he to-day that sheds his blood with me
> Shall be my brother; be he ne'er so base,
> This day shall gentle his condition:
> And gentlemen in England, now a-bed,
> Shall think themselves accurs'd they were not here;
> And hold their manhoods cheap, whiles any speaks
> That fought with us upon Saint Crispin's day. IV, 3, 35

Our failure to capitulate may be due to the fact that we have lost our taste for the pageantry of war; it may be that we see so little of Henry, the man, as against Henry the King, and the Prince Hal we used to know seems to bear little relation to this fighting monarch. But actor and producer will have to use every device they can jointly evolve to save our hero from his own glory.

The minor characters are scattered with a liberal hand and vividly portrayed. Shakespeare is once more moving freely among the soldiers and men-at-arms whom he met in the taverns of Thames-side. The French Princess is delicate, precise, filled with gaiety and grace; the fiery, loyal Welshman, Captain Fluellen, is instantly endearing; Bates and Williams are the eternal English Tommy, almost unbearably up-to-date. In fact, the wealth of minor characters, following a track of their own, sometimes threaten to overwhelm the play, unless they are kept very skillfully within its pattern. This will be a large part of our problem. Shakespeare must have known it. For he had promised, in the Epilogue to HENRY IV, PART II, to put another character into this sequel and must subsequently have realized that, if he did so, both the English victors and the French vanquished would fade like mist from the field of Agincourt, and, between the wraithlike armies, Falstaff would stand alone.

The two plays which come between RICHARD II and HENRY V, both historically and in the order in which Shakespeare wrote them, constitute a special problem and are radiant with a particular glory. HENRY IV is no more than a label. They are FALSTAFF, PARTS I and II; and the difference between the two parts is notable. In PART I, Shakespeare still has his colossal Galatea in hand; he holds the balance between the Boar's Head and the scenes of politics and war by throwing into the scale against Falstaff the magnificence of Hotspur and by setting Prince Hal pretty squarely between the two of them. But in PART II he cannot stop Falstaff. The Tavern scenes are richer than ever and are amplified by the gaudily vital creation of Doll Tearsheet, the fuller treatment of Mistress Quickly, and the subsidiary help of Ancient Pistol and Falstaff's new page. Even when the reluctant warrior leaves for the wars, he gets little further than Justice Shallow's orchard, and there conjures up another world of the most entertaining civilian companions to keep himself and us from the military history of the play's original design.

Of this ingredient, Shakespeare uses as little as he can, and that is a good deal too much for us. The remnants of the Hotspur rebels are a tame, colorless lot; as one of them says, describing Hotspur's death:

> In few, his death, whose spirit lent a fire
> Even to the dullest spirit in the camp,
> Being bruited once, took fire and heat away
>
> I, I, 112

The King's side finally overcomes the last flicker of rebellion by a mean and shabby piece of trickery, and this poor business Shakespeare turns over to Hal's younger brother, Prince John of Lancaster, of whom Falstaff says: "Good faith, this same young sober-blooded boy doth not love me, nor a man cannot make him laugh, but that's no marvel, he drinks no wine."

The military scenes are dead wood in the play. Hal cannot be mixed up in them; and Shakespeare is in a great difficulty with Hal. Henry V is already in his mind. At the end of the play, Hal is to disown Falstaff utterly, and the ties between them are already so loosened that they appear together only in one scene, of which Hal has a very minor share. To bridge the gap, Shakespeare gives Hal the moving scene with his dying father; but Henry IV himself has preserved no more than a melancholy sonority, in our remembrance, and, though we are moved, we are still Falstaff's, heart and soul; so that when Hal, at his coronation, utterly rejects his old companion, we are not at all appeased by the high-minded moral precepts which father and son have interchanged to prepare us for this denouement.

We are left, therefore, with two thirds of the play Falstaff's, incredibly rich, brimming over with life and gusto. Of the remainder, the rebellion scenes are something of a weariness, and the King's scenes a dignified interlude from laughter, while the final curtain is bound to leave us with a sense of frustration and dissatisfaction.

The presentation of PART II by itself is therefore a puzzling task. There have been attempts to make a Falstaff play out of a compressed version of the two parts together. But this is not entirely satisfactory. Shakespeare himself knew that it was dangerous to give us too much Fat Knight at a stretch without a change of diet. When PARTS I and II are done successively, as they were by the Old Vic Company in 1946, they emerge as the logical entity Shakespeare planned. But it is hard to interpret PART II without the memory of Hotspur, Douglas, and the rest to lend proportion and significance to the rebellion scenes; and we lose the sense of continuity and development in Hal and in King Henry. As a result, the great wealth of the Falstaff scenes has been largely lost to us because PART II is so seldom presented in the theater.

It would seem that Falstaff is like Hamlet in that a very great deal of scholarly toil, amateur psychology, and printer's ink have been expended on him; and the two characters are certainly equal in the towering superiority they enjoy in their respective spheres. Many commentators have been at great pains to analyze just why the world should have taken Falstaff to its heart. "Why," asks one of them, "should we laugh at an old man with a huge belly and corresponding appetites," a coward, a boaster, a thief, a liar, a man untroubled by the smallest moral principle or scruple? Falstaff himself gives the best answer:

> The brain of this foolish compounded clay-man is not able to invent anything that tends to laughter more than I invent, or is invented on me; I am not only witty in myself, but the cause that wit is in other men.   II-I, 2, 5

Perhaps it is partly his refreshing freedom from all the limitations of conventional behavior, from the tyranny of "honor," from the load of moral obligations under which the lesser man staggers, together with his unquenchable zest for life, which gives him such unequaled power in raising our fullhearted laughter. When Shakespeare balances him with Hotspur, the embodiment of all the high romance of medieval chivalry, with its daredevil fearlessness and its pursuit of personal honor as the most glittering of all the world's prizes, he gives us what is perhaps the fullest and richest of all the histories, HENRY IV, PART I.

This play has never received in the theater the popularity that has been accorded the "star vehicles," RICHARD III, HENRY V, and, more recently, RICHARD II, simply because it has no single leading part. Honors are fairly equally divided between Falstaff and Hotspur, with Hal a very close third, and star actors have appeared in all three of the parts. But the ten-week run it received in New York in 1939 with Maurice Evans as Falstaff, Wesley Addy as Hotspur, and Edmond O'Brien as Hal proved its power to hold modern audiences. A fraction of the problem which the play presents was eased in this production because Mr. Evans's RICHARD II was still a recent memory to the audiences who saw it, and the political background supplied by the events of the earlier play was therefore familiar to them. Further evidence of the play's popularity was, however, afforded by the Old Vic revival with Ralph Richardson as Falstaff and Laurence Olivier as Hotspur.

As always, Shakespeare gets the necessary political groundwork done with as quickly as possible and settles down, as we do, to the fascination of watching character in action. Again, according to his habit, he besprinkles the political scenes liberally with the names of off-stage personages, a complication

which once caused an absent-minded "King Henry" to declare
in perfect pentameters that

> The Earl of Whatsisname, Lord Something Else,
> Some kind of Bishop and two other guys
> Capitulate against us, and are up.

But in this play the balance between military and civilian
activity is much more evenly held than in most of the other
histories. Even the Hotspur scenes are packed with comedy,
from Harry Percy's opening speech about the "certain lord,
neat and trimly dressed," who came with such elegant in-
solence to demand the prisoners after the battle of Holmedon,
to the warmth and mischief of his scene with his wife, and
the impish caricature of Glendower. Hotspur is always kept
alive and burning; he is no puppet warrior. On the other
side of the picture, Falstaff and Hal, whose story at the outset is far removed from any theme of war, seldom stray for
long from the sound of the distant trumpets. At the close of
the second Boar's Head scene they too are for the wars. Hal
strides off with a martial flourish. Says Falstaff wryly:

> Rare words! Brave world! Hostess, my breakfast come!
> O, I could wish this tavern were my drum!   III, 3, 205

The minor characters, all richly painted, complement the
strength of their leaders in the two halves of the play. The
satellites of the Falstaff scenes need some help from their
actors, especially Peto and Gadshill, who seem to be sketches
for an actor's personality to amplify. The tiny portraits of the
two Carriers who are robbed by Falstaff's gang come instantly
alive, however, with their "gammon of bacon and two razes
of ginger to be delivered as far as Charing Cross," and their
comment on the lately deceased ostler: "Poor fellow never
joyed since the price of oats rose, it was the death of him."
To the Hotspur side come the lively wit and grace of Lady
Percy, the fiery Glendower, and, late in the play, Sir Richard

Vernon, who bursts upon us with a blazing description of
Hal and his companions:

> Glittering in golden coats like images,
> As full of spirit as the month of May,
> And gorgeous as the sun at midsummer.   IV, 1, 100

The balance is the more remarkable in that Falstaff and
Hotspur hold credos as opposite as the poles, and yet, in
voicing them, they complement each other and bind the play
as indivisibly as the two sides of a shield. Says Hotspur:

> By heaven, methinks it were an easy leap,
> To pluck bright honour from the pale-fac'd moon,
> Or dive into the bottom of the deep,
> Where fathom line could never touch the ground,
> And pluck up drowned honour by the locks,
> So he that doth redeem her thence might wear
> Without corrival all her dignities.   I, 3, 201

Says Falstaff:

> Can honour set to a leg? no: or an arm? no: or take away the
> grief of a wound? no. Honour hath no skill in surgery, then?
> no. What is honour? a word; what is in that word honour?
> what is that honour? air. A trim reckoning! Who hath it? he
> that died o' Wednesday. Doth he feel it? no. Doth he hear it?
> no. 'Tis insensible then? yea, to the dead. But will it not
> live with the living? no. Why? detraction will not suffer it,
> therefore I'll none of it, honour is a mere scutcheon, and so
> ends my catechism.   V, 1, 131

Hotspur is killed, dying with bitterness on his lips:

> But thoughts the slaves of life, and life time's fool,

and Hal, his conqueror, speaks for him a bitter epitaph:

> When that this body did contain a spirit,
> A kingdom for it was too small a bound,
> But now two paces of the vilest earth
> Is room enough.   V, 5, 89

But Falstaff, having politicly saved his own life by counterfeiting death, survives to take up Hotspur's body and drag it ingloriously from the field; a sour conclusion, which we must suppose Shakespeare fully intended. He has given us life, at its fullest and most red-blooded, and he gives us death like a sudden blow between the eyes. He gives us all the panoply of war, but he is not finding much to commend the spurious glamour of battle. We shall miss the play's meaning if we lose ourselves among the banners.

As we have seen, in the following play, PART II, he turns entirely away from war to follow Falstaff; and in HENRY V he cannot go back to his fighting scenes until he has disposed of the figure who might so easily make them seem ridiculous and pitiful. So Falstaff, too, must die, Shakespeare's loving tenderness for the broken old rascal flowing through every word of Mrs. Quickly's description of his passing:

> He's in Arthur's bosom, if ever a man went to Arthur's bosom. A' made a finer end, and went away an it had been any Christom child: a' parted e'en just between twelve and one, e'en at the turning of the tide: for after I saw him fumble with the sheets, and play with flowers, and smile upon his fingers' ends, I knew there was no way but one; for his nose was as sharp as a pen and a' babbled of green fields. "How now, Sir John?" quoth I: "what, man? be o' good cheer:" so a' cried out, "God, God, God!" three or four times: now I, to comfort him, bid him a' should not think of God; I hop'd there was no need to trouble himself with any such thoughts yet; so a' bad me lay more clothes on his feet: I put my hand into the bed, and felt them, and they were as cold as any stone: then I felt his knees, and they were as cold as any stone, and so upward and upward, and all was as cold as any stone.   II, 3, 11

No wonder we have a hard time, after this, in working up an interest in the men of war.

There remains one play, isolated in historical position, which was written before Shakespeare started on the HENRY IV's; he had already turned from his single-character focus, and he had not yet arrived at the superb triple-protagonist achievement which was to follow. KING JOHN, therefore, presents some special difficulties, and its merits have been theatrically subject to undeserved neglect. It shares, with the other plays which have dropped out of stage use, the lack of any focal point. It is significant that both KING JOHN and RICHARD II were revived, after lengthy periods of oblivion, on the English stage around the turn of the last century by Sir Herbert Tree; but while RICHARD has held its own ever since, KING JOHN has once more practically disappeared, despite a fine revival by Robert Mantell in New York shortly afterward.

For King John himself falls, so to speak, between two Richards. He is a "villain," but an uncertain one, liable to panic when the tide turns against him; he is a weak monarch, but there is little we can discern of the man behind the façade. From the beginning he seems to have a fever in his veins; he grasps at the stronger wills of his mother and his illegitimate brother, Faulconbridge. He can rant with the best of Shakespeare's early reciting monarchs, but these tirades, though richer, are not more revealing than theirs. Shakespeare is still clinging to something of the pageant method. But his doubts about the dramatic potency of the war theme are stronger. He had begged the question in RICHARD II. Through John's mouth he voices disillusion:

> There is no sure foundation built on blood,
> No certain life achiev'd by others' death.   v, 2, 104

In two scenes, John comes fully alive: first in the devious fascination he exercises over the blunt-minded Hubert in order to incite him to the murder of young Arthur; when he suddenly breaks the oily, inferential speech he has so far used with the single command, "Death," the effect is as startling as a flash of forked lightning from a heavy sky. But, like the Thane of Cawdor, "nothing in his life became him like the leaving it." It is a great death scene. The fever rages through his veins, the poison he has eaten brings him to a tortured, writhing, ugly end:

> There is so hot a summer in my bosom,
> That all my bowels crumble up to dust:
> I am a scribbled form drawn with a pen
> Upon a parchment, and against this fire
> Do I shrink up . . .
> And none of you will bid the winter come
> To thrust his icy fingers in my maw;
> Nor let my kingdom's rivers take their course
> Through my burn'd bosom; nor entreat the north
> To make his bleak winds kiss my parched lips
> And comfort me with cold. I do not ask you much,
> I beg cold comfort; and you are so strait
> And so ingrateful, you deny me that.   v, 7, 30

Here is fine material for an actor, but still we have no pattern for a play.

Shakespeare seems curiously ill at ease. Perhaps it is that he is being forced to adapt and telescope an old play, THE TROUBLESOME REIGN OF KING JOHN, without his heart in the work. He does not transform his material with his usual freedom. Perhaps he has grown weary of the old iteration of defiance and lament, without as yet discerning the way of freedom which Falstaff, and even the "little men" of HENRY V, were to bring him.

The play looks backward, with its high, heroic, overembroidered verse; with the verbose peerage; and with the character of Constance, another Margaret, with a mellower tone and some strain of moving nobility, but an equal tendency to dull our ears and hearts with repetition of her griefs. It looks forward with the character of Faulconbridge, who has independence, humor, stature, and a dimension all his own.

He steps out of the play like a flesh-and-blood actor from a puppet stage; he interprets to us and for us; he is most particularly ours. Falstaff would know him; their minds would meet. Hotspur would know him by the flash of his sword, and the resounding clarion of his concluding lines:

> This England never did nor never shall
> Lie at the proud foot of a conqueror,
> But when it first did help to wound itself.
> Now these her princes are come home again,
> Come the three corners of the world in arms,
> And we shall shock them. Nought shall make us rue,
> If England to itself do rest but true.   v, 7, 112

KING JOHN is one of the plays which should be revived; there is a turbid power in it. It is also one of the plays which, as the theater stands today, could only repay revival as part of a repertoire, perhaps then only "on Saturday nights," proverbially reserved by the old actor-managers for the plays which could never draw an audience on a Monday. There are half a dozen other plays like it. They are too dangerous a gamble for the commercial manager of today; and we have succeeded in evolving no substitute for him, no answer to the question of how to be daring yet solvent. There is an audience for KING JOHN, but not one which will repay us an investment of $35,000; it will therefore probably remain unproduced for many years to come. Something seems to be wrong somewhere.*

* This was written in 1941. In 1955 the required sum would be about three times as great. Something seems to be still wronger.

9. The Comedies

BY THE TIME Shakespeare came to write the HENRY IV's, he had already produced the first of the group of comedies with which he gloriously rounds out his first ten years as a playwright. Indeed HENRY IV, PART II is perhaps more purely a comedy than THE MERCHANT OF VENICE, which preceded it. Next comes MUCH ADO ABOUT NOTHING, probably in the same year as HENRY V, and, in 1599–1600, AS YOU LIKE IT and TWELFTH NIGHT. The date of THE MERRY WIVES OF WINDSOR, like everything else about the source, plot, and textual aspects of that play, is the subject of much discussion. General agreement assigns it to the period immediately following the other Falstaff plays, but Sir E. K. Chambers, whose chronology I have elsewhere accepted, puts it three years later, contemporaneously with HAMLET, on evidence which I think inconclusive.

At all events, by the time Shakespeare brings the fantasy of Illyria to its golden close, he is already wrestling with the stern realities of ancient Rome; and, from the intermediary form of JULIUS CAESAR, he will take the leap straight into the finished greatness of tragedy. Not the least astounding feature of his career is that he must have made for himself four distinct and separate reputations as a dramatist: first, as a writer of chronicle histories, with some deviations to romantic comedy and one poetic tragedy to grace his poet's reputation; then, as a writer of comedies, and an extremely successful one. Suddenly, when his fellows must have thought the bent of his genius fully settled, came HAMLET, and for six or seven years they settled down to being tragic actors when Shakespeare's work was in rehearsal. But from Stratford in the evening of his days came scripts which were not tragedies at all; he had come back to a form of romantic comedy, but of a mood and design so different from THE MERRY WIVES that the new actors in the Globe Company, who had never known Shakespeare, must have thought it barely conceivable that the same man could have written them.

All of the comedies have held the stage continuously. As with his other theatrically successful plays, they contain wonderful acting parts and must have rejoiced the hearts of the boy actors of the Globe, who as yet had had nothing except Juliet to compare with the plums which had fallen to the leading men. But the full-length Shrew, and many slighter sketches, had shown what Shakespeare could do for women in comedy; and now came, in swift succession, Portia, Beatrice, Rosalind, and Viola, with Mrs. Ford and Mrs. Page thrown in for good measure. The boy actors must have prayed that Will would stick to writing comedies; and leading actresses ever since have kept his radiant, witty, gracious heroines continually before the public.

THE MERRY WIVES OF WINDSOR is, of course, another Falstaff play. Long-established tradition has it that Elizabeth, reflecting the popular taste as usual, was a Falstaff fan and demanded another play about the Fat Knight in love. Possibly the Globe Company felt it had disappointed its public in giving them a HENRY V without Falstaff and knew he was still excellent box office. At all events, the text as we have it, from the evidently patched-up Folio printing and a pirated "bad" Quarto, shows distinct signs of having been written in a hurry and without very much heart. Falstaff has fallen from his former high estate: the penetration, the ironic understanding, the rapier thrusts of philosophy are gone; he is a butt and a dupe, an old, fat fool in love.

But this declension is of more moment to the fireside critic than to the occupant of a balcony seat at THE MERRY WIVES; for the play is a farce, and pretends to be nothing else; it has gusto and facility and momentum; and, if we had not known the earlier Sir John, we should not grumble about this one. The actor, however, who has the good fortune to play both will find the clay on which he works changing curiously under his hands to a softer, spongier texture. He will not be able to mold from it a second figure of a stature equal to the first.

Shakespeare, turning out the play in two weeks according to the traditional account, sits down to his task and starts it off with a flourish and the impetus of a writer to whom the humors of the English middle class come easily. He has some old friends whom he had by no means exhausted at their earlier appearances: Justice Shallow, Nym and Pistol, Bardolph, who he doesn't apparently think will be of much use to him, and Mistress Quickly, younger, fresher, and sprucer than her namesake. He creates some new friends immediately: the Justice's ineffably foolish cousin, Slender; Sir Hugh Evans, the Welsh parson; and Dr. Caius, the French doctor. Wales and France are always good for comedy.

Mine Host of the Garter Inn is a breezy, beery, hail-fellow-well-met kind of a figure, who can be relied upon to kick the plot into action if it threatens to languish; Page is an honest, worthy, sufficient yeoman who will give the piece ballast, and Ford the usual jealous husband, who will be used for the comic possibilities of jealousy and perhaps will touch a chord in the depths of Shakespeare's subconscious mind which, years later, will provide the thematic base for Leontes. The Merry Wives themselves are new figures in his gallery; they are coarser in grain than the heroines who will follow, near in blood to Emilia and Paulina of the later plays, but more independent and set in quite different surroundings. They will never quite recur; and Shakespeare takes pleasure in them from the beginning and treats them to a brilliant duologue scene together.

So far he is not disliking his enforced task; but he is shirking the Falstaff business, which is just what he has been commanded to write, and dallies with these new creatures as if he would really like to explore them further and see what happens. When he at last buckles down to Falstaff in love he seems to put aside Sir Hugh, Dr. Caius, Shallow, and, to a certain degree, Slender with an apologetic shrug to them and an irritated bow toward the royal command.

His invention does not fail him for the incidents of plot, which are hilarious enough in their kind, and his dialogue does not lose its salt; but the richness of enjoyment is no longer present. Final proof of the mechanical nature of his labor may perhaps be found in the young lovers, Fenton and Anne Page, to whom, alone among all his romantic youth, he does not give one line to stir or lift the heart with music. Fenton is amiable cardboard; Anne has spirit, especially in her comment on the suggestion of Dr. Caius for a prospective husband, the flashing:

> Alas, I had rather be set quick i' the earth
> And bowled to death with turnips.   iii, 4, 84

The romance between them, and the consequent confounding of Caius and Slender, are necessary to the plot, but the poet in him does not once rise in their defense.

Finally he winds up the play rather like the writer of a

musical-comedy book when he finds that it is nearly eleven o'clock; in honor of the royal performance that is to be given for the court at Windsor he puts in a masque, gracefully salutes the Knights of the Order of the Garter, and sends his characters thankfully home to "laugh this sport o'er by a country fire, Sir John and all." He slams the manuscript down on Burbage's table with an enormous sigh of relief and rushes back to the unfinished script which all this time has been waiting in his heart; we cannot tell for certain which it is; perhaps MUCH ADO, perhaps JULIUS CAESAR, perhaps HAMLET.

Our main difficulty in producing the play lies exactly parallel to Shakespeare's in writing it. We have to supply all the warmth, humanity, and mellowness of which the script runs short. There is plenty of pace in the action; we have only to keep up with it. There are endless possibilities for comic business, some of them so obvious in the script that we cannot miss them, some more subtly implicit in a turn of phrase. We shall have to accept a few editorial emendations where the text, though conceivably correct, is too obscure to make immediate auditory sense. There are some problems of staging where the concurrent plots have to be kept going simultaneously, and Shakespeare has been in too much of a hurry to do more than make one set of characters "retire" to discuss one plan in private while another set discusses the other plan in full hearing.

There are many instances, especially in the middle of the play, where one or more characters are left carelessly standing around while the subject of the scene swings away from them, and we shall have to fill in the gaps for them as unostentatiously as possible. Sometimes their presence is fruitful of comedy even though they have not a line to speak. At the end of Act III, scene 3, after Falstaff has been rescued under the very eyes of the jealous Ford by being carried off in a buck basket, Mrs. Ford, the injured wife, is left during thirty lines of general commotion without a word to say, and Mrs. Page, "a very tattling woman," is similarly silent; but there are indications that the sobs of the one, apparently heartbroken, and the righteously indignant ministrations of the other form a continuous part of the general confusion which swirls around the bewildered Ford. We must read with our eyes in all the general scenes, and play for the comedy of speed and high spirits.

THE MERCHANT OF VENICE, the earliest of the comedy group, ranks among the most continuously performed of all the plays; the elements of successful theater are felicitously present, contrasted and combined with almost arrogant skill, and their dramatic potentialities and relative importance have been treated by producers in every imaginable way. The Venetian world which Shakespeare created with such opulent facility has remained fairly stable, though variously taken for granted, enhanced, or overlaid with scenic interpretation according to the resources of the producer and the convention of the time. We have had three-ply Bridges of Sighs and painted-drop Grand Canals faithfully reproducing everything but the well-known Venetian odors; and we have had expressionistic treatments, with the Senators of the Doge's Council represented by red-robed figures in sheeplike masks.

Fortunately the theater has produced a regular supply of magnificent Shylocks and Portias, but it has seldom realized the necessity for producing magnificent Salanios and Salerinos and has generally thrown onto the stage two callow and underpaid young men in wrinkled tights to deal as best they know how with this supposed pair of notorious bores. Lorenzo has fared a little better, for the exquisite poetry of his last-act speeches at least rates a fine speaker of verse; Gratiano, whom Shakespeare himself has allowed to degenerate as the play proceeds in the quality both of his social status and of his wit, has been pretty handsomely cast; Antonio is frequently treated with insufficient imagination. The actor is prone to take a dangerous cue from the opening lines:

> In sooth I know not why I am so sad,
> It wearies me, you say it wearies you;

and to neglect the dignity, courtesy, and courage implicit in Bassanio's description of:

> The dearest friend to me, the kindest man,
> The best-condition'd and unwearied spirit
> In doing courtesies; and one in whom
> The ancient Roman honour more appears
> Than any that draws breath in Italy.   III, 2, 292

His behavior at the Trial scene has a quiet truth and steadfastness which are not unworthy of the finest actor's service.

Bassanio, being the romantic lead, has been more generally justified by the theater than by the critics, who analyze him into an ineffectual fortune hunter. Shakespeare, if he did not take much trouble to deepen the character, is not so foolish as to bother with this academic interpretation of plot exigencies. He gives his juvenile lead noble verse from the outset and knows he will have the services of an actor whose appearance will justify Nerissa's "he, of all the men that ever my foolish eyes look'd upon, was the best deserving a fair lady."

These characters between them will carry the Venetian scene, and not least the easy, carelessly arrogant Salanio and Salerino, with their lavish richness of phrase and gilded metaphor. They are lords of the European metropolis, masterfully at home in a city of legendary glamour, endowed with all the wealth of the Italian Renaissance civilization. At the play's first beginning they anatomize Antonio's sadness into a fantasy of dream-world misfortune:

> I should not see the sandy hour-glass run
> But I should think of shallows and of flats,
> And see my wealthy Andrew dock'd in sand
> Vailing her high-top lower than her ribs
> To kiss her burial. Should I go to church

> And see the holy edifice of stone,
> And not bethink me straight of dangerous rocks,
> Which touching but my gentle vessel's side
> Would scatter all her spices on the stream,
> Enrobe the roaring waters with my silks,
> And in a word, but even now worth this,
> And now worth nothing?   I, I, 25

We should think again of this metaphor of "enrobe the roaring waters with my silks" when the two elegant young men stand aghast and helpless before the torrent of Shylock's outpoured hatred and, sobered by this contact with an unbelievably harsh reality, go, not without dignity, one to stay by the doomed Antonio and the other to fetch Bassanio from Belmont.

They form part of the delicate, invisible links forged by Shakespeare between the fabulous atmosphere of Venice and the fairy world of Belmont; for the story of the three caskets is pure fairy-tale, and the encircling air must not blow too roughly upon it. Belmont is the eternal Xanadu of the poet's imagining, from its first foreshadowing in Bassanio's

> In Belmont is a lady, richly left,
> And she is fair and, fairer than that word,
> Of wondrous virtues . . .
> Nor is the wide world ignorant of her worth,
> For the four winds blow in from every coast
> Renowned suitors, and her sunny locks
> Hang on her temples like a golden fleece,
> Which makes her seat of Belmont Colchos' strand,
> And many Jasons come in quest of her.   I, I, 161

The enchanted Princess, at her first appearance, will prove, however, that a fresh, light wind of wit breathed through the scented gardens; the breeze must be kept gentle; Nerissa, if she is brash or labored, may shake the heavy blossoms from the trees.

Only when we have done with the dusky, sonorous Morocco and the fantasticated Aragon will the Princess ripen into full, sure womanhood with the grave beauty of her surrender to Bassanio. The shadow which immediately falls on the lovers with the news of Antonio's danger matures her to authority, understanding, and deep tenderness. For Belmont must be guided back toward the Venetian dimension, where its Princess is to meet Shylock on his own plane and vanquish him. She who plays Portia will be unwise to neglect this steady deepening of strength in the development of the character in order to skip too skittishly after the easy comedy of the scene with Nerissa where she plans her boy's disguise.

At the play's finish, with Venice once more in the distance, Shakespeare will bring back the enchantment of Belmont, this time through Lorenzo and Jessica's famous antiphonal lyric, through the "still" music which is commanded for them, and through the quiet, spellbound duet of peace which Portia and Nerissa play at their first entrance, broken so delicately when Portia sees the two lovers:

> Peace, ho! the moon sleeps with Endymion,
> And would not be awakened.   v, 1, 108

"Music ceases," says the stage direction, and Portia's very next line,

> He knows me as the blind man knows the cuckoo,
> By the bad voice,

swings the scene to the mood of gay comedy, one might almost call it comedy of relief, after the tension of the trial, in which the rest of the action is to be played. For the whole play is smoothly and beautifully locked together, reconciling apparent irreconcilables with matchless skill and precision. It is our business to preserve this unity of texture by weaving personal color of high contrasting value into an undisturbed harmony.

The black figure in the picture is, of course, Shylock, the alien in these linked worlds, the "outsider" in every spiritual sense, whose single-purposed force nearly shatters them both. The storms of controversy have swept Shylock to the crest of the popular wave, and kept him there. Actors and critics have contributed alike.

His stage history is marked with epoch-making performances breaking through a supposedly established tradition, to become traditional in their turn. Dogget, at the beginning of the eighteenth century, made a comic figure out of him, with the aid of an appalling "adaptation" by George Granville. Macklin restored him to a forceful reality and was so afraid of his own daring that he never rehearsed the interpretation he intended to give, but sprang it as a complete surprise on his thunderstruck fellows at the opening performance. Edmund Kean, penniless and starving, got his first chance in the part in 1814 and electrified London, not only by the savagery of his reading, but by wearing, for the first time in recorded history, a black wig. Even Burbage, according to extant memoirs, had worn a red one. Edwin Booth later made the interesting suggestion that Kean wore the black wig simply because a "black-bald" was part of every stock actor's essential equipment, and he had no money to buy a new "red." Sir Henry Irving played Shylock for all the pathos of the despised and downtrodden Jew, with the dragging, broken exit from the Trial scene which is so enormously effective, and so great a distortion of Shakespeare's intention.

For Shakespeare saw Shylock under a brilliant light; he realized to the full what the pressure of the Venetian world would do to a man of Shylock's race and trade and did not soft-pedal the issue. But the celebrated "hath not a Jew eyes" tirade has tended to falsify our vision of Shylock, the individual, with generalized partisanship; for there is little that is sympathetic about this particular Jew. He loved his wife, Leah;

he loves his daughter, Jessica, though Heaven knows why, for she is a little baggage. But he loves them as his, his possessions, like his turquoise and his ducats and his race and his revenge. His, his, his. It is the keynote of the man; the passion of possession raised to demonic power, driven by the circumstance of his world to the snarling, merciless defense of the cornered rat. His very speeches choke with suppression, with poison. There is tragedy in the stripping from him of everything that is his, daughter, ducats, revenge, religion, everything but the burden of continued, unvalued life. But it is not a "sympathetic" tragedy, and there is more terror than pity in it.

There are no rules for Shylocks; we can hope that traditions will be made and broken as often as great actors arise to play the part. There is, I think, a rule for directors, which is, here as always, to try to realize the wholeness of Shakespeare's dramatic intention, of which each separate character forms a part. The attempt to twist and stretch both characters and plot to fit a preconceived formula of one's own devising is neither good drama nor good sense. In this day and age we flatly refuse to accept in fiction or on the stage the attempt to arouse hatred or prejudice against the Jewish race. It would, however, be absurd to maintain that every Jew in literature must be a hero or a saint. Shylock, certainly, is far too much alive to be crammed into the strait jacket of theory. He is far too savage for laughter, too tragic for hatred; but he rejects, equally, the justifications of sentimentality. He is not a martyr. He must be interpreted courageously and whole. If you distort Shylock you will also wreck the play.

Shakespeare was not anti-Semitic. Indeed he was not anti-anything in terms of generalizations about races or creeds. He wrote about human beings, each of them an individual and not a "type." They are rarely all of a piece, all black or all white, nor are they puppets manipulated to point a moral. It is precisely for this reason that his plays have never dated and are still applicable to ourselves, because the springs of individual human behavior have altered very little. But they are too powerful to be reduced to the purposes of contemporary special pleading. It is not surprising that THE MERCHANT OF VENICE still holds the stage as one of the most popular of his plays; despite the charges so frequently and mistakenly brought against it, it remains a human document in superb dramatic terms.

The remaining comedies contain no Shylock to rock their equilibrium, and, though their balance is thereby more easily obtained, they lack, perhaps, the same thrill of tension. MUCH ADO has a villain, Don John, whose machinations will provide the intricacies of the plot; he is a monosyllabic fellow, whose brief lines strike like single harsh notes through the first half of the play, leaving a faint dissonance in the air. His work done, and Hero delivered to shame and dishonor, he disappears with the sardonic:

> Thus pretty lady,
> I am sorry for thy much misgovernment.

But Shakespeare, in this case, is not mainly interested in the plot. He uses it like a frame within which he places the people in whom he and we are really interested: Benedick, Beatrice, Don Pedro, and the humble, solemn, pompous little constables whose simplicity is the means whereby intrigue is brought to destruction.

Dogberry and Verges have been among the most misused of Shakespeare's comics. They have been provided with layers of "character" make-up, and Dogberry has made much ado indeed at forcing his verbal mistakings over the footlights as if they had to be spelled out before the audience would get the point. He and Verges have frequently played with a ruthless determination to be funny or die and have consequently met the latter fate. But the constables are quiet, fearfully earnest,

proud of their office, stubborn in its defense, and, in the arrest
of Conrade and Borachio, they obstinately pursue the right
people for the wrong reasons until truth is brought to light.
Dogberry's first exhortation to the citizens of the "Watch,"
those volunteer keepers of their neighbors' peace, sets the tone
for all of them, if it be played simply and fervently, without
caricature:

> DOGBERRY: [to *"George Seacoal"*] You are thought here to be
> the most senseless and fit man for the constable of the watch;
> therefore bear you the lantern. This is your charge: you shall
> comprehend all vagrom men; you are to bid any man stand,
> in the prince's name.
>
> SECOND WATCH: How if a' will not stand?
>
> DOGBERRY: Why, then, take no note of him, but let him go, and
> presently call the rest of the watch together, and thank God
> you are rid of a knave.
>
> VERGES: If he will not stand when he is bidden, he is none of
> the prince's subjects.
>
> DOGBERRY: True, and they are to meddle with none but the
> prince's subjects. You shall make no noise in the streets; for
> the watch to babble and to talk is most tolerable and not to
> be endured.
>
> SECOND WATCH: We will rather sleep than talk, for we know
> what belongs to a watch.
>
> DOGBERRY: Why, you speak like an ancient and most quiet
> watchman, for I cannot see how sleeping should offend: only,
> have a care your bills be not stolen . . .   III, 3, 21

It is much more important that the audience should love Dogberry, and little Verges, "honest as the skin between his
brows," than that the actor should concentrate on extorting a
forced laugh with his celebrated "comparisons are odorous."

Beatrice and Benedick are, of course, the glory of the play,
and on their two actors its success will largely depend. The
flexibility and brilliance of their prose gave the English lan-

guage a new dramatic weapon; Shakespeare himself never surpassed it, and perhaps only Congreve and Sheridan at his height were ever to set a greater luster upon the form. It needs brilliant speaking, extreme lucidity of analytic thought, and phrasing which will exactly correspond to this analysis, precise enunciation, and, above all, speed. Even Ellen Terry, the happiest and most irresistible of Beatrices, said of herself that she was never swift enough. For if Beatrice's railing against husbands in general and Benedick in particular does not bubble as lightly as champagne, it may become tedious and sententious. The following extract may exemplify the danger, and the opportunity:

BEATRICE: Lord, I could not endure a husband with a beard on his face. I had rather lie in the woollen.

LEONATO: You may light on a husband that hath no beard.

BEATRICE: What should I do with him? Dress him in my apparel, and make him my waiting-gentlewoman? . . . he that is less than a man, I am not for him: therefore I will even take sixpence in earnest of the bear-herd, and lead his apes into hell.

LEONATO: Well, then, go you into hell?

BEATRICE: No, but to the gate, and there will the devil meet me, like an old cuckold, with horns on his head, and say "Get you to heaven, Beatrice, get you to heaven, here's no place for you maids:" so deliver I up my apes, and away to Saint Peter for the heavens; he shows me where the bachelors sit, and there live we as merry as the day is long.   II, i, 26

Shakespeare uses a new and daring device when Beatrice has overheard Hero and Ursula discussing Benedick's love for her; the little soliloquy which follows is not merely in verse, but in rhymed verse, as formal and simple as that of the earliest of the heroines. But its apparent stiffness provides the actress with a golden opportunity to show the flashing, self-sufficient Beatrice as humbly, softly, sentimentally in love as any milkmaid; and from here on the softness must never be lost. All through the play Beatrice must remember that she was "born in a merry hour," not a quarrelsome one, so that her interchanges of wit never become rasping. Beatrice has "dancing feet"; she runs "like a lapwing"; a star danced at her birth; the part is featherweight.

Benedick is of rougher stuff; his speeches have a broader sweep, if his speed in repartee is half a jump behind Beatrice. He is gifted with an inexhaustible wealth of metaphor and imagery: "Hang me up in a bottle like a cat," "an oak with but one green leaf on it would have answered her," "I will fetch you a toothpicker now from the furthest inch of Asia." Love does not reduce Benedick to verse, for he "was not born under a rhyming planet." But the surge of love does somehow simplify his speech to a greater directness; his finest declaration to his lady has an accent inescapably his own; it is not merely the language of love, but the language of Benedick in love. "Will you go hear this news, signior?" says Beatrice; and he answers, "I will live in thy heart, die in thy lap, and be buried in thine eyes; and moreover I will go with thee to thine uncle's." Exit. For, among other things, he has a masterly talent for the exit line, until he finishes the play with the impudent "Prince . . . get thee a wife, get thee a wife!" to Don Pedro, the promise to "devise brave punishments" for Don John, and the flourish "strike up, pipers!"

So Shakespeare disposes of a plot which he has never taken very seriously. It has never been merely silly, and we must see that it never becomes so. None of the characters in it, especially Hero, lacks validity. Claudio, unlike Bassanio, is rather shabbily treated; we are angry with him for being taken in to begin with, and angrier at his wooden repentance afterward. We feel a little mollified by the fact that Don Pedro, one of Shakespeare's most gorgeous Renaissance princes, is equally deceived. But we have known that it must all come out right in the end; and even while the drama of the Church scene holds us, mainly through the way in which it brings out unsuspected qualities in its participants, we know that the little constables are blindly plodding along the road which will lead us all to a happy ending.

The plot has held the shadow which gives depth to the whole picture; no one in the play is left untouched by it; no one is quite the same at the end as he was at the beginning, and we must emphasize this line of personal development. Shakespeare is drawing closer, perhaps unconsciously, to the theme of man under the pressure of circumstance; this undertone, barely audible, gives a depth we must not lose to the gaiety and swinging movement of MUCH ADO.

AS YOU LIKE IT, however, is the most cloudless of the comedies. It has been described as the most English, but I do not feel this to be true. The yokels of the wood near Athens, its very flowers and trees, are more English than the Forest of Arden, where the pastoral life conducted by the banished courtiers has a quality of playing at rusticity, like a Fête Champêtre by Watteau. There are no dangers in this Forest and not the mildest inconvenience to the progress of mellow thoughts, sweet speech, and gay, fullhearted loving, predestinate to happiness. Danger is the mere painting of itself; the "green and gilded snake" glides into a bush at the hero's approach; the lioness has a "royal disposition" and can do no more than scratch his arm; one generous action will win the implacable Oliver to unstinted response, and even the black-hearted Frederick will meet "an old religious man," and, "after some question with him," be "converted both from his enterprise and from the world."

There is magic in this wood, too, but the magic of the sun, and it is a more constantly effulgent planet than ever shone in the uncertain English summer. The very prose of the play is shot with poetry, as the shade is checkered with sunlight.

The irony of Touchstone's shafts is nowhere tipped with malice; and Jaques, the philosopher whose blood is as cold as his mind is clear, arouses not cynicism but compassion. This is the play of harmony. It is not England, nor any part of the known world; it is a part of the happy man's dream, the man who trusts and loves mankind.

If we can reproduce this quality in the theater, we shall have succeeded. The problem is as simple and as difficult as that. The actors will need a gaiety of soul more even than they will need technical equipment. The play must be lovingly performed. Even Audrey and William, who have so often gaped and yammered through their scenes, are in love, and it is the most important thing about them. Even Touchstone decides, with a wholly conscious dissection of his motives, to submit to the prevalent emotion. Only Jaques disdains it, so off he goes to the Duke's "abandoned cave," an appropriate refuge. It seems to be the people of the outside world, Duke Frederick and Charles the Wrestler and the Oliver of the early scenes, who are bemused among false perspectives. The little time-server Le Beau betrays a wistful sense of it, when he takes leave of Orlando with:

> Hereafter, in a better world than this,
> I shall desire more love and knowledge of you.   1, 3, 296

The comedy is so simple, so straightforward, and also so well known, that we are tempted to think it will necessarily need embellishment. The Forest of Arden, we are prone to think, is as much in need of scenic elaboration as is the wood near Athens. Actually, it needs only a sense of sunshine and greenness, of pleasure and peace. Nor need the director beat his brains out devising comic business for the actors, so long as the heart of laughter is in them. At the World's Fair performances in 1939 we found, slightly to our surprise, that AS YOU LIKE IT proved far stronger in the warm regard of our audiences than did THE SHREW and THE DREAM, though it was the least embellished with directorial invention and we did not have the assistance of any scenic background whatever.

Rosalind, setting the pace and pitch for the whole, is subject to similar temptations. She has probably more "sides," and possibly more puns, than any other of Shakespeare's women; sometimes the actress affects a "swashing and a martial outside" to an extent that gives a brassy quality to her scenes. But all the way through there is tenderness as well as ardor in her loving. Edith Evans, in a recent production at the Old Vic, managed to discover moments of a melting sweetness which no one who saw them will forget. She proved that, if Shakespeare's boys had an easier task in the matter of disguise, the modern actress has a chance to achieve a modulation which can be immeasurably valuable.

Like Beatrice, Rosalind demands great swiftness; there is also, frequently, an extremely subtle interplay of thought behind, in contradiction to, the spoken word. Rosalinds do not grow on every theater bush, nor are they manufactured in drama schools; for Rosalind must put the audience in love with all the gaiety and sweetness of life. If they leave the theater with sour faces, we shall have failed to translate Shakespeare's intention. If we are merely "bright" about it, we shall be simply unbearable.

TWELFTH NIGHT is the last of the great comedies; the sun of AS YOU LIKE IT shines more softly in the Illyrian air, the beams growing long and level toward sunset. Even the music with which the two plays are saturated has a different note. In AS YOU LIKE IT, everybody sings, men and women and boys, and the play harmonizes like a madrigal or a rondo. But Orsino's musicians play him melodies with a "dying fall," and even Feste's love song ends:

> What is love? 'tis not hereafter;
> Present mirth hath present laughter;

What's to come is still unsure:
In delay there lies no plenty;
Then come kiss me, sweet and twenty,
Youth's a stuff will not endure.

We feel that the world of AS YOU LIKE IT will abide our return. But TWELFTH NIGHT is filled with impermanence, fragile, imponderable.

Yet it has in it a set of characters and a sequence of plot more robust and coarser in grain than anything in the other play; our theater problem becomes, in consequence, the blend and balance of disparate elements.

These elements are not portioned out into watertight compartments of character or class. Sir Toby carries the broadest of the comedy; but he is more than a drunken roisterer; he is a gentleman, Olivia's cousin, not so far removed in rank from the Duke. He is the younger son, the professionless gentleman who hunts and shoots and trades smoking-room stories at his club and lives shamelessly on his relatives and, a little, by his wits. Sir Tobys have supplied a steady counterpoint to English history; until September, 1940, you could have walked into any club on Pall Mall and found him sitting in a leather armchair.

His associates are not boors or rustics either. Maria, though she carries more than a little of the "soubrette" tradition along with her, is Olivia's gentlewoman and confidante; and in the great households of Shakespeare's day such positions were filled by girls and women who were themselves of the lesser nobility. It will, further, be a mistake to cast Sir Andrew as several feet of lank, dank dolt. He is a figure of some importance in his own home town, "the glass of fashion and the mould of form" to some Illyrian Podunk; he is simply out of key with the manners of the great world, overzealous in everything, from his clothes to his French tags, his eager little mind hopelessly outdistanced by Toby's broad and easy jests. Fabian is a superior servant, and a clever one, not much more. He is one of the characters to whom we must be especially careful to give some distinguishing mark by which a modern audience may place him recognizably in the hierarchy. It is a little puzzling to decide why Shakespeare put him in at all, unless he felt the need of another note in the comic chord.

Olivia and Orsino are at the other end of the scale. They live in an unreal world of their own imagining; they are in love with love and with all the trappings of love, phrases and pictures and music. Orsino is brought to a sense of real values before he himself knows it; the presence of "Cesario" has an astringent effect which he would be the last to admit; but when, in the last scene, he comes to suspect and to receive apparent proof of the love between Olivia and his page-boy, a psychologist might find his furious jealousy to be caused as much by the faithlessness of "Cesario" as by the cruelty of Olivia. If he plays the scene too heavily, he may upset the balance of comedy and romance which it is to resolve.

Olivia will similarly put the play out of gear unless she is willing to play the spoiled young girl, flattered and pampered all her life long, kept from every contact with reality, thinking in terms of the legendary "Fairy Prince" in humble disguise, confident that every love story will have a happy ending, and that she, in particular, could not possibly be denied the love of her capricious choice. A staid and dignified matron, playing earnestly, and unwilling to be affectionately laughed at, will, again, rend the delicate fabric of fantasy, by causing us to interpret the mistaken-identity plot in terms of a realism which will immediately nullify its charm.

The links between the earthy comedy of Sir Toby and Co. and the lovelorn picture-book world of Olivia and Orsino are Viola herself and Feste. Both bring a highly realistic sense of values to the artifice of their masters; both can readily appreciate a good joke, and Viola can even be made the dupe of one without any lessening of our regard for her; both can spin a web of music in song and speech to catch the very essence of loving, and hold the reflection of man's evanescence; both have the gift to soften laughter with compassion. These seem to be the reasons for which Fabian is substituted for Feste in the more ruthless part of the Malvolio plot, for Feste is not to be identified with any single faction in the play but is part of the alchemy which blends them all. For the same purpose, Viola will be involved in the rich clowning of the duel, for she is to be no lovesick Victorian maiden but an inhabitant of all the play's imagined dimensions.

Malvolio is the solitary figure of the comedy, as alone in this fantasy of artifice and song and cakes and ale as Shylock has been in Venice. Illyria is hostile to Malvolio, and he is perpetually at odds with it, because he cannot make it make sense. And to Malvolio everything must make sense: literal sense, pettifogging sense, hierarchic sense, the sense of moral justice and the rewards of virtue. But life itself perpetually conspires to dupe and disillusion its Malvolios through their very adherence to arithmetical values and brutally tears down the edifices of convention. So, Toby and his fellows embody for this Malvolio the Nemesis of ridicule which awaits those who are strong in principles but weak in tolerance and imagination. Whether we shall pity the man, hate him, despise him, or all three together, and in what proportionate degree, depends on the actor and, to an equal degree, on the balance of all the other actors.

For here is a play which illustrates beyond all the rest the importance of the human element to our theater pattern. No two TWELFTH NIGHT's could ever be exactly alike, even if they were produced from identical prompt copies. The delicate adjustments between the component elements in the play must necessarily vary with every set of actors; here, the comics will tend to be preponderant; there, the Viola-Olivia scenes will embody our acting high lights. The director will have to balance and combine his ingredients in carefully graded proportions, compensating for weaknesses, keeping a moderating hand on excessive strength. This play, above all, he must treat with a light touch and a flexible mind, keeping the final goal clearly in sight. He must be prepared to reach it by devious paths, around obstacles he had not foreseen, and through short cuts he had not anticipated. For there are no frontiers to Illyria, and its inhabitants will forever elude the totalitarian method of theoretical regimentation.

"A great while ago the world begun," and few things in it have remained immutable but the wind and the rain and the sighing echo of a song. If you do not like the title TWELFTH NIGHT, you may call the play WHAT YOU WILL; and, if, striving to please you, we fail of our purpose, we will lift the curtain another day, upon a different world. "Man, proud man" will be our theme, if we are to follow Shakespeare; man, and the immortal gods; men set against each other; the single man's soul set against itself. The conflict will never be resolved; its progress will be labeled "tragedy."

10. The Tragic Essence

NORTH'S TRANSLATION of Plutarch's *Lives* exercised, perhaps, a greater influence over Shakespeare than any of his other source material. He never respected Holinshed as he respects Plutarch, who opens to him a new world and a new race of characters. He is not, at first, wholly at ease among the Romans, and he relies greatly on Plutarch's reports of their actions and even their words; his imagination is not confined, but it is disciplined. In this discipline he feels his way to a new style, firmer and more muscular than before; and in the men who move among the streets of Rome he finds a new type of conflict and a new way of thinking. JULIUS CAESAR is his transition to the tragedies, and Brutus the first of his new tragic heroes.

Like most pioneers, Brutus is not, in himself, fully successful. Shakespeare dissects him and puts together the component parts again—nobility, integrity, Stoicism, sensitivity of mind; he gives us the mental conflict, the confusion of personal and public loyalties, the high intention and the disparate deed; but somewhere the fire is lacking. Antony is freer and far showier; the mixture of warmth and shrewdness, impulsiveness and opportunism, directness and demagogy, are admirably done. Every scene of Brutus is a hard one for the actor, for Brutus is not a man who reveals himself easily; every word of Antony, and they are magnificent words, is a showpiece in itself.

Cassius is no less successful; the twisted, indriven bitterness of the beginning, resentment raised to the status of a social cause, blends to the loneliness and yearning of the end so inexorably that we are touched to compassion. This man "thinks too much," dangerously to others, destructively also to himself. This is the man who braves tyranny with the fearless brag:

> Nor stony tower, nor walls of beaten brass,
> Nor airless dungeon, nor strong links of iron
> Can be retentive to the strength of spirit;
> But life, being weary of these worldly bars,
> Never lacks power to dismiss itself.   I, 3, 93

and who will, indeed, dismiss his own life at the last with the very sword which had killed Caesar, because his fears are greater than his courage to abide the issue of the battle. Brutus is not the only tragic hero in JULIUS CAESAR.

The play is more a conflict between these three contrasted men than it is an onslaught on dictatorship. The dictator himself is a question brilliantly begged; and the new order which is to succeed his fall is to be governed not by the enfranchised people, nor by the confused liberalism of such men as Brutus, nor even, in the final event of which ANTONY AND CLEOPATRA is the analysis, by the popular arts of Antony, but by the cool, keen ruthlessness of Octavius. In this play Shakespeare has not much time for him; but his every line is a power and a portent; the character has taken root, and it is he, because of his unity of purpose and undivided heart, who is to inherit the earth.

The dramatic quality of the play has made it eternally

acceptable in the theater. It shares with the greatest plays that spaciousness of conception which enables any one of twenty interpretations to be applied to it; its political implications can be, and have been, brought into conformity with current issues over the period of more than three hundred years since it was written. At the end of the Nineteen Thirties, Orson Welles took the text of JULIUS CAESAR by the scruff of its neck and beat it into submission to his own purpose, which was to contrive a melodrama about the murder of a dictator, Mussolini model. The result was a brilliant and "timely" piece of theater, but it was fraudulent Shakespeare. The characters of Brutus and Cassius emerged as only fragments of themselves, quite dwarfed by that of Caesar, and the last third of the play disappeared almost completely, Octavius included.

No such mutilations are necessary to bring CAESAR up to date. In 1950, playing a very faithful text but using a modern costume scheme, we found that its impact on young audiences was immediate. College and even high school students started writing theses about its relation to current problems: about civilian authority in the hands of an ambitious general, about demagogy and crowd psychology, about totalitarian ruthlessness as opposed to the free, if fumbling, processes of democracy. The play cannot fail to raise in the mind of any thinking man some of the abiding questions: what choice is the "confused liberal" to make between his personal loyalty and his social conscience, between acquiescence in tyranny and a rebellion which involves murder? is the resort to force and violence ever justifiable? or ever, in the last analysis, successful? can there ever be a "sure foundation built on blood"?

Such are the problems which Caesar and Antony, Brutus and Cassius and Casca, so vividly raise. They remain themselves and yet they are a part of our own world. They lead Shakespeare to his most universal men and his most ageless dramatization of the spiritual conflict in the soul of man;

the heroes will always go down before an Octavius or a Macduff or an Iago, not because of any superior quality in these
men, still less through any extrinsic circumstance, but because
of the "perilous stuff" within their own hearts.

HAMLET, the first of the four great tragedies, stands apart
from the others in conception and treatment, but the essence
of Shakespeare's tragic theme has been stated. OTHELLO, KING
LEAR, and MACBETH will raise it to a poetic power which is
beyond the range of the normal man and give it the dimension of poetic drama on a plane above the level of life. This
will set us, in the theater, a problem different from any which
we have before encountered or are to meet again.

In producing any one of the four great tragedies the director
and his actors may be forgiven for feeling a trifle overwhelmed.
The greatest minds in literary criticism have weightily pre-
stated the case in a continuous march of finely pondered
judgments. The greatest actors, designers, directors, and producers have said their theater say. The majority of any audience to whom the play is presented will have their own ideas
about Othello, their particular form of worship for King
Lear, and, most decisively, their own especial Hamlet in the
mind's eye, with whose beloved lineaments the new Hamlet
will tamper at his peril.

Very much that has been written on the four plays will
open new angles of vision to the persevering if affrighted
director. But he may, after a time, find it hard to preserve his
theater common sense suitably blended with a becoming
humility in the presence of so many pundits, and his brain
will reel with the effort to assimilate and reconcile their conflicting views. For, on the whole, they tend to make things
look much more difficult and alarming than they really are.
Perhaps the director will finally be forced to clear himself of
all the theories about Hamlet's madness, all the speculations
about the double-time scheme of OTHELLO, all the superlatives

which have been lavished darkly upon KING LEAR, and simply consider the prosaic business of presenting to an audience the texts as we know them.

This can be in no sense a belittling of the greatness of the material in the plays; for in them the actor will have need of a kind of inspiration. The word genius, so carelessly traded these days over the counters of an artistic ten-cent store, will not be too great in its true essence for the man who can fully measure Shakespeare's Othello or his Hamlet or his Lear. We are growing unaccustomed to the actor whose spiritual caliber enables him to make of himself the medium for a greater power. Perhaps we are afraid of him, or he of himself. We accept instead a set of variations on competence, personality, sweet reason, and sex appeal. We say, half apologetic and a tiny bit relieved, that Duses are not born any more. Perhaps not. But we no longer demand them; we do not seem to miss them. Shakespeare misses them, for in these tragedies of his there is a greater stature than mere skill will ever reproduce; in them the actor may, as the author did, open the floodgates to the power and the glory which transcend the appraisal of the logical analyst.

Skill, however, will do much. We cannot know whether Burbage gave wings to the parts he played; but we do know that Shakespeare so fashioned his plays that their melodramatic theater quality carried them to the tumultuous favor of an Elizabethan audience. It may be well for us to start by getting their theater structure soundly based and built, to try to recapture their firm, free craftsmanship, their enormous tempo, their passion, their delicate dramatic inflection of stress and relief, and their sweeping impetus of sound.

The director cannot manufacture wings, but he can give the actor space and scope in which to put them on. If the production is planned and patterned to Shakespeare's measurements, it will hold in the theater under a diversity of different psychological interpretations, for in all of the tragedies there is a universality from which actors and audience may draw just as much or as little as is in themselves. But without theatrical validity a welter of fine mystic or philosophic forethought may totally fail of its effect.

Shakespeare, however startling it may be to remind ourselves of the fact, started with the story. In HAMLET and in LEAR, he had an old play upon which to work, in OTHELLO an Italian romance, in MACBETH the chronicles of his old friend Holinshed, who had seen him through so many medieval battles. The amazing poetic and dramatic genius which enabled him to transform his story material into the essentials of pity and terror is a commonplace of critical praise. But let us remember that he never lost the story.

For about a hundred and fifty years after the first production, nobody saw anything particularly difficult or obscure in the character of Hamlet; they accepted him, dovetailed, as in fact he is, with a thousand invisible links to the dramatic action of the play which bears his name. Gradually, however, critics began a separate analysis of the man himself, growing more obscure and more entangled as he became to them a distinct entity, having a life of his own, related only distantly to the dramatic purpose he serves in the dramatic world which he inhabits. Cut versions, all soliloquies and no plot, added to the murk of conflict. Of recent years, producers have rediscovered HAMLET in its entirety, and it has been hailed with some surprise for what it is, an extraordinarily finely jointed piece of theater craftsmanship from which no part, other than a few isolated speeches, can be removed without some loss. It has been proved, moreover, that Hamlet himself emerges with infinitely greater clarity among the fuller contour of his fellows, that audiences will actually feel the play to move more swiftly in four hours than it does in two and a half, and that the actor who plays Hamlet has, by the universal testimony of those who have played both versions, an easier time in the full one than he has in the compressed tension caused by cutting.

Surprising things have emerged from these recent treatments of the play. Rosencrantz and Guildenstern, long supposed the two prize bores of all Shakespeare's characters, have acquired identity and purpose; the little scenes in which they are concerned, between Hamlet's exit from his Mother's closet and the "How all occasions do inform against me" soliloquy, have been found to quicken the play's movement, clarify its plot, and provide Hamlet with an invaluable ease from strain by the employment of some beautifully pointed ironic comedy. Polonius has regained almost his richest comedy in the brief scene with Reynaldo, and in so doing restores to the play, still reeling from its ghostly visitation, the proportion and accent of the humdrum world where Hamlet's "strangeness" will be so inevitably misinterpreted. Claudius, in lines and half speeches usually dispensed with, in the sequence after the Play, and even in the scene in which he tempts Laertes to the murder of Hamlet, takes on a new gloss, a new subtlety of shading; he becomes a man we understand because the light is turned on every facet of his thinking, and he is not left half effaced in the gloom, with nothing of his features distinguishable except the brand of Cain. Fortinbras rounds out the play, by reference at the beginning and in his own person at the end, with the vivid value of the man who is all that Hamlet is not.

When I staged the uncut text for Maurice Evans in New York in 1938, we had had no intention of playing the entirety version eight times a week; we had felt that most audiences would prefer the more usual brevity of playing time and had planned to give at least half of our performances in a cut version, using, however, a fuller and differently adapted text from the one generally employed. But the demand to see the play that Shakespeare wrote and the response of the public toward it caused us to drop all cut performances and concentrate exclusively on the full text. The play was the thing. Shakespeare received universal applause for the scope and sweep of his drama, its impetus, simplicity, and clarity. Evans's Hamlet was hailed with relief as being bewilderingly unbewildering. John Anderson wrote in the *Journal American:*

Instead of being a distorted, overly concentrated study of one character, the play becomes a dilated chronicle of melodramatic proportions, fastened securely to its central figure and carried with him in the flooding tide over overwhelming tragedy. The smaller eddies of its plot move inward on a vast centrifugal power until the whole, with all its thrilling momentum, reaches its momentous climax.

Yet Evans himself, around whose performance the whole production revolved, would be the last to claim any part of it as definitive. We aimed at certain specific values which seemed to us to have become obscured in the course of time, and these were not abstract, but concrete. We were fortunate in our interpreters, particularly in Mady Christians, who made of the Queen a clearly understandable woman whom everyone in the audience could recognize, caught by her very weakness in a web of circumstance far beyond her control. It was our intention to bring the play close to its hearers, even to lead them by inference to believe that in this palace of Elsinore people led everyday lives much like their own, ate and slept and dressed and listened to music and took an interest in the theater and in the skill of riding and horsemanship. Behind this façade of familiar things moves the spiritual and emotional conflict of the play.

Within the frame of Shakespeare's dramatic structure, here as in all his greatest plays, imaginative and psychological values can be differently related. The actor, however, must necessarily choose one clear line of interpretation and follow it in detailed application; he may lose, and consciously lose, some particular high light for the sake of integrity in the whole. The director, too, must choose his pattern, and most carefully in the relation between one character and another: the interpretation of the actor who plays Claudius cannot be determined apart from that of the actress who plays Gertrude. The director, like the actor, may be forced to some sacrifice of his pet theories in achieving a homogeneous entity. The whole must be indivisible; but there will be freedom of choice for both of them in determining what line of interpretation to pursue. Shakespeare, however, constructed his plays with the utmost theatrical skill and care in order that their higher implications might have dramatic cogency. The craft of their structure is mathematical; it is not capable of variation according to taste.

MACBETH, whatever the spiritual or abstract significance with which it has been variously endowed, has always been played for its tremendous dramatic impact. The structural basis of OTHELLO ensures a sweep of movement which, in the theater, overwhelms all theoretical debate as to the motivation of its principal characters. And it is the lack of this fundamental theater economy, rather than any insuperable difficulty in the playing of the leading part, that makes KING LEAR, for me, the least actable of the four plays.

Of them all, it is probably the most hypnotic to the reader. In the theater also there are scenes which stir the heart and trouble the blood, especially the last of them, whose poignant beauty effaces much that has gone before, for it remains vivid and unspoiled in the audience's recollection. There are, moreover, lines and speeches of such magnificence that one's reasoning faculty is stunned by them. If the Lear, and not only the Lear but the Edgar, the Edmund, the Kent, the

Gloucester, all three of the women, and indeed practically the whole cast, are superlative actors of superhuman power, they may catch us wholly into a realm of high poetic frenzy, in which we shall gladly abrogate the prerogative of intellectual judgment. Nevertheless, and with infinite respect to the serried ranks of opposed opinion, I cannot believe that KING LEAR ever was or ever will be a good play in the sense of "a theater piece."

Professor Bradley, whose lectures on the four tragedies remain among the most profound Shakespearean criticism, has this to say about it:

> When I read KING LEAR two impressions are left on my mind . . . KING LEAR seems to me Shakespeare's greatest achievement, but it seems to me *not* his best play. And I find that I tend to consider it from two rather different points of view. When I regard it strictly as a drama, it appears to me, though in certain parts overwhelming, decidedly inferior as a whole to HAMLET, OTHELLO, and MACBETH. When I am feeling that it is greater than any of these, and the fullest revelation of Shakespeare's power, I find I am not regarding it simply as a drama, but am grouping it in my mind with works like the PROMETHEUS VINCTUS and the DIVINE COMEDY, and even with the greatest symphonies of Beethoven and the statues in the Medici Chapel.

Granville Barker has devoted one of his most trenchant prefaces to disproving this point, and indeed he does most admirably demonstrate that the stage which Shakespeare used helps us enormously to reproduce the dramatist's true intentions. We will then realize, Barker alleges, that KING LEAR is a fine play in the theater also, quite as satisfying as the one we read in the library. This may be true in theory; I can say only that I have never seen it demonstrated, nor have I read of a production which seemed to me as if it had proved Barker's contention. For I do not think that our basic difficulties in accepting KING LEAR "strictly as a drama" are simply a matter of staging, nor that we can dispose of them by changing our production methods.

We are forced to clear our minds, to begin with, of the fascination and awe which echo through the writings of poets and critics when they confront KING LEAR and consider just what are the difficulties with which the plain man in the balcony, as well as the plain actor behind the footlights, are faced. Audiences do not, as a whole, react on the lines of "I do not understand it, so I suppose it must be great"; their emotions are seldom engaged without a sympathetic collaboration of the mind; the greatest actors and the greatest plays have not seized upon their hearts by baffling them, but by illuminating them.

Yet KING LEAR seems to me baffling from the very begining. There is about the first scene, says Mr. Barker, "a certain megalithic grandeur, Lear dominating it, that we associate with Greek Tragedy. Its probabilities are neither here nor there. A dramatist may postulate any situation he has the means to interpret, if he will abide by the logic of it after."

If we grant this, we are still faced with a play which is to describe the tragic progression of retribution and, if you like, the spiritual rebirth of an old man who has behaved like an arbitrary, stupid despot, adding to an admittedly improbable course of action in abdicating his kingdom, a rejection of the one daughter whose love is immediately patent to the dullest of us and of the one subject whose courage and faithfulness are instantly beyond doubt. That he is megalithic about it does not make him any the more understandable.

The plain man in the balcony will start, almost inevitably, with the conviction that Lear is a pigheaded old tyrant who will deserve whatever he gets. I have only once seen an actor successfully counteract this very reasonable reaction, and this was Michael Redgrave at Stratford-on-Avon in 1953. He played the first scene very simply, as if the old man were frozen, immobilized, isolated within the towering walls of great age and the absolute power and grandeur of royalty. Cordelia's "Nothing" struck at the whole basis of his existence; where everything had been immovable and rocklike, the very foundations seemed to dissolve and he was left looking into a black void of "nothing." The rest of the scene he played with a dreadful quiet, not so much in rage as in unendurable pain, as if he were compelled to banish, to expunge from existence, every trace or reminder of Cordelia, who had caused it.

There are, of course, many other ways of interpreting the scene, and no absolute "right" or "wrong" may be pronounced on them. It may well be argued that we are not meant to feel any sympathy toward Lear at the beginning—quite the contrary; that we are intended to be repelled by what he does and that the actor need not, perhaps should not, try to make us understand him. Certainly the succeeding scenes are calculated to deepen the audience's first reaction. Lear behaves like a choleric, self-willed megalomaniac, whose presence in the home would be intolerable even to the most dutiful of children. Goneril's actions may lack charm, but she has had ample provocation.

The gigantic folly of Lear's behavior begins to grow beyond all bounds; his mind lurches wildly toward the abyss of madness. In turn, the pitiless nature of his daughters, the ruthless cruelty of Cornwall and his henchmen, gather in violence and power. Lear, finally, is thrust out into the storm. To this point, perhaps, an audience may be held, fascinated by the sheer size of the play. Its crisis comes now, when Lear confronts the furious onslaught of the heavens. Granted that he himself has invited the wrath of the gods, now we are to see him as their victim; he is to be stripped to the naked soul.

The arguments as to whether or not KING LEAR is an actable play center around the storm scenes. Can the cataclysmic convulsions of nature be reproduced in the theater? The answer, of course, is no. Thunder-sheets and wind-machines, rain "effects" and stereopticon lightning, make a niggardly mockery of Lear's "cataracts and hurricanes," his "sulphurous and thought-executing fires." They succeed only in drowning out the actor's voice without arousing either pity or terror. Shakespeare must surely have relied on the actor to show us the tempest and convulsion of Lear's soul. Yet if he is called upon to do this while standing upon a stage where no wind stirs a hair of his wig, no drop of moisture falls upon his cloak, and the accompanying storm-sounds barely reach voice-level, he is asked to perform an almost impossible creative feat. Perhaps it can be done; I have never yet seen it.

As I read the scene to myself I am moved by Lear's senseless, pitiful arrogance, his hopeless, even ludicrous defiance, his challenge to the unchallengeable. But most of all I am moved by the great, surging, battering words, the enormous images, full of doom and fury. They unseal the springs of terror, they even touch the impulse of compassion; logic and reason recede. In theory this should also happen in the theater, but in my experience it does not. The actors contend in vain with the reality which surrounds them. Reason and logic are never silenced. Lear's own self-pity negates our own. Why should we think him "a man more sinn'd against than sinning"? The "poor, infirm, weak and despis'd old man" has too much to answer for. It is here, I believe, that Shakespeare's unsparing treatment of Lear in the early scenes does him, and us, the greatest disservice. We, in the theater, cannot be brought to ignore the shortcomings of the stage illusions because we are not swept away by the man himself; we stand aloof from him; we will not yield him our separate identity.

Once we are out of the storm, huddled in the little hut with Lear and his few, faithful companions, the illusion may recapture us. We are, perhaps, bludgeoned into compassion.

But it is hard to refrain, even yet, from sitting in judgment on Lear, just as he sits in judgment on his imagined "daughters." In the following sequence, and especially in the scene with Gloucester, we are to remark, or so the critics tell us, a "deep repentance" in him, a "compassion for sin" by which we are to be greatly moved. But to the plain man the change is more likely to seem a gigantic swing of the pendulum of wrath, so that he, the despot who has had no thought for the poor and wretched among his subjects, now rails with equally insensate fury against every representative of riches, authority, or power. We are aghast at the glorious frenzy of his speeches; but do we, truly, care? When it comes to his scenes with Cordelia, we shall care; their very quietness, the exquisitely simple writing of them, the touching, homely images, the tender feeling of familiar things—these will at last bring us to capitulation. But it has been an immensely difficult road.

If the dramatic structure of the play had stood, clean and firm, around its central character, it would still be actable; Lear himself would be upheld by it. But, in my view, he is not. The subplot of Gloucester and his two sons loads the play with complicating horrors; and, though Shakespeare develops their story with masterly economy, the characters seem at once too fierce and full for the space within which they are confined, and yet too insistent in their interruption of the progress of the main plot. The pattern of Gloucester's folly and its Nemesis, paralleling the story of Lear, may indeed enforce with savage fury the picture of a dark, relentless world, where "machinations, hollowness, treachery and all ruinous disorders follow us disquietly to our graves"; but the compression necessitated by the handling of the two plots adds to the many conflicting complexities of the play.

The subplot is especially full of developments inadequately prepared, or arbitrary twists of circumstance, including the major puzzle as to why Edgar does not reveal himself to his blinded father when there is no reason whatever for further concealment, and why he further indulges in a series of differing impersonations which usually defeat the hardiest young actor and bedevil the audience entirely. There surely never was such a young man for burning down the house in order to roast the pig.

With the exception of Lear and Gloucester, and of Albany, who is sparsely but subtly developed, every one of the dramatis personae steps upon the stage pure white or dead black and continues along a vigorous but all too apparent way, so that we cannot take refuge in the delayed tension which accompanies the gradual revelation of character, or the unsuspected development of it, as in HAMLET or MACBETH. Kent, superbly drawn in the first half of the play, is more or less dropped in the last third of it. The Fool is dismissed unexplained and apparently unlamented. He has served his purpose in lightening the gathering strain with a wistful and touching lyric of fragility; but he has also touched our hearts; quite simply, we want to know what happens to him. Shakespeare, perhaps, has no more need of him for the purposes of the play, but we resent his disappearance.

How are we, in the theater, to compensate for or to conceal the fissures and enormous rifts in the structure of this dinosaur of a play? The practical objections which I have here outlined may seem picayune to the enthralled and worshiping reader, but I believe they have almost always proved fatal to the play in performance. Why is it that the theater can add depth and color to an extremely mediocre play like HENRY VI and yet fail to translate a magnificent epic like KING LEAR? How can it create belief in the one case and destroy it in the other? Mr. Gian-Carlo Menotti has given a definition which seems to me to be pertinent to the problem. "There is only one kind of bad theater:" he says, "when the author's imagination steps outside the very area of illusion he has created. But as long as the dramatist creates within that area, almost no action on the stage is too violent or implausible."

The magic of the theater is a duality. It can evoke and sustain illusion or it can be as revealing as a microscope or an X-ray photograph, searching and merciless. The bedrock substance of an acted play is the basic stuff of its human characters. If you overload them with more than they can contain, if you overload the actors with more than flesh and blood can convey, then you overload, in turn, the capacity of an audience to absorb or ultimately to believe. What the theater adds to a flat and wooden piece is the human dimension; when the human dimension is surpassed, the dreadful realism of the theater will destroy what you are trying to create. There is space for the abstract and the transcendental in great poetry, perhaps also in great novels; but they do not have to put on human flesh before our eyes.

LEAR can well be considered the greatest of Shakespeare's dramatic poems, but in the theater it has never proved the equal of OTHELLO or MACBETH. In these plays the capacities of actors and audience alike are put to the highest test, but they are not strained beyond the limits of the theater medium. In many lesser plays Shakespeare has swept us past improbable plots on the wings of fantasy or passion; he has cajoled us with his theater sleight-of-hand into accepting the most unrealistic hypotheses. But in LEAR the magnitude of the attempt will not let us smile indulgently and accept a let's-pretend; you cannot smile at LEAR; either it is sublime or it is incredible. Nor is Lear's Britain a let's-pretend world. Men are savage, lustful, greedy, evil with a senseless, insatiate appetite; they set the world spinning toward eternal chaos. But every one of their actions brings retribution, not exact or just, but magnified to a vast and horrible doom.

Every character makes some reference to the gods, the heavens, the eternal vengeance, the justicers above, the stars which govern our conditions. But it is the wheel of human action which comes a full and terrible circle. The play has been called one of capricious cruelty; Shakespeare is said to have been thinking himself in terms of Gloucester's famous:

> As flies to wanton boys are we to the gods;
> They kill us for their sport.

But it is as arguable that he is thinking, now as almost always, primarily in terms of humanity, but that here, as very seldom, he is passionately out of love with humanity and supremely doubtful of the civilized veneer with which mankind has succeeded in covering its primeval instincts. The evil in Lear's world is a force liberated by mankind to destroy itself. We may more readily identify Shakespeare with Edmund than with Gloucester, possibly as to his own thought, certainly as to his dramatic credo:

> This is the excellent foppery of the world, that when we are
> sick in fortune—often the surfeit of our own behaviour—we
> make guilty of our disasters the sun, the moon and the stars:
> as if we were villains by necessity, fools by heavenly com-
> pulsion, knaves, thieves and trecherers by spherical predom-
> inance, drunkards, liars and adulterers by an enforced obedi-
> ence of planetary influence, and all that we are evil in by a
> divine thrusting-on: an admirable evasion of whoremaster
> man, to lay his goatish disposition to the charge of stars!
>
> I, 2, 120

Perhaps LEAR must be interpreted as a gigantic attack upon humanity itself, and we are too squeamish so to accept it. Certainly it is also a bitter and terrible cry against the overwhelming power of the gods. The play is dominated by them. Shakespeare seems to have been moving steadily nearer to this terrible confrontation between his tragic "heroes" and the cosmic forces beyond mortal knowledge. In CAESAR there have been portents and ghostly visitations. In HAMLET it is the

Ghost who fires the train of action. Through Horatio, Claudius, and Hamlet himself we see the strong background of superstition and fear with which the supernatural was regarded, even by the most enfranchised Renaissance minds. Yet the play is not, in any primary sense, a conflict between man and the invisible powers nor even between man and the larger designs of fate. The division is in the heart of the protagonist; the struggle is between him and his own soul.

But in the later "tragedies of passion" there is an ever-present sense of some terrible force which can be unleashed by man's weakness or his capacity for evil. Once set in motion, he is powerless to control its direction or its effect; it becomes incarnate in human beings, the servants of the devil. Long before, in RICHARD III, Shakespeare seems to have approached this theme. Now he returns to it with tremendously increased force and penetration.

In MACBETH, the subtle power of darkness becomes all-pervading; it takes the form of "supernatural soliciting," it employs "instruments of darkness," it drenches the play in blackness and in blood, poisons the air with fear, preys on bloated and diseased imaginings, turns feasting to terror and the innocent sleep to nightmare, and employs a terrible irony of destruction in the accomplishment of its barren ends. Yet MACBETH contains no villain, no Iago, no Edmund. Evil is alive of itself, a protagonist in its own right.

In the greatest of his plays, especially the tragedies, Shakespeare spends little time on exposition. The Prologue to TROILUS AND CRESSIDA frankly announces that the author proposes to "leap o'er the vaunts and firstlings of these broils, Beginning in the middle"; and in MACBETH he fairly hurls his characters at the crisis of the action. His source book, the *Chronicles* of Holinshed, gives plenty of facts from which he might have built up a case for the Macbeths, had he wished to do so. For instance, Macbeth was Duncan's cousin, and, since the Crown of Scotland did not at that time descend by right to the King's eldest son, he had every right to suppose that he would be elected to the throne after Duncan's death. The old man's attempt to "establish our estate upon our eldest, Malcolm" was, in fact, highly unconstitutional. There was the further consideration, not altogether trivial, that Macbeth's father, and Lady Macbeth's grandfather, brother, and first husband had all been slain in varying circumstances of treachery and violence by Duncan's unamiable predecessor, Malcolm the Second. Between the two houses there was, accordingly, a blood-feud of long standing. But Macbeth had served Duncan loyally and with great ability. He had truly saved the country in spite of its King.

But Shakespeare was evidently not interested in the turbulent politics of eleventh-century Scotland, nor even in presenting evidence to excuse or explain the Macbeths themselves. The moment we see them is itself the moment of decision. We never know them under conditions of normality. It is perhaps for this reason that both characters have been interpreted by critics and depicted by actors in widely different and contradictory ways. Lady Macbeth has been described as a "fiend incarnate" or as a wife who dares all for love, a remorseless woman ridden by ambition, or a helpless dupe of the devil. She has been played with eagle eye and raven (or flaming) hair, tragic and imposing of mien, or as fair, delicate, and fragile.

There have been as many contrasting conceptions of Macbeth, depending on whether the emphasis was laid on the soldier or the poet. Critics have tended to assume that "Bellona's bridegroom" must necessarily be a burly ruffian, muscular, hirsute, and encrusted with hardware. But Bellona, that much-married lady, apparently neglected these qualifications in espousing such warriors as Napoleon, Attila, Alexander Hamilton, or Frederick the Great. Personal valor does not seem to have been the prerogative of the physically bulky. As to Shakespeare's own intentions in the matter, we may usefully remember that the actor who originally created Hamlet was also, only four or five years later, the original Macbeth. In writing the part, Shakespeare would hardly have forgotten that Burbage was to play it, and if he was a little heavy for the modern notion of Hamlet, he must have been a good deal lighter than some of our recent Macbeths.

The duality of Macbeth's nature is, of course, undeniable. He has enormous physical courage; war is his trade; he excels at it and is proud of it. Yet he has a sensitivity of soul which makes him a prey to every trick of the imagination. His senses are preternaturally sharp; sights and sounds translate themselves into images, vivid, surrealist images of a dream, or a nightmare. But he is not an intellectual, nor a poet, as Richard II was, who delights in words for the pleasure of playing on them. The magnificent verse which Shakespeare gives him is the expression of a man who is almost psychically receptive to every vibration of the atmosphere around him. It is absurd to suppose that such a temperament is incompatible with military valor. The veterans of two wars should have shown us this with searing clarity.

Lady Macbeth, on the other hand, is completely devoid of imagination; and there is almost no music in the writing of the part. It is sharp, incisive, purposeful. It is precisely when she sees the thing she has never imagined that the purpose shatters in horror. These two, the man and the woman complementing each other, are the ideal instruments for the dreadful power which takes possession of them.

There is a long theatrical tradition of disaster behind MAC-BETH, dating back, it seems, to the earliest productions of the play. A theater superstition makes it unlucky even to quote MACBETH inside a theater, and no actor who believes in this but can quote you a long string of supporting evidence proving the play's fatal influence. Anyone who believes in the darker powers, in whatever form, cannot be wholly incredulous; for no play ever written has more powerfully invoked them.

Yet MACBETH is the best melodrama of them all; and, if you prefer your murders "straight," you can so take them. Its construction is as tight as LEAR's is vast and spreading. Its shortness has led many critics to suppose that the Folio text, which is the only one we have, has been much cut. Yet its design is exact, its pattern as precisely balanced as a Bach fugue, its action taut and muscular, its poetry many times magnificent. As Bradley says of it: "Shakespeare has certainly avoided the overloading which distresses us in KING LEAR, and has produced a tragedy utterly unlike it, not much less great as a dramatic poem, and as a drama superior."

The producer's problem is therefore a very different one and centers upon three protagonists, the two Macbeths and the power which is behind them. We must at every point be made conscious of the pervasive power of evil suggestion; most clearly we shall feel it through Macbeth himself, so reluctant at first to "yield to that suggestion," yet committed to it more and more deeply, more and more fiercely, as if in action, in blood and more blood, he could kill forever the reproaches his conscience had once heaped upon him. As the quality of his imagination had first shown him the cosmic horror which would follow Duncan's murder in the daring and terrible images of

> . . . pity like a naked new-born babe
> Striding the blast, or heaven's cherubin hors'd
> Upon the sightless couriers of the air,

so this same faculty of perception stretching far behind the concrete aspect of material things is increasingly obsessed by images of blood and death. But now there is no pause between the image and the deed which translates it into action. The tempo increases to the speed of a nightmare; Macbeth cannot stop nor pause in this doomed frenzy of murder lest his imagination should come alive again and significance should flood back over the ashen, relentless path he is traveling. There is no end, any more; there is only the driven, hunted slavery of one who has indeed given "his eternal jewel" to "the common enemy of man."

Through Lady Macbeth we shall be made equally but quite differently aware of the third protagonist. In her very first scene—and it is one of the problems of the part that we neither see nor hear anything of Lady Macbeth before the pressure of climactic circumstance begins to work on her—she reads Macbeth's account of the witches' prophecies, and immediately afterward comes the news of Duncan's approach.

> The raven himself is hoarse
> That croaks the fatal entrance of Duncan
> Under my battlements.

We can almost hear the soft beat of wings. At once she begins the terrible invocation:

>   Come you spirits
> That tend on mortal thoughts, unsex me here,
> And fill me from the crown to the toe top-full
> Of direst cruelty . . .
>   . . . Come to my woman's breasts,
> And take my milk for gall, you murdering ministers,
> Wherever in your sightless substances
> You wait on nature's mischief. Come, thick night,
> And pall thee in the dunnest smoke of hell,
> That my keen knife see not the wound it makes,
> Nor heaven peep through the blanket of the dark
> To cry "Hold, hold!"   1, 5, 38

And they come, these sightless substances; there should be no smallest doubt about that. They use her, possess her, just exactly as she had prayed them to do; they make of her a creature as relentless as she had desired, they shroud the stars and charge the blackened night with terror. And, when the murder is once accomplished, Lady Macbeth is exhausted, used up, the vitality and spring of life drained out of her. She will still summon all the remnant of her power to help Macbeth when he sees the ghost of Banquo; but he has gone beyond her, obsessed, blinded, bound to the treadmill on which she had first set his feet. There is no contact between them any more, only the feel of the blood between their hands. The last part of Lady Macbeth is filled with echoes, ironic echoes, terrible echoes, inescapable, even through the thick, haunted nights from which sleep has forever gone.

Toward the end of the play the accelerated pace and spreading effect of evil are apparent in every scene. All of the minor characters begin to apprehend it: the uneasy guests at the banquet; the mysterious Messenger who comes to warn Lady Macduff but dare not stay to protect her; Ross, describing Scotland as "almost afraid to know itself"; the Doctor and the Gentlewoman, frightened of finding out more than they dare know; the succession of terrified servants who bring to Macbeth the news of Malcolm's approach. Fear is in the ascendant, fear and hate, under whose banners evil has always triumphed. With the victory of Malcolm's army, and Macbeth's death at the hands of the man he had most feared, the spell is broken, suddenly and completely, as the dawn dispels the nightmares of Walpurgis Night.

Every sign and signal of this progression may be carried out in clear theatrical terms, yet it is only in the witches that the evil force is ever actually incarnate, and they present us with the most difficult problem in the play. Shakespeare seems to have taken both the description of their appearance and the abracadabra of their incantations almost verbatim from a contemporary book on witchcraft, and with these generally accepted features his audience was familiar. He was using a symbol of great potency of which there appears to be no equivalent today. Only the most intelligent and enlightened members of his audience would have claimed that they no longer believed in witchcraft, and in doing so they would have rendered themselves suspect. For common belief credited these old hags with undisputed powers. King James himself wrote a treatise against them and encouraged their persecution and savage punishment. It was widely believed that two hundred of them had set out in sieves to try to sink the ship which had brought his Queen from Denmark.

It was not difficult to bring an Elizabethan audience to a state of terrified acceptance before the figures of the Three Weird Sisters. Long after 1606 the average man would still, however hotly he denied it, have felt distinctly uncomfortable had he met three strange old women on a lonely heath. He would have been unable to dismiss a "witch's" curse or blessing freely from his mind. But the most terrifying thing about these old women, especially at their first appearance on the "blasted heath," would have been their apparent harmlessness. Three old women—as simple as that. And suddenly they vanished into air—as incredible as that. What ineluctable force of doom might not lurk behind this phenomenon? A man is paralyzed with fear not so much by some colossal and unheard-of monstrosity as by the more dreadful horror of feeling a familiar thing melt and change beneath his hand.

It is probable that, deep in our hearts, we "moderns" are as vulnerable to superstition as our Elizabethan ancestors, though we deny it more strenuously. But it is almost impossible to find for a modern audience a symbol which will have the effect that Shakespeare's witches had on his. Orson Welles, in his Negro MACBETH, found the perfect equivalent in voodoo; but obviously this is no solution of general application. Gypsies and fortunetellers come somewhere near the mark but not quite up to it. Spiritualist mediums have occasionally been substituted. Other producers have employed mechanical apparitions of grotesque appearance, like the fancier flights of Walt Disney's imagination.

I do not believe Shakespeare's intention to be truly carried out by such devices, which have, in fact, more often induced laughter than terror in the spectators. I believe that we should see as little as possible of the Witches in the flesh of actors or actresses. The unseen voice of evil, its imminence, its very facelessness, these things have a chilling power; we can use shadows or twisting silhouettes, the glimpse of hands, the outline of a head, shifting, hovering, formless; their voices should echo from the hollow rocks and stream away against the wind. We should see them by reflection, through the human beings who come so terrifyingly close to the unknowable. We must make sure that the influence which governs them is never absent, for it is implicit or expressed through all the fabric of the play. We shall believe in the Witches only so far as we believe in the more terrible Presence whose ministers and mouthpieces they are. A lot of elaborate hokum about their appearance—or disappearance—will only distract our attention with speculation as to how the trick is done.

In MACBETH, even more explicitly than in LEAR, Shakespeare brings the supernatural within the walls of the theater; but this time he does not violate the governing principle that drama, whether of thought, of passion, of poetry, or even of metaphysics must be expressed on the stage in terms of human beings and a story. The essence of his tragedies has been described as "character under the pressure of circumstance"; the conflict between man and man, man and himself, man and fate. In this conflict he may boldly ask us to accept an improbable series of events as the basis of the plot; or he may require our belief in the intervention of the supernatural;

or he may present us with one or more characters who are larger than life-size. His mastery lies in compelling our acceptance of the initial hypothesis and in keeping faith both with us and with his characters thereafter. Nowhere does he demonstrate it more clearly than in OTHELLO.

OTHELLO is the most human of the four great tragedies. There are no ghosts, no inexplicable convulsions of nature, no imagery even, as there is so strongly in LEAR, of the primeval characteristics of the animal world to which the world of man is so nearly akin. There is human passion, of which the germ is in each one of us, raised to its highest pitch and forged to a white heat of dramatic action. The play is an astounding extension of normal humanity to the level of high, poetic tragedy.

There has been much literary argument over the nature and the credibility of its two principal characters, Othello and Iago. Even Professor Stoll, who disclaims as "neither here nor there" the psychological explanations with which critics have tried to codify Shakespeare's tragic heroes, feels that we shall need "that willing suspension of disbelief which constitutes poetic faith." I would suggest that in the theater we do not even experience the alleged disbelief; not, at least, if the actors know their business.

It is true that Iago is presented to us full-grown and we are asked to accept him whole, exactly as we were with Richard III. Like Richard, he is a brazen "villain." Critics have probed and strained for the logic of his motivation, echoing in fretful bewilderment Othello's agonized question:

> Will you, I pray, demand that demi-devil
> Why he hath thus ensnared my soul and body?

and getting in answer nothing more than Iago's own reply:

> Demand me nothing; what you know, you know.

Early in the play he himself has avowed a number of rather shadowy motives, his resentment over the promotion of Cassio, his suspicions about Othello and Emilia, his even more perfunctory suspicion regarding Emilia and Cassio. It has been agreed that none of them fully account for his hatred of the Moor. He has been described as a man who loves evil for evil's sake; or, more convincingly, as a man with a superiority complex reveling in his power to destroy someone whom the world has set above him. But Shakespeare is bolder than his apologists, and Iago states the initial premise without equivocation: "I have told thee often, and I re-tell thee again and again, I hate the Moor." The pure venom of this chills the blood; it also compels us to belief as it compels Roderigo, to whom it is spoken. In the theater we do not stop to fuss for the reasons. We accept the terrifying fact.

We accept also, despite critical admonitions to the contrary, the façade of "honest Iago" which he so successfully presents to the rest of the world. The actor must, obviously, take the very greatest pains to preserve it. There must be no suggestion whatever of the sly Italianate villain, the insinuating, sneaking rogue from whom any sensible housewife would hide the silver spoons the moment he came in. The theatrical appurtenances of villainy, however sly and sidelong, will be fatal to Iago and everybody else. For Othello believes him to be honest. So does Emilia, his wife; she is no fool, indeed she is the only person in the play who comes very close to guessing the truth; but she fails to identify her husband as the author of the villainy she divines, because she is in love with him. Cassio trusts him; so do his brother officers. We hear no rumor or suspicious word against him from any of the camps or guardrooms where he has served. Even Roderigo, to whom he reveals himself fairly recklessly, is long in coming to any realization of what he really is. They accept him, one and all, as "honest, honest Iago." Believe that they do, says Shakespeare, and imperiously at that.

And we do believe it, so long as the actor does not interfere. We, too, accept Iago hook, line, and sinker. This is partly because he dominates us with his own assurance from the beginning and partly because Shakespeare's writing of the character is at its most dazzling. The brilliant speed of his small, unscrupulous thinking, the dash of recklessness, the complete worldly armory of his mind, the plenitude of will and the absolute lack of imagination are all full and clear and contrasted unerringly with Othello's utterly alien temperament. The contrast between them is, of course, the crux of the play.

The very quality of Iago's speech is differentiated from Othello's by every possible means. Except for the soliloquies, it is almost all in prose, light, acute, beautifully phrased, every cynical, easy turn of it unerringly directed. It needs polish, precision, and extreme lucidity in the speaking, little music. Othello, who early says of himself "Rude am I in my speech," is to run an orchestral gamut, always spiced with the flavor of strangeness and enriched with the color of the East and the burnished sun. He is to talk of "antres vast and deserts idle," of sibyls "that had numbered in the world the sun to course two hundred compasses," of Arabian trees and turbaned Turks and Ottomites and anthropophagi. The measured gravity of his first address to the Senate,

> Most potent, grave and reverend signiors,
> My very noble and approved good masters,

will change to a passionate agony of tumbling phrases, to the almost unintelligible ravings of "Lie with her! lie in her! —We say lie on her, when they belie her.—Lie with her! 'Zounds, that's fulsome! Handkerchiefs—confession—handkerchiefs!" And it will change again, under the sway of a great and noble sorrow far transcending the initial passion of jealousy, to the sacrificial majesty of:

> Put out the light, and then put out the light:
> If I quench thee, thou flaming minister,
> I can again thy former light restore,
> Should I repent me: but once put out thine,
> Thou cunning pattern of eternal nature,
> I know not where is that Promethean heat
> That can thy light relume.   v, 2, 7

It is commonly, and as I think erroneously, supposed that Othello must carry us on a torrent of sound past some intrinsic improbabilities of characterization. George Bernard Shaw has said: "The words do not convey ideas—they are streaming ensigns and tossing branches to make the tempest of passion visible . . . Tested by the brain it is ridiculous; tested by the ear it is sublime." It is, of course, the fury of Othello's so-called "jealousy" that strikes Shaw as ridiculous, which, in Shaw, can hardly be regarded as surprising.

Many critics have, however, stressed the factual improbability of the situation, the impossible shortness of time, the intervention of fortuitous events, such as the dropping of the handkerchief, which alone makes possible the success of Iago's scheme. They have agreed with Shaw that Othello is incredibly gullible and that all the glory of his spoken music cannot evoke our compassion, that we remain aloof from him, as we do from Lear, and echo in our hearts Emilia's "O gull! O dolt!" "What should such a fool do with so good a wife?"

It is true that many cultured and gentlemanly actors, reluctantly and faintly disguising from us their familiar features under a layer of becoming coffee-colored grease paint, rather as if they had recently returned from Palm Beach, have seemed to us possessed of far too much intelligence, restraint, and self-control ever to be swept by an uncontrollable passion which is not from the mind at all and only a little from the heart, but principally from the bowels. Mr. Knight says of this emotional situation that "it does not mesh with our minds." But then cool reason was not intended to be the arbiter, and Othello himself is not of our breed.

He is more somber, profound and dangerous, primitive in simplicity, primitive also in violence, alien in blood. The gulf which divides him from Desdemona, once their first concord has been broken, is much more than a difference of pigmentation, though this is an essential part of it. It is a gulf between two races, one old and soft in the ways of civilization, the other close to the jungle and the burning, desert sands. It divides him from his officers and men, from his Senatorial superiors, from the whole society by which he is surrounded, its religion, morals, conventions and habits of living. It is the vital point of weakness on which Iago fastens, knowing every twist and thrust of the knife which he can inflict upon the Moor because of his alien and "inferior" race. But even Iago does not reckon on the full, primitive passion which he arouses in Othello's soul.

This question of racial division is of paramount importance to the play, to its credibility and to the validity of every character in it. There has been much controversy as to Shakespeare's precise intention with regard to Othello's race. It is improbable that he troubled himself greatly with ethnological exactness. The Moor, to an Elizabethan, was a blackamoor, an African, an Ethiopian. Shakespeare's other Moor, Aaron, in TITUS ANDRONICUS, is specifically black; he has thick lips and a fleece of woolly hair. The Prince of Morocco in THE MERCHANT OF VENICE bears "the shadowed livery of the burnished sun," and even Portia recoils from his "complexion" which he himself is at great pains to excuse.

Othello is repeatedly described, both by himself and others, as black; not pale beige, but black; and for a century and a half after the play's first presentation he was so represented on the stage. But after this the close consideration of nice minds began to discern something not quite ladylike about Desdemona's marrying a black man with thick lips. They cannot have been more horrified than Brabantio, her father, who thought that only witchcraft could have caused "nature so preposterously to err," or more convinced of the disastrous outcome of such a match than Iago, who looked upon it as nothing but a "frail vow between an erring barbarian and a supersubtle Venetian" and declared, with his invincible cynicism, that "when she is sated with his body, she will find the error of her choice: she must have change; she must!"

Whether Othello came from the shores of the Mediterranean, the Atlantic Ocean, or the Red Sea is not a matter of paramount importance; and it has been pointed out, with perfect justice, that an actor of any race can play Othello if he is good enough. But the fundamental sense of racial difference must never be lost. Just as a thin actor playing Falstaff must "act" fat through his whole being and not merely put on some padding, so the white actor playing Othello must blacken the very marrow of his bones. The conviction of difference must be instant and all-pervasive. When Paul Robeson stepped onto the stage for the very first time, when he spoke his very first line, he immediately, by his very presence, brought an incalculable sense of reality to the entire play. Here was a great man, a man of simplicity and strength; here also was a black man. We believed that he could command the armies of Venice; we knew that he would always be alien to its society.

The values of the play fall miraculously into place when this perspective is established rightly; every character in it takes on an added dimension. We see the true quality of Desdemona's courage in daring a marriage which the ladies of polite society would universally condemn, the steadfast strength of her love and loyalty, from the moment she faces the Venetian Senate to the moment of her death. We are fascinated by Iago's unerring, devilish skill in manipulating the weaknesses of another human being. We divine the tinge of mistrust and resentment which, from the first, colors Emilia's attitude toward Othello and appreciate better the generosity of Cassio's devotion.

We understand Othello himself, how well he must be aware of the world's judgment on his marriage, how easily he could be persuaded to believe that Desdemona was unfaithful. Once convinced of this, the passion which overwhelms him goes far beyond the "jealousy" of a deceived husband. To him, chastity is not just a word, and there is no such thing, in the tribal world to which he belongs, as the tolerance of infidelity. The man whose wife betrays him is himself tainted and dishonored. He owes expiation to the gods; the sin destroys him as well as her and must be utterly wiped out. The shedding of her blood is not revenge or murder. It is a terrible sacrifice offered by the Priest-King to the primal gods, ordained and ineluctable.

It seems to me that in OTHELLO Shakespeare's genius is at its height; his understanding is nowhere more penetrating nor his compassion more profound. This is a document of the human race, not of individuals named in the play and bounded by it, not limited to any age or country. It stands alone. Never again will Shakespeare take us into this realm of music and madness, of terror and pity and glory. He comes back to the real world. He will require passion from his actors, but never so complete a release; he will give his hearers superb speeches, but never pound them into submission by the sheer power of language. He will show us a jealous man in Leontes, an ambitious one in Octavius, an embittered outcast in Timon, but it will not be the sacrificial jealousy of Othello, the haunted ambition of Macbeth, or the madness of Lear. Nothing that happens in the later plays will carry us beyond the sphere where reason is still a comfortable guide. Nor will man ever again cry with such anguish to the stars to shield him from the unbearable responsibility of the world he has fashioned. The theater will revert to its normal self, its walls solid and comfortably bounding the two hours' traffic of make-believe. There will be plenty of technical problems to be faced. ANTONY AND CLEOPATRA especially will call for a width and range of vision; many of the plays to come will need adroit and lavish handling. But never again will the hearts of players and audience be so swept with the mystery of life and the bitter release of death.

11. Plays Unpleasant

UNDER THIS TITLE I have grouped four plays which the stage has virtually lost, and partly on account of their "unpleasant"-ness. They are ALL'S WELL THAT ENDS WELL, MEASURE FOR MEASURE, TROILUS AND CRESSIDA, and TIMON OF ATHENS. The dates of their composition are in every case uncertain, though we have limiting evidence. It would seem that the first three were written in the period immediately following HAMLET and before OTHELLO and the other tragedies.

TIMON appears to belong some two or three years later, but its spiritual sourness makes one feel it as nearly akin to the other three. The text we have is so garbled and filled out by other hands than Shakespeare's that it is hard to assign it to any definite period of his development. Certainly he left it unfinished; probably his collaborator never fully completed the job; much of the verse is in a rough and chaotic condition, as if it were taken from unfinished notes and first drafts; and there is evidence that it was not originally intended for publication in the complete Folio but was inserted to fill a gap caused by a temporary difficulty in obtaining the rights of TROILUS AND CRESSIDA.

The disintegrating critics have a wide field of conjecture in all these plays and have done some brilliant bibliographical reconstruction on them. ALL'S WELL bears clear marks of some very early work, and editors conjecture that original material for MEASURE FOR MEASURE and TROILUS was composed some time before either play was finished; all seem to have been cut, revised, and added to at successive times, both by Shakespeare and by collaborating authors.

The texts are certainly corrupt and the dramatic qualities of the plays are not completely satisfying. It is unlikely that TIMON or ALL'S WELL will often be seen in the theater. ALL'S WELL does acquire a certain warmth in performance; faults in it that seem glaring to an analytic student are not so apparent to an audience. The English director, Tyrone Guthrie, chose it for the opening season of the Stratford, Ontario, Shakespeare Festival in 1952 and gave it a production of imagination and life. The casting of Alec Guinness as the King of France revealed once more what an actor's personality and temperament may do to revitalize a supposedly dull part.

Helena has strength and beauty in the writing itself and some most happy lines of verse such as the famous:

> Shall I stay here to do't? no, no, although
> The air of paradise did fan the house,
> And angels offic'd all.   III, 3, 125

and

> But with the word that time will bring on summer,
> When briers shall have leaves as well as thorns,
> And be as sweet as sharp.   IV, 4, 31

She has dignity and, in a rare moment of softness, a really moving scene of abandoned grief when she reads Bertram's letter to his mother, "Madam, my lord is gone, forever gone." But she is dreadfully strong-minded in her pursuit of the wretched young man, tool of the plot as well as of his own folly, upon whom she has unaccountably set her heart.

Shaw thinks highly of Helena for being a good doctor and having more brains than most of the heroines. But she is altogether too Shavian, in the manner of Ann in MAN AND SUPERMAN, to warm our hearts. The extremely dubious stratagem by which she eventually secures her husband leaves us coldly incredulous. Nor does poor Bertram seem a particularly desirable prize. An actor with charm and personality will have to come to his rescue.

Other characters come out well upon the stage. The Countess of Rossillion is an altogether charming old lady, with the mellow wisdom of age, and the elderly Lord Lafeu, who plays very much better than he reads, partners her with his shrewdness and understanding. He has a trick of very simple speech, which is rare when Shakespeare writes, as he does in this play, without heart. After a scene with the Clown, a rather tedious, acid pensioner-punster, Lafeu comments "A shrewd knave, and an unhappy." And to the disgraced and discountenanced Parolles, whose pretentious nothingness he had been the first to suspect, he still shows kindness without sentimentality: "Though you are a fool and a knave, you shall eat; go to, follow."

"I praise God for you," replies Parolles. We may deduce the infinite relief behind the words. For Parolles is a weakling in his own braggart kind, a thinly flashy sort of rogue. He, too, emerges with more substance on the stage than in print. The episode of the drum which his company has lost in battle and which he boasts of being able to recover, to his own ultimate confusion, is vivid and amusing and distracts us from the unbearable Bertram story, but Shakespeare dismisses it perfunctorily, without caring much what happens. The best thing about Parolles is his appearance before the King in the last scene, in which the mixture of fear and bravado, sycophancy and tattered pride, offer more to the actor than to the casual reader.

TIMON OF ATHENS seems to be less playable than ALL'S WELL. Mr. Guthrie's production of it at the Old Vic in 1952 served to point up its intrinsic weakness despite the resourcefulness of the director's craft. For one thing, the part of Timon falls into two distinct halves which Shakespeare seems to have made little attempt to reconcile. Perhaps he intended to, and wrote the two extremes, but never worked on the play to the point where he could achieve the gradations. In the first half everybody flatters Timon, and he is witlessly generous to each and every comer. In the second half everybody deserts him, except his steward, and he is as witlessly bitter to and about the whole of mankind. The normal man will be equally mistrustful of him at both times.

Indeed the flood of bitterness in the second half of the play is so relentless that our ears and minds grow dulled to it. The characters vie with one another in cursing mankind and themselves; Apemantus, whose acidity has never changed, does not soften to Timon in misfortune; "a madman first, now a fool," he calls him; and, when he is asked what he would do with the world if it lay in his power, he replies succinctly "Give it to the beasts, to be rid of the men." The servile little Painter, with his friend the Poet, who have flattered Timon in his heydey, come to him again, hearing he has found gold, and even they have disillusion on their lips: "I will promise him an excellent piece . . . To promise is most courtly and fashionable; performance is a kind of will or testament which argues a great sickness in his judgment that makes it." Timon's comprehensive curses blaze through the last two acts like a destructive fire; Shakespeare seems to be unleashing all the tortured hatred of the world; it is magnificent, incomparable rhetoric:

> Rascal thieves,
> Here's gold. Go, suck the subtle blood o' the grape,
> Till the high fever seethe your blood to froth,
> And so 'scape hanging. Trust not the physician,
> His antidotes are poison, and he slays
> Moe than you rob: take wealth and lives together;
> Do villainy, do, since you protest to do't,
> Like workmen. I'll example you with thievery:
> The sun's a thief, and with his great attraction
> Robs the vast sea. The moon's an arrant thief,
> And her pale fire she snatches from the sun.
> The sea's a thief, whose liquid surge resolves
> The moon into salt tears. The earth's a thief,
> That feeds and breeds by a composture stol'n
> From general excrement: each thing's a thief,
> The laws, your curb and whip, in their rough power
> Has uncheck'd theft. Love not yourselves, away,
> Rob one another, there's more gold, cut throats,
> All that you meet are thieves: to Athens go,
> Break open shops, nothing can you steal,
> But thieves do lose it: steal no less for this
> I give you, and gold confound you how soe'er:
> Amen.   IV, 3, 429

Timon is a great operatic part; but the mind of the plain man recoils before the pitiless, raging bitterness of the play. It is surmised that Shakespeare, with all these "plays unpleasant," was going through some experience of extreme personal disillusionment and that with TIMON he reached the breaking point. There can be very little doubt that he was in some way spiritually and intellectually rudderless when he wrote it; and this lack of mental stability deprived him of his sure dramatic sense.

TIMON is bad philosophy and bad theater, however brilliant the writing. It seems, not surprisingly, that the Globe Company never performed it; and, though the eighteenth century made some halfhearted attempts at adaptations, the first recorded performance of the Folio text did not come till 1851 at Sadler's Wells, London, by Samuel Phelps. It is a pity that we cannot ever hear the great speeches greatly spoken; but we simply cannot take the play, for it never arouses us to participation or to compassion; only very occasionally can we discern a rift in the clouds, as with the fragmentary gleam of:

> Then, Timon, presently prepare thy grave:
> Lie where the light foam of the sea may beat
> Thy grave-stone daily, . . .   IV, 3, 378

and we realize, with a lifting of the heart, that the sea will not always be so savage as it has been, and that Shakespeare will presently wake from this nightmare and find himself once more among his fellows at the Globe.

TROILUS AND CRESSIDA has in it a good deal of the turbulence of TIMON; it is diffuse, incoherent, difficult to trim to a recognizable dramatic pattern. A lot of people are piled into it, and not a single one of them is wholly likable, with the exception of Troilus himself. The scurrilous Thersites smears the play with scabrous jests, though many of them have a good salt sting that we cannot help appreciating; again, the iteration of invective is apt to pall. "How now, thou cur of envy," says Achilles to Thersites. "Thou crusty batch of nature, what's the news?" And Thersites replies: "Why, thou picture of what thou seemest, and idol of idiot worshippers, here's a letter for thee." And later in the same scene Thersites and Patroclus interchange the following pleasantries:

PATROCLUS: Why, thou damnable box of envy, thou, what mean'st thou to curse thus?
THERSITES: Do I curse thee?

PATROCLUS: Why, no, you ruinous butt, you whoreson indistinguishable cur, no.

THERSITES: No? Why art thou then exasperate, thou idle immaterial skein of sleave silk, thou green sarcenet flap for a sore eye, thou tassel of a prodigal's purse, thou?

v, 1, 24

Shakespeare is not in the romantic vein, certainly. Achilles is a sulky lout who finally kills Hector by a cowardly betrayal; Patroclus is a sycophant, Ajax a boor and a fool, Menelaus a stock cuckold, and Diomedes a "smoothy." Agamemnon comes off rather better. Ulysses, upon the slightest provocation, will out with thirty or forty lines of complex trope and metaphor; for Shakespeare is in his overwriting period, his mind fecund of pentameters, his heart troubled and unsure. We may have to use a blue pencil with Ulysses, but he has some magnificent things to say. His great speech which begins

> Time hath, my lord, a wallet at his back
> Wherein he puts alms for oblivion,   III, 3, 145

is studded with famous maxims. "Perseverance, dear my lord, Keeps honour bright." "The welcome ever smiles, And farewell goes out sighing." "The present eye praises the present object" and, startlingly familiar, "One touch of nature makes the whole world kin." This is brilliant but extravagant. Ulysses' powers of observation and his judgment of people must, however, have been of the greatest value to the Greek diplomatic service. This is his analysis of the newly arrived Cressida:

> There's language in her eye, her cheek, her lip,
> Nay, her foot speaks, her wanton spirits look out
> At every joint and motive of her body.
> O, these encounterers, so glib of tongue,
> That give a coasting welcome ere it comes,

And wide unclasp the tables of their thoughts
To every ticklish reader! set them down
For sluttish spoils of opportunity,
And daughters of the game.   IV, 5, 56

This is recognizable, vivid; the mind engages with it; but it
is also a description of "our heroine" and illustrates the problem which confronts us in the play.

We start off, firmly enough, with Troilus in love; he is
clearly, maturely drawn, and there is music in him, if, like
all the music of the play, it is too elaborately orchestrated. We
see Pandarus, lively enough in print but capable of far more
likable comedy in the playing, and Cressida, whom we are
never led to trust. She is too beautiful, too assured, too "glib
of tongue."

Here, with the background of war, are the elements of
tragedy. But with the scene of the Greeks in council, Act 1,
scene 3, we realize how easy it may be for the lovers and their
story to get lost among these "cogging Greeks." For Shakespeare is not in love with war; he is not in love with the men
who make wars; he is intent on dissecting, not the bright, flat
tapestry heroics of the English chronicle wars, but the battle
of power politics, personal jealousies, and faction fights, confusion of issues, confounding of order and sanity, the seamy
side of valor.

Having thoroughly discredited the Greeks with one of the
least amiable Thersites scenes, he returns to the Trojans in
council, discussing a peace proposal. The Trojans are more
likable than the Greeks and not quite so long-winded. If any
one of them comes near Shakespeare's own thoughts, it must
be Hector, who, greatest fighter among them all, uses the
most common sense and is the strongest for peace. But Hector-
Shakespeare is won over, although his judgment is entirely un-
convinced by the arguments in favor of refusing the peace
terms. To Troilus and Paris he says that they have argued

```
                    . . . not much
Unlike young men, whom Aristotle thought
Unfit to hear moral philosophy.
The reasons you allege do more conduce
To the hot passion of distempered blood,
Than to make up a free determination
'Twixt right and wrong; for pleasure and revenge
Have ears more deaf than adders to the voice
Of any true decision.                    II, 3, 165
```

But the war must go on, and so must the play; and all the
way through it Shakespeare seems to be struggling with an
infinite contempt for the whole business of fighting, and the
story of Troilus and his false Cressida struggles for breath
too, choked with disillusion, occasionally rising to the surface
for a long breath of magnificent poetic air. To the facile
Cressida, who is fully and unsparingly drawn, he gives one
of the most beautiful of his singing speeches:

```
If I be false, or swerve a hair from truth,
When time is old or hath forgot itself,
When waterdrops have worn the stones of Troy,
And blind oblivion swallow'd cities up,
And mighty states characterless are grated
To dusty nothing, yet let memory,
From false to false among false maids in love,
Upbraid my falsehood!                    III, 2, 179
```

But, if the song is sweet, the irony lies heavily upon it.

Neither the love story nor the war story is ever fully resolved. There is no "pay-off." Cressida is false, Troilus dis-
covers her falsehood; he seeks death in battle but does not find
it; he finds Diomedes, his successful rival, but does not kill
him. Hector is slain not in fair fight but in ambush by Achilles
and all his gangsters, and Achilles goes off with a couplet of
such incredible banality that we cannot help feeling that
Shakespeare is nauseated with the whole business. Both sides

claim the victory in battle, Thersites threads in and out discrediting everything and everybody, and Pandarus ends the play with some obscure and bawdy rhymed verse; or, rather, the play stops because it has already gone on a long time and there doesn't seem to be much left to write about.

All of this leaves us, in the theater, faced with very great difficulties: the problem of imposing a recognizable form on this shapeless play, of cutting the verbiage away from it, of presenting some sort of conclusion. It might well be worth trying; for there is much fine stuff in the text and much that is possibly closer to our thinking today than it has ever been to any audience before. I feel that we should have to do some very free editing and make a decision, which Shakespeare himself never clearly made, as to whether we are presenting satire, caricature, or a genuine, if caustic, commentary on love and war. The experiment would be worth making. But since, in America, the commercial theater no longer dares to produce any but the most popular of Shakespeare's plays, we are faced with our usual problem: we have no place for professional experiment.

The last of the four plays, on the other hand, is overripe for revival. MEASURE FOR MEASURE is a strong piece of work, less informed with music than the greatest plays but brimming with life. It is not polite life, nor disciplined life; the comedy characters from the stews of Vienna would not get past Hollywood censorship, but there is no question as to their reality. Pompey is a fine, fat part, and Elbow, the constable, is in the best Dogberry-and-Verges tradition. Lucio, described in the Folio list of actors as "a fantastic," has a light, showy impudence and a quick tongue.

One of the sourest things in the play is the savagery of the punishment which the Duke imposes on Lucio at the end. They would never have treated him so in Arden or Illyria. But this is not a dream world; it is a hard one, peopled by men and women in the grip of strong, difficult emotions. Spirit and flesh are at war with each other, and their conflict is no more resolved than is the conflict of war in TROILUS AND CRESSIDA. The pattern imposed for its resolution is an arbitrary one. We feel Shakespeare thinking contemptuously that life doesn't solve things so easily, but this is the theater, and here is your deus ex machina and your last-act curtain, so make the best of it.

There is no doubt that the trick by which one woman substitutes herself for another in a man's bed, always with the noblest intentions, as Helena did in ALL'S WELL and as Mariana does for Isabella in this play, was an accepted artifice with Elizabethan audiences, however difficult we may find it. The impenetrable-disguise business is also put to use, this time by the Duke; and, in reading, we find the Duke's procrastination in revealing himself and meting out the necessary rewards and punishments more than a little irritating. This device, also, is much more acceptable in the theater; in recent stage revivals it has been proved that the Duke, humanized and strengthened by an actor's personality, may be given a variety of thought and feeling which is not immediately apparent from his actual words and may become much more than "a tall dark dummy," as Van Doren calls him.

Shakespeare knew, and no doubt counted upon, the interpretative possibilities of silence. The Duke does quite a lot of listening and quite a lot of learning as he listens; there is, further, much ironic humor implicit in his actual lines. He is dispassionate; he has the power to end all the threatened evils of the play or, rather, to resolve its immediate problems in terms of a pattern roughly just. Over the dark emotions which have caused these problems he has no power. When Shakespeare is writing full tragedy, there will be no Duke to say "Thus far, and no further"; but this play is to be insulated from a consummation of pity and terror, and the Duke will do it for us, interpreting between the audience's normal pulse of thought and the underground currents of emotion which the play so nearly lets loose. He is, supremely, a part for an actor of imagination who has the ability to project unspoken thought.

Angelo is the medium of that ungovernable passion of which Shakespeare wrote in the sonnets with a force that can come only from personal experience:

> The expense of spirit in a waste of shame
> Is lust in action; and till action, lust
> Is perjur'd, murderous, bloody, full of blame,
> Savage, extreme, rude, cruel, not to trust;
> Enjoyed no sooner, but despised straight;
> Past reason hunted, and no sooner had,
> Past reason hated, as the swallowed bait,
> On purpose laid to make the taker mad.
>
> Sonnet 129

The degrees of Angelo's yielding to a passion he hates and fears are brilliantly dissected; they carry the first two acts on a flood tide. But in the third act he drops unaccountably from the play and becomes merely the tool of its plot. His last scene is as difficult as ever an actor can have been called upon to play; it can only be redeemed by the whole-souled truth which he can bring, after the ultimate breaking down of all his stratagems, to the complete repentance of

> I crave death more willingly than mercy;
> 'Tis my deserving, and I do entreat it.   v, 1, 472

There can be no question of making Angelo "sympathetic"; but we must feel that here is a man who has been "sick unto death" with a fever so terrible that it has left him shriveled to the bone of what he had been, and that clean flesh must grow in the slow process of healing. Shakespeare is not even sure, I think, that this spiritual regeneration can take place; but the artificial devices of the happy-ending plot have at least opened the way for it, and the whole play must be motivated not to the finality of a last-act curtain but to this speculative conclusion.

For Isabella, swept by the passion of chastity as Angelo by the passion of lust, must also be healed; and the Duke's gentleness to her gives promise that she will be. Diverse judgments have been passed on Isabella, arising, as Dr. Ridley says, "from the diversity of the critics, not from inconsistency in the character." Any attempt to smooth her into a "straight" heroine, any lapse into a smug self-righteousness, will be disastrous.

For the interest, in the play's second half, swings dangerously away from the Isabella-Angelo story toward the comedy of the prison scenes. Lucio, Pompey, and Abhorson threaten to carry it away, with their pungent vitality. To preserve the balance, Isabella and Angelo must have brought the original theme to a pitch of tension which will not cease to tingle in our minds. But only the Duke can hold the two elements together, according to the measure of his authority, penetration, and humor. There should be some support from Mariana, who, having only a few lines, must nonetheless contrive to inform them with the stress of grief and hope, faith and desperation; and the smaller parts, Escalus and the Provost, must never become placid or sententious.

MEASURE FOR MEASURE is an adult play. The writing of its emotions is less forthright and more indriven than in almost any other. There are inconsistencies of a minor nature in the text, which skillful staging will easily smooth out. But there is also a feeling of fundamental unease in Shakespeare's mind. At times he seems to be forcing himself to write a comedy. Perhaps the company had begged him for one, thinking back to the prosperous days of AS YOU LIKE IT. But there is no harmony in his soul now, and the comedy he produces is a little acrid and almost too realistic. For this very reason, however, it may be the more easily blended with the turbid emotion of the thematic material. This, again, is a play which has possibly grown more comprehensible as audiences have become educated to some small appreciation of the importance and complexity of the subconscious mind.

Like the other "unpleasant" plays, it lacks music. There are a few notes of harmony: the beautiful song "Take, O take those lips away"; occasional lines, such as the Duke's "Look, the unfolding star calls up the shepherd"; Claudio's famous outburst upon death, which lifts fear of the unknown into pure poetry, and catches at our hearts with swift and beautiful imagery. We cannot, however, take refuge in melody nor be swept beyond logical analysis, as we are by Othello's "Wash me in steep-down gulfs of liquid fire." We face life and people at their least charming and a dramatic design at its most stubborn. But, in my judgment, the modern theater is admirably equipped to grapple with this play, and it might prove an extremely rewarding attempt.

12. "Sad, High, and Working"

I come no more to make you laugh: things now,
That bear a weighty and a serious brow,
Sad, high, and working, full of state and woe:
Such noble scenes as draw the eye to flow
We now present.   HENRY VIII, Prologue

IT SEEMS that in writing the triple magnificence of
OTHELLO, MACBETH, and LEAR Shakespeare had freed himself
from the uncertainties which clog TROILUS and MEASURE FOR
MEASURE. We cannot tell when he finally cleared his mind
of the poison which runs through TIMON. The suggestion
that he wrote it almost simultaneously with LEAR, as if he
were peeling emotional vegetables and throwing all the husks
into TIMON and all the good feeding into Lear, is not wholly
convincing. But at any rate he did at last succeed in purging
his mind and heart, and brought back to his work an even
increased degree of sanity and compassion.

With ANTONY AND CLEOPATRA his intellect is at work on
the problems of high tragedy compressed into the dramatic
form which his stage demanded, and he produces what is perhaps his most impressive piece of theater craftsmanship in the
tragic vein. He is free of the over-elaborate and decorated
writing of his middle period; his verse is more flexible and
more subtly adapted to the rhythms of speech than ever before.

The form remains basic to the end of his life, more involved
in CORIOLANUS and THE WINTER'S TALE, softened to a gentler
modulation in THE TEMPEST. CORIOLANUS follows ANTONY;

Plutarch is still in his pocket; it has authority, discipline, little compassion, and no mystery. HENRY VIII brings him back to England. Its characters are nearer home than they have been in the Roman world of CORIOLANUS, which, for the first time, has assumed an almost coldly classical air. The Roman plays steadied his mind; the English one, even though it is written in collaboration with another playwright, warms him again.

The glories and the dramatic problems of ANTONY AND CLEOPATRA, like those of the other great tragedies, defy the easy analysis of a few sentences. The play has been denied a rank with the other four, not because it is inferior, but because it is different in aim and texture, different in the tragic conception, ostensibly less unified. Yet many commentators have written about it in unrestrained superlatives, profoundly moved and even awed by the majesty of their subject.

The unerring power of the text is of such unflagging beauty and of so sure an aim that we may open the play at any point and fall instantly to quotation, from the opening lines, as inescapably thematic as the first bars of the Fifth Symphony:

> Nay, but this dotage of our general's
> O'erflows the measure; those his goodly eyes,
> That o'er the files and musters of the war
> Have glow'd like plated Mars, now bend, now turn
> The office and devotion of their view
> Upon a tawny front. His captain's heart,
> Which in the scuffles of great fights hath burst
> The buckles on his breast, reneges all temper,
> And is become the bellows and the fan
> To cool a gypsy's lust,   I, I, I

to Octavius' epitaph on Cleopatra herself at the play's end:

> . . . she looks like sleep,
> As she would catch another Antony
> In her strong toil of grace.   v, 2, 345

The aptness and beauty and precision never falter. But of all the great speeches and famous passages with which the play is filled, not one may justly be isolated from its context or from the character who speaks it, for every line both reveals the speaker and furthers the play's design.

It is not an easy play to produce in the modern theater. Now, as always, star actors are attracted by the dangerous magnetism of the two name parts; but a really fine production, such as the one directed by Glen Byam Shaw at Stratford-on-Avon in 1953, can never be achieved by treating the play as a vehicle for the leading players. We must always follow and endeavor to re-create its original stage design.

An unfortunate production on Broadway in 1937 furnished melancholy but convincing evidence that it is fatal to ignore this necessity. The text was extensively "adapted," supposedly in accordance with modern needs. The self-styled editors laid violent hands upon this, the most subtle and complex example of Shakespeare's later art. In this play the delicate steel of his dramatic craftsmanship is welded into a machine of tremendous power, each tiny wheel engaging smoothly and beautifully with the main driving shaft. Throw in one monkey wrench, and the machine will run amok and destroy itself. But the editors thought, and the impulse behind their thinking is still widely shared, that the play as it stood was impossible for reproduction on the modern stage. They evidently felt that a process of compression would be beneficial; so they put together lumps of Roman scenes, alternating them with lumps of Egyptian scenes like an endless club sandwich. On the contrary principle they committed several atrocious scene changes in the very middle of a flow of action, even in the midst of Cleopatra's lament over the dead Antony. The result, naturally, was that the actors were blamed for failing in a task which Burbage and Bernhardt together could not have accomplished successfully.

I do not think that the right lessons were learned from this unfortunate episode. It is true that we must have great Antonys and brilliant Cleopatras; it is also true that we must have Shakespeare; and in this play no part will stand unless in its just relation to the whole. If we fear the breadth of its scope and want only the story of how Antony lost all for love of an Egyptian queen, we had better produce Dryden's ALL FOR LOVE, as the eighteenth-century producers did, embellishing the easier story with dollops of Shakespeare's verse. For he tells us a different kind of story; he shows us exactly how and why Antony lost the world, what sort of world it was that he lost, how it was governed and by what caliber of men, and by what process their disciplined strength prevailed over the effete Egyptian civilization, and over the hopelessly unsound resources of Antony.

There is little to take us by surprise in the development of Antony himself. The actor who studies carefully his first two scenes will find the character fully shaped between his hands. Nothing that follows will come upon us unexpectedly, as Cleopatra constantly flashes into new and astonishing self-revelation. The disintegration of Antony is inevitable; it is implicit in the play's very first lines; Enobarbus specifically forecasts it; Antony himself knows in his own heart from the beginning that it is already undermining his greatness. He is the "lion dying" who has cast himself out from the Roman conventions and abrogated the right to rule among them. Yet the old habit is strong; he can never, in his heart, belong to the soft Egyptian world.

Antony is a hard part to "act"; the actor must give us, through his own personal quality, a similar abundance of strength from which he can continuously discard as its foundations are sapped by sensuality and passion and as the old strength of the Roman general softens into confusion and ruin. The actor must never have to "play for" power; he must have it in himself and let us see the gradual wrecking of it.

Volumes have been written about Cleopatra; she is described in the play, commented upon, discussed, praised, disparaged, loved, hated. No character in any of the plays is more fully analyzed in words or more comprehensively revealed in action. No commentary could amplify that which the text itself provides. There is no mystery here except the high mystery of the attempt to interpret, to convey through the medium of one human being, the "infinite variety" of a being unique in drama as in historical fact. This indeed calls upon the innermost art of acting; and here it must be fortified by the greatest fund of technical and imaginative resource.

But, it cannot be too strongly emphasized, an Antony and a Cleopatra are not enough. "The wide arch of the ranged empire" is the frame within which they move and the action of the play strides the width of it. If ever Shakespeare's imagination wore seven-league boots, it is here.

There is little verbal scene painting, little even to enhance with poetry the wheeling cycles of light and darkness. This is not Romeo's world, star-governed, or Titania's, enchanted by the moon. It is a world of men; the discipline and daring of man have discovered it, know it, move free and unafraid throughout its vastness. There are no dark corners, no unguessed terrors; light informs the play with reason; there are causes and effects, and they lie in character itself, and character in action.

For this purpose Shakespeare uses a spaceless stage; the thirteen scenes of the third act and the fifteen of the fourth, so marked by the editors, make nonsense of his intention. Heavy scenic settings must drive us away from his extreme flexibility, and we shall lose the careful interlocking of each unit in these scenes, carefully pieced together for the dramatic effect of juxtaposition and contrast. We must recapture this freedom if we are to allow the play unfettered scope. He does not localize, not from carelessness but from extreme deliberation and by right of careful choice. He is arrogant in his demands on actors and audience; from the scene designer he demands, more than anything else, the ability to resist temptation.

But we can supply something, and we should; nothing we can achieve with paint and canvas will follow Shakespeare fast enough if we attempt to pin him down to local geography; but we can supply a background to his spirit, a wide sky to his wide empire. We can emphasize the contrast between Egypt and Rome, for it is important and vital to the play's meaning. There must be differences of costume, of color, of atmosphere, of "temperature."

Granville Barker, in what I judge to be the greatest of his prefaces, supplies a detailed analysis of how we may translate this mighty design into the action of the theater. Any such attempt is outside the scope or purpose of this book. It is easy to fail in a production of ANTONY AND CLEOPATRA, for the enterprise is a tremendous one, perhaps more difficult than any other except LEAR. But it is not impossible if we will trust the text and follow it with vision and devotion. Shakespeare, however, is adamant; he will allow no tampering with his craftsmanship, no evasion of his demands, no substitution or "improvement." We must rise to his level, not try to reduce him to our own.

In CORIOLANUS, the arch of the Roman world, which we have seen stretched to meet and melt into the infinity of space, becomes a tangible stone structure which we can reproduce as easily as we can photograph Trajan's Column. The passions which move beneath it are as simply analyzed, tabulated, and codified as the episodes of warfare carved on the Trajan monument. We are in no trouble over space and time. They are marked down and divided up. Some simple pillars, some steps, a rostrum or two with a suitable air of immutable Romanness, a set of curtains, a campfire, and we are ready for the actors. They march on; they stride off; they stand and argue; they strike poses and orate; they salute one another, kneel to one another, fight one another; they hardly ever sit down. Somehow, we feel unaccountably disappointed. So, presumably, does Shakespeare; and when he has rung down a grandiloquent last curtain, he throws Plutarch into the River Avon for cold food to the fishes and goes for a long walk through the fields. He will not pass Plutarch's way again. As his hero has said: "There is a world elsewhere."

We wonder what Burbage made of this script. He must have realized that the responsibility lay on him and that it would be no easy task. Whoever was assigned the part of Volumnia had a valiant, heroic, grim time of it. We guess that "Menenius" chuckled to himself at the first reading and began counting the possible laughs. "Aufidius," not altogether displeased, tentatively tried out his chest notes; the musicians, who hadn't had much fun for a long while, just sighed and went home, all but the trumpeter. The smallest part actors, however, were vastly pleased, for they realized that the burden of the play would lie between themselves and Mr. Burbage, and that whenever the text said "Hoo! Hoo!" for the Citizens, they might look forward to an ad-libbing field day.

Because plays are not usually produced for the benefit of the extras, this one has had a sparse history in the theater. "Not worth a damn," said Irving, and generations of actor-managers endorsed his view and left the play alone. But to a world deeply engaged in an armed appraisal of totalitarianism and democracy CORIOLANUS does have something to say.

Our rage for "timeliness," however, is not entirely satisfied by this play. It is useless for us to try to make Coriolanus a dictator. He hates and mistrusts the people and the people's tribunes, but he has no wish to rule them. He is content to serve under another general; he runs from public commendation of his own deeds and worth; he is not especially elated over the offer of the consulship; and he cannot bring himself to purchase it by any truckling to the voters or exercise of the demagogic arts. He is a "lonely dragon," glorying in his own power as a fighter and willing, for no reward but the satisfaction of his own pride, to serve in the most austere tradition of the military caste.

He is not a very satisfactory hero for us. The description

> His nature is too noble for this world:
> He would not flatter Neptune for his trident,
> Or Jove for's power to thunder: his heart's in's mouth:
> What his breast forges, that his tongue must vent,
> And, being angry, does forget that ever
> He heard the name of death   III, 1, 254

might fit Hotspur but for that ominous "his nature is too noble for this world." We cannot feel that Shakespeare liked him much, and we are enough of the people to resent him, however illogically. Music is seldom wrung from him, save, briefly, in the scene where his wife and mother come to plead for Rome; but even the love and yearning of the greeting to his wife is steeled with his obsessing purpose: "O, a kiss, Long as my exile, sweet as my revenge!" Almost the most touching thing about him is the line and the rare stage direction which follow Volumnia's plea: (*After holding her by the hand, silent*) "O, mother, mother! What have you done?"

He fails us as a human being, and he does not provide us with any material for a dictator either. He does, however, voice a potent case against the rule of the many, as against the rule of the few, which is the ground base of the play.

> . . . They choose their magistrate,
> And such a one as he, who puts his "shall,"

His popular "shall," against a graver bench
Than ever frowned in Greece. By Jove himself,
It makes the consuls base; and my soul aches
To know, when two authorities are up,
Neither supreme, how soon confusion
May enter 'twixt the gap of both, and take
The one by the other.   III, I, 104

And, of "democratic" government:

                    . . . This double worship,
Where one part does disdain with cause, the other
Insult without all reason: where gentry, title, wisdom,
Cannot conclude, but by the yea and no
Of general ignorance, it must omit
Real necessities, and give way the while
To unstable slightness. Purpose so barr'd, it follows,
Nothing is done to purpose.   III, I, 142

The argument is not for one man, but for an all-powerful
oligarchy, especially in time of war. It is of the highest interest
to us, and the whole of the second and third act is vibrant
with the sway of power between the senators and the people's
tribunes, who are two opportunist politicians, sharply and
sardonically drawn. It is the personal quality of Coriolanus
himself, however, which decides the issue and precipitates the
crisis.

The people are nowhere, and by nobody, considered as an
entity worthy of reason or regard. Coriolanus despises them,
Volumnia advises him simply to deceive them with words that
are not from his heart. The demagogic tribunes, intent on
personal power, openly use them with methods no less blatant.
And they themselves deserve no better treatment; they show,
in the scene where Coriolanus begs their "voices" with a
sting of contempt behind the words, a kind of blunt, bewildered common sense. But they are, throughout, fickle,

stupid, won and lost by the wrong people for the wrong reasons. Coriolanus, banished, cries at them:

> You common cry of curs, whose breath I hate,
> As reek o' the rotten fens . . .
>   . . . I banish you,
> And here remain with your uncertainty.
> Let every feeble rumour shake your hearts:
> Your enemies, with nodding of their plumes
> Fan you into despair: have the power still
> To banish your defenders, till at length
> Your ignorance (which finds not till it feels,
> Making but reservation of yourselves,
> Still your own foes) deliver you as most
> Abated captives, to some nation
> That won you without blows!   III, 3, 122

Reading such scenes as these, we are not surprised to remember that some years ago a production of the play at the Comédie Française caused such a storm that rioting broke out and the theater had to be temporarily closed; the possible truth behind Coriolanus's taunts was too close to be comfortable.

There is, then, power and excitement to be derived from this part of the play if we keep the balance accurate and do not try falsely to weight one scale. The handling of the crowd will be extremely important. Shakespeare always seems to make his Roman citizens unusually articulate. Here, as in JULIUS CAESAR, many of the citizens have individual lines and individual characteristics. For the rest, the director will have to invent both. A crowd must never be treated in lumps, with lump emotions. Every member of it must feel his own life and be as conscious of himself as the center of surrounding events as is the citizen of today who cheers for the Republican or Democratic candidate with a wholly personal ardor, and for reasons which he at least supposes to be entirely his own. This crowd needs actors; the director conducts the orchestra, but every instrument has its own value, and none of them is easy to play.

The little people in this play are certainly as much alive as its protagonists, with the exception of Menenius, who lives up to his own rich description of himself:

> a humorous patrician, and one that loves a cup of hot wine, with not a drop of allaying Tiber in't . . . hasty and tinder-like upon too trivial motion: one that converses more with the buttock of the night than with the forehead of the morning. What I think, I utter, and spend my malice in breath.

Volumnia, like her son, is noble, but not likable; she is a woman and a mother-in-law in the most blood-curdling tradition, though it must be admitted that the milky Virgilia would irritate a far more tolerant woman than Volumnia. Both of them will take a good deal of humanizing by the actress. Valeria is lightly but incisively sketched, graced most by Coriolanus's exquisite greeting:

> The noble sister of Publicola,
> The moon of Rome; chaste as the icicle
> That's curded by the frost from purest snow
> And hangs on Dian's temple: dear Valeria! v, 3, 64

There are, however, many ripe plums for the small-part actors. The little scene between Aufidius's servants flashes suddenly into vibrant life:

> SEC. SERV'T: Why, then we shall have a stirring world again. This peace is nothing, but to rust iron, increase tailors, and breed ballad-mongers.
> FIRST SERV'T: Let me have war, say I, it exceeds peace as far as day does night: it's spritely, walking, audible and full of vent. Peace is very apoplexy, lethargy, mull'd, deaf, sleepy, insensible, a getter of more bastard children than war's a destroyer of men.   IV, 5, 222

We can still feel the stress and tension of the conflicts between the factions and classes of ancient Rome, the aristocrats, the military men, the politicians, and the common people; the hostilities and unholy alliances; the pressures of ambition, pride, patriotism, greed, jealousy, and fear—all these things are still real to us, more so than the lofty, unlovable figure of Coriolanus himself. John Houseman's New York production of the play in 1954 proved that the modern producer is wise to seek out these living values, rather than to try to re-create the classical façade of the Roman world.

HENRY VIII occupies a curiously anomalous position in the canon. It has had a continuous stage history, as full as that of CORIOLANUS is meager. Its processions, banquets, halberdiers and citizens and bishops have provided flourishing, colorful theater spectacle, with some rough, lively comedy in between, and plenty of pathos in the Queen Katherine scenes. Yet the consensus of scholarly opinion, much more unanimous than usual, admits only four and a half scenes as being wholly Shakespearean. Whoever wrote the rest of the play, Fletcher or, less probably, Massinger, was certainly inspired beyond his usual form. For, though the smoothness of the verse has been criticized as lacking Shakespeare's muscular flexibility and the conception of the play condemned as lacking in continuity, there is a great deal, even in the non-Shakespearean portion, that is of sure theatrical effectiveness.

Katherine is the most memorable figure in it; and, indeed, if we may judge by the authors' own epilogue, they relied upon her being so. Some of Shakespeare's finest writing is in the courage and emotional strength of her trial scene. It is something of a shock to be reminded that her last two scenes are Fletcher's, including the famous song "Orpheus with his lute." But they are fine ones; her confrontation of the Cardinals has dignity and integrity, and any actress who plays the death scene with austerity and truth will find herself well rewarded.

Wolsey provides an equally rich opportunity for an actor. Again, we are a little startled to discover that it was Shakespeare's collaborator who wrote the most quoted passage in the play, Wolsey's "Farewell, a long farewell to all my greatness." Fletcher (supposing it was he) appears to have taken a rather more sentimental view of the great Cardinal than did Shakespeare, who laid down the first design for the part. The change of heart which marks his downfall comes very suddenly and is inadequately prepared. But the two sides of the man's nature are very fully described by Katherine and Griffith in Act iv, scene 2. They are not irreconcilable. The actor must never forget that, despite all the arrogance and ostentation of the triumphant Wolsey, there still exists in his heart the other self he could have been, the man of whom Griffith says:

> His overthrow heap'd happiness upon him;
> For then, and not till then, he felt himself,
> And found the blessedness of being little.

This inner quality he must never lose, however few opportunities he may find to express it.

Henry himself is a little disappointing. He never quite reaches the stature of these two. This may be because Fletcher found the Tudor zest a little too much for him, and the Henry of the later scenes never lives up to the vigorous life of the early ones, except for the brief moment when he hears of his child's birth. Here Shakespeare brilliantly brings him alive again, together with the inimitable Old Lady, who is one of the raciest and sharpest little sketches ever written within so small a compass. There are other good parts from both authors, notably Buckingham, full of salt in his first scene (Shakespeare) and of sugar in his last (Fletcher), facing life and death with equal courage.

Too much stress has, I think, been laid on the play's inconsistencies of style and too little on its highly dramatic scenes, its irony and humor. There are many opportunities to enrich the script with music and dance, heraldic ritual, pageantry and color. These assets are largely lost to the legitimate theater nowadays and have become the prerogative of musical comedy or operatic drama. There is no reason why we should not reclaim them when we get the chance, for they are very properly a part of the theater's glamour and audience appeal. But the over-all design of HENRY VIII is not so tightly integrated that we need fear to take some liberties with it. The sequence concerning the conspiracy against Cranmer, which drags out the last quarter of the play, is usually, and I think rightly, omitted on the stage. It has been argued that these scenes are essential because they show the completion of Henry's break with the Church of Rome through his championship of the first "Protestant" Archbishop of Canterbury. But I do not believe that Shakespeare, left to himself, would have killed off his two main characters and then turned the play over to a long, political controversy concerning a minor one.

For his theme, as always, is expressed in personal and human terms. It is precisely stated in the Prologue: it is to be "sad, high and working, full of state and woe." The spectators are promised a rich shilling's worth of entertainment, which indeed they get, and are then adjured thus:

> Therefore, for goodness' sake, and as you are known
> The first and happiest hearers of the town,
> Be sad, as we would make ye: think ye see
> The very persons of our noble story
> As they were living; think you see them great,
> And follow'd by the general throng and sweat
> Of thousand friends; then, in a moment, see
> How soon this mightiness meets misery.

The statement of theme is explicit at the beginning, and so is its resolution at the end. It is that out of all this welter of "mightiness" and "misery," this whirlpool of ambition and devotion, love and lust, undeserved suffering and insecure triumph, emerges at last the predestinate figure of the little child whose baptism ends the play. It is she to whom men's eyes will turn when all the rest are dust.

> . . . Truth shall nurse her,
> Holy and heavenly thoughts still counsel her:
> She shall be lov'd and fear'd. Her own shall bless her;
> Her foes shake like a field of beaten corn,
> And hang their heads with sorrow. Good grows with her:
> In her days every man shall eat in safety,
> Under his own vine, what he plants; and sing
> The merry songs of peace to all his neighbours:
> God shall be truly known, and those about her
> From her shall read the perfect ways of honour,
> And by those claim their greatness, not by blood. v, 5, 28

Shakespeare (or Fletcher) may simply have contrived this ending as an exaggerated tribute to their recently dead sovereign. We have yet to see the prophesied Utopia realized in fact. But the trumpets of the last scene still ring in the ears of Englishmen, together with the Garter King-of-Arms' resplendent salutation: "Heaven, from thy endless goodness, send prosperous life, long and ever happy, to the high and mighty Princess of England, Elizabeth!"

13. *"Music at the Close"*

SHAKESPEARE was undoubtedly influenced toward the end of his life by the romantic comedies of Beaumont, Fletcher, and their contemporaries, which were becoming increasingly the fashion. Also, the Burbage syndicate was now working at the indoor theater at Blackfriars, as well as at the old Globe, and demanded an increase of masques, processions, and other spectacular aids to the drama. In consequence, the stage directions of the last plays are unusually full, and the spectacles unusually elaborate.

Some of them, such as the vision in CYMBELINE, may be regarded as playhouse additions to Shakespeare's text; we should be grateful to get rid of this particular excrescence with such an excuse. The dumb shows in PERICLES are certainly not his, but the whole text of PERICLES is open to grave question. With THE WINTER'S TALE, he had more fully mastered the new form with which he was experimenting, and by the time he wrote THE TEMPEST he had sublimated it to a use exquisitely and unmatchably his own. The four plays are closely knit together as a group, and in them Shakespeare is fancy-free, using the license of the romantic form to give wings to his imagination and to let it roam the "cloud-capp'd towers, the gorgeous palaces" where Fortune is a capricious but kindly deity and man need never resolve unaided the dreadful conflict with his own soul.

In THE TEMPEST, so the scholars tell us, Shakespeare wove the last of his great dramatic dreams: after this play we have only disconnected fragments of his craft, even less of his mind. It is commonly assumed that he settled down in Stratford, peacefully intent on acquiring real estate and debating to which of his relatives he should leave his second-best bed. Perhaps this is an erroneous assumption. It may be that the path of his mind traveled a region at once too ample and too rare to be confined within the walls of the Blackfriars or to attract the rough and avid audiences of the Globe. We have no record of his spirit's journey; we know only that he traveled alone.

If THE TEMPEST is inimitably his own, "full of grace and grandeur" as Hazlitt said, PERICLES has only intermittent flashes of these qualities. It is generally agreed that the first two acts of it are by another playwright, though in fact they do not seem markedly inconsistent with the rest. If Antiochus is a slightly wooden tyrant, Pericles's descriptions of him are pertinent:

> With hostile forces he'll o'erspread the land,
> And with ostent of war will look so huge,
> Amazement shall drive courage from the state,
> Our men be vanquish'd e'er they do resist,
> And subjects punish'd that ne'er thought offence.
>
> I, 2, 24

> To lop that doubt, he'll fill this land with arms,
> And make pretence of wrong that I have done him.
>
> I, 2, 90

The formulas of tyranny have not greatly changed.

Our one glimpse of the "little men," in the Fishermen who rescue Pericles, is lively. But the episode in which Pericles disguises himself as a poor knight and wins the hand of the Princess Thaisa is pedestrian writing and altogether too naive for the modern theater.

With the shipwreck in Act III, matters improve considerably; there is music and true emotion in the scene where Pericles and the old nurse with the honey name, Lychorida, cast the coffined Thaisa into the sea. The opening of the coffin by Cerimon gives us another authentic sequence. He describes himself as "made familiar" with

> . . . the blest infusions
> That dwell in vegetives, in metal, stones;
> And I can speak of the disturbances
> That nature works; and of her cures; which doth give me
> A more content in course of true delight
> Than to be thirsty after tottering honour,
> Or tie my pleasure up in silken bags,
> To please the fool and death.   III, 2, 35

And of course he revives Thaisa.

The story moves on, through Tarsus with its Queen, the "jealous step-mother," Tyre, which stands "in a litigious peace," and Mytilene, where are placed the brothel scenes which Victorian commentators so self-righteously denied to Shakespeare. Thinking back to MEASURE FOR MEASURE, we may be absolved of any serious doubts; they are not pretty, they are extremely outspoken, they sound a harsh discord in the lyric of the play; but it is a Shakespearean dissonance. Marina, decked, like Perdita, with flowers of springtime delicacy, moves through them with a white ardor. When, at last, she and Pericles are reunited, the play is swept up with music, grace, and "all simplicity." The second reunion, between Thaisa and her husband and daughter, is perfunctory by comparison.

The story has meandered a long way; it has been, of itself,

consciously artificial; and, worst theater fault of all, its diverse episodes, separated widely in space and time, are bridged by no such dramatic scheme as Shakespeare has been at pains to devise for his great plays. They are arbitrarily linked by a narrator, who describes the intervening events in deliberately archaic octosyllabic couplets. If the play is done at all, it must have the quality of an idyll of the golden age and be set luminously and richly. It was a hit, apparently, throughout its early career and retains at least some of the essential elements which made it so. But we should have to cut and tighten, drench the scenes with music, and play it like a decorative tapestry for the eye. It is a play for a relaxed and leisured audience, not too demanding, ready to accept make-believe. Until such time as we evolve a company and an audience who take pleasure in Shakespeare for Shakespeare's sake, we are unlikely to see much of PERICLES.

CYMBELINE is beloved, and rightly so, for Imogen's sake. Imogen is she whom every woman in love would wish to be —free, generous, sane, miraculously happy in the expression of her love. Over and over again she puts feeling into words so just that she seems to express the emotion for all time:

> I did not take my leave of him, but had
> Most pretty things to say: ere I could tell him
> How I would think on him at certain hours,
> Such thoughts and such; . . .
> . . . or have charg'd him,
> At the sixth hour of morn, at noon, at midnight,
> To encounter me with orisons, for then
> I am in heaven for him;   1, 3, 25

with the ominous letter whose contents, as yet unread, are to lead her toward unsuspected death:

> O, learn'd indeed were that astronomer
> That knows the stars as I his characters;

> He'ld lay the future open. You good gods,
> Let what is here contain'd relish of love,
> Of my lord's health, of his content, yet not
> That we two are asunder; let that grieve him;
> Some griefs are medicinable; that is one of them,
> For it doth physic love; of his content,
> All but in that!   III, 2, 37

and, having read the letter,

> O for a horse with wings! Hear'st thou, Pisanio?
> He is at Milford Haven: read, and tell me
> How far 'tis thither. If one of mean affairs
> May plod it in a week, why may not I
> Glide thither in a day? Then, true Pisanio,—
> Who long'st, like me, to see thy lord; who long'st
> (O, let me bate) but not like me; yet long'st,
> But in a fainter kind:—O, not like me;
> For mine's beyond beyond.   III, 2, 49

Even when she is told of Leonatus's command to have her killed, the music of love is unsilenced:

> . . . Come, fellow, be thou honest,
> Do thy master's bidding. When thou see'st him,
> A little witness my obedience. Look,
> I draw the sword myself, take it, and hit
> The innocent mansion of my love, my heart:
> Fear not, 'tis empty of all things but grief:
> Thy master is not there, who was indeed
> The riches of it.   III, 4, 65

In the disguise of Fidele, Imogen keeps all her own matchless quality, but unfortunately she no longer holds the play, except in the last scene, where she again glorifies it with her integrity and honor; and for the last two acts we are in very serious trouble.

It is difficult to define the reasons for which this play is so extraordinarily unsatisfactory on the stage. The first three acts go with dazzling assurance. It is true that we have to accept a slightly wooden king and a cruel stepmother who reminds us rather too forcibly of SNOW WHITE, though we are mollified by her magnificent speech on the invasion of England, on which subject the ineffable Cloten also has some heart-warming remarks. The rest is brilliant: Iachimo springs alive like coiled steel; in the scenes of his wager with Leonatus, the prose writing is as supple as anything Shakespeare ever wrote, and the character of the two men is unerringly differentiated in it. We are, perhaps, made a little uneasy by the old fairy-tale trick, but we forgive Leonatus for being duped, because Iachimo has engineered his plot with such skill. His speech in Imogen's bedroom while she is asleep is matchless in dramatic poetry. The action moves compactly and surely. If Shakespeare keeps this up, he will give us a masterpiece.

But in Act III, scene 3, the warning lag begins. It lies, I think, in those two terrible young men, Guiderius and Arviragus. They are, perhaps, part of the romantic convention in which Shakespeare is still not completely at ease. They are the noble savage, but tutored to an unbearable civility by their old guardian, the verbose and pompous Belarius. They go on getting nobler and nobler, and, in case we should miss anything, Belarius stops at regular intervals to tell us just how noble they are. Even their exquisite elegy over the "dead" Fidele leaves us with unforgiving hearts.

To make matters worse, we have lost Iachimo, one speech of whose villainy is worth all their stainless operatic Aryanism; Leonatus is fossilizing slowly but surely, and our old black-and-purple friend, the Queen, is sick unto death in her dressing room. Finally, we are disgusted to discover ourselves launched on an Anglo-Roman war, whose military strategy and fortunes are described in lengthy, complex dumb-show stage directions, with an enormously long narrative speech about the off-stage battle from the unfortunate Leonatus. What a job for a hard-pressed hero! The war business concludes, moreover, in a blaze of appeasement, which inevitably makes us think of the old epitaph,

> Since I was so quickly done for,
> I wonder what I was begun for.

In the last scene, with the utmost dexterity and every resource of the old theater craftsman, Shakespeare rescues himself from the various complications which he has allowed to pile up around the play. We are left enraged that he should have buried our Imogen beneath all this farrago of fairy-tale picture books. Perhaps there is a way to rescue her, mercilessly blue-penciling the whole fourth and fifth act, cutting the episode of Leonatus in prison entirely out, and leaving the audience to make the obvious assumptions about the battle. If we had much less of the noble twins we should like them much more. And we shall have to get an actor who can carry us with him for the shabbily treated Leonatus and another who can make Iachimo's manufactured end join with his admirable beginning.

The mood of the play is evident Renaissance, despite its ostensible setting in ancient Britain; Iachimo is an Italian, not a Roman, and says as much. Togas and woad will be perfectly hopeless for this piece of gilded artifice. "The Family of Darius Kneeling to Alexander" will be nearer our mark, if a little over-ornate. It is a pretty problem for a producer, but surely there will still be found some knight of the theater to flaunt Imogen's lovely sleeve upon his billboard.

Both CYMBELINE and THE WINTER'S TALE have suffered long periods of neglect in the theater; but the latter has been seen of recent years both in New York and London, where John Gielgud staged an exceptionally fine production, cast with great acting strength. This is essential to the play. It has no great star part, but several exceptionally fine ones which are worth the best talent the theater can bring to them. Autolycus, for instance, is a smooth, assured, accomplished clown, last exemplar of the fool-and-commentator tradition; he is skilled in song and dance and is always on the best of terms with the audience. Camillo, Polixenes, and Antipholus have authority and depth; Paulina and Hermione are in the front rank of Shakespeare's mature women. But the first half of the play is the tragedy of Leontes, the second the romantic comedy of Perdita; and in the violence of the contrast, deliberately contrived, lies our difficulty in the theater, a difficulty further complicated by the fact that the end of Act IV and the first two scenes of Act V move at a snail's pace.

The final reconciliation scene, moreover, depends upon a device much more artificial than anything we have encountered in the play and touches no one of the principal characters to any fresh or profound revelation of emotion. But it has gentleness and dignity and, since it depends on visual effect, is far more moving in the theater than in the study. The conclusion comes with formalized grace, the lines chiming quietly and rhythmically, like bells. The actors can inform them with an inner truth.

The first three acts move in a real world, and a harsh one, far distant from those realms of romance where a happy ending provides every cloud with a discernible silver lining. Sicilia is no Utopia. But in the very first line of verse in the play Polixenes lets slip the fact that there is such a kingdom in his own Bohemia:

> Nine changes of the watery star hath been
> The shepherd's note, since we have left our throne
> Without a burden.   I, 2, I

Presently we are to see the stars and the shepherds; but for three acts they are forgotten in the swirling torrent of Leontes' jealousy, which overwhelms everybody within its reach.

The part is one of the hardest ever written; with almost no preparation, the emotion of it is at flood height. It is an obsession, feeding itself, tortured of itself, relentlessly lashing itself to an insane and superhuman power. We see nothing of what the normal Leontes is like, and almost nothing of the incidents which give rise to this fever in his brain; it is postulated that Hermione and Polixenes are innocent and that Leontes is already nearly helpless in the grip of a passion that no reason can control. Camillo realizes it at once. He thinks for us in deciding that there is no way of sanity or logic by which this torrent may be dammed.

Polixenes must escape or be destroyed; he escapes, leaving Hermione to her fate with no more than an ineffectual wish that everything may come out all right in the end. Leontes alone can make us appreciate the inevitability of Polixenes' flight, and it will take an actor supremely able to liberate passion. The verse in which the part is written is half the actor's battle; it is tormented, twisted, involved, sometimes deliberately senseless, driven pell-mell from the seething insanity of Leontes' fevered mind. Only an actor who can use the instrument of speech with virtuoso technical command will be able to encompass the reiterated chords of

>   . . . Is whispering nothing?
> Is leaning cheek to cheek? is meeting noses?
> Kissing with inside lip? stopping the career
> Of laughter with a sigh (a note infallible
> Of breaking honesty)? horsing foot on foot?
> Skulking in corners? wishing clocks more swift?
> Hours, minutes? noon, midnight? and all eyes
> Blind with the pin and web but theirs; theirs only,

That would unseen be wicked? Is this nothing?
Why, then the world, and all that's in't, is nothing,
The covering sky is nothing, Bohemia nothing,
My wife is nothing, nor nothing have these nothings,
If this be nothing.   I, 2, 284

Paulina's outbursts feed Leontes; they have an equal power but a direct and forthright aim. Hermione, in character and speech, holds the play within bounds; her trial scene reminds us a little of Queen Katherine, but with equal dignity it combines a greater beauty of soul, and the verse is level harmony:

                    . . . But thus, if powers divine
Behold our human actions (as they do)
I doubt not then but innocence shall make
False accusation blush, and tyranny
Tremble at patience. You, my lord, best know
(Who least will seem to do so) my past life
Hath been as continent, as chaste, as true
As I am now unhappy; which is more
Than history can pattern, though devis'd
And play'd to take spectators . . .
                    . . . For life, I prize it
As I weigh grief, which I would spare: for honour,
'Tis a derivative from me to mine,
And only that I stand for.   III, 2, 28

The part is not a long one, but it is deeply felt and purely written.

Actresses and producers have occasionally agreed to have it doubled with Perdita, a proceeding which seems to me to do great violence to Shakespeare's intention, and to have nothing to recommend it save the possibility that audiences may want to see one woman star through the whole play instead of two in half the play each. The fact that Perdita is "her mother's glass" is the least important thing about her. She brings with her a new world, as far from Leontes' Sicily as May from December. She is sixteen or she is nothing.

With her, the play takes on, quite literally, a new life of shepherds and rustics, and sun and flowers and ribbons and spices and songs; it has dew upon it, and so has Perdita herself. She is the unclouded spirit of youth unstained by sorrow upon which Shakespeare so loved to dwell in his last plays. Florizel too, like Ferdinand, beautifully rounds the picture, gracing her and himself with the exquisite

> . . . What you do
> Still betters what is done. When you speak, sweet,
> I'd have you do it ever: when you sing,
> I'd have you buy and sell so; so give alms,
> Pray so; and, for the ordering your affairs,
> To sing them too: when you do dance, I wish you
> A wave of the sea, that you might ever do
> Nothing but that.   IV, 4, 135

This is as fresh as it is lovely; this is the daughter Hermione would have prayed to have; but it is not Hermione in little. The actress "playing for" youth cannot, however greatly gifted, achieve the poignant, transitory loveliness of youth itself.

It is argued that because Perdita at the first meeting with her father is almost mute, and has only two short speeches in the scene with her mother, Shakespeare must have had this doubling in mind. But it is hard to believe that he would have admitted so clumsy a device; nor do I think we shall better the disappointing lameness of these last scenes from Perdita's point of view by substituting a back-to-the-audience dummy for the actress who has now reverted to her first role as Hermione. We shall only add to the handicaps already in the script.

A garland of flowers weaves these last plays together, link-ing them with the fragrance of springtime, summer, and autumn, in the eternal fields where they are set. There is a curious chime of death behind their sweetness. In PERICLES, Marina strews Lychorida's grave with flowers:

> . . . the yellows, blues,
> The purple violets, and marigolds,
> Shall, as a carpet, hang upon thy grave
> While summer days do last   IV, 1, 14

In CYMBELINE, Fidele's grave also is to be decked with a blossoming echo:

> . . . With fairest flowers,
> While summer lasts, and I live here, Fidele,
> I'll sweeten thy sad grave; thou shalt not lack
> The flower that's like thy face, pale primrose, nor
> The azur'd harebell, like thy veins.   IV, 2, 220

And Perdita has flowers of winter, flowers of middle summer; lacking flowers of spring, she brings them beautifully close to our remembrance:

> . . . daffodils
> That come before the swallow dares, and take
> The winds of March with beauty; violets (dim,
> But sweeter than the lids of Juno's eyes,
> Or Cytherea's breath); pale primroses,
> That die unmarried e'er they can behold
> Bright Phoebus in his strength (a malady
> Most incident to maids); bold oxslips, and
> The crown imperial; lilies of all kinds,
> The fleur-de-luce being one! O, these I lack
> To make you garlands of, and my sweet friend,
> To strew him o'er and o'er!
>   What, like a corse?
> No, like a bank for love to lie and play on;
> Not like a corse . . .   IV, 4, 118

Shakespeare seems to come back from the fields by the green and quiet Stratford churchyard, where deep bells answer the hour, yet time slips by uncounted as the flowers bloom and die and bloom again with the returning spring.

THE TEMPEST lifts us to another dimension, unique, and last, of Shakespeare's worlds. Ceres' "proud earth," flowers and "turfy mountains," "windring brooks," and "unshrubbed down" is visioned for us, but the play is air and water, always within sound of the sea, always eluding the touch of mortal hands because it belongs to the spirit alone. In LEAR, Shakespeare's overmastering daemon had driven inexorably through the wooden boundaries of his theater even when they were his daily horizon. In THE TEMPEST we feel that he reminded himself, with an effort, of the requirements of show business. The indoor theater at Blackfriars was well equipped to provide complicated effects for a shipwreck or the "quaint device" of a vanishing banquet. He put in some fat scenes for the comics and plenty of chances for music and dance. The old theater magician is as lavish and deft as ever; but the spell has a new and luminous quality and, in the end, it dissolves the very walls of the theater into nothingness:

> Our revels now are ended. These our actors,
> (As I foretold you) were all spirits, and
> Are melted into air, into thin air,
> And like the baseless fabric of this vision,
> The cloud-capp'd towers, the gorgeous palaces,
> The solemn temples, the great globe itself,
> Yea, all which it inherit, shall dissolve,
> And like this insubstantial pageant faded,
> Leave not a rack behind: we are such stuff
> As dreams are made on; and our little life
> Is rounded with a sleep.   IV, I, 148

It has been very plausibly contended by some scholars that this speech may once have formed the conclusion not of the

Masque, but of the play itself. The whole scene of the Revels, with its goddesses and nymphs and reapers, was quite probably added, by request, for a special performance at court. The occasion was the marriage of King James's daughter, Princess Elizabeth, to the Elector Palatine, and the Masque would have been a graceful tribute, certainly, from the company of the King's Men; but it can be lifted right out of the play without damage to the structure. I should like to believe that Prospero's beautiful speech was, in fact, originally written to end the play, for I had the temerity to use it there in my New York production of 1945 and I have seen the profoundly moving and satisfying effect it made on an audience.

The lines are, in any case, the perfect resolution to a play or to a lifetime of playwriting. If they were indeed Shakespeare's farewell to the traffic of the stage, or to the traffic of the world, they could not have held a more lovely final harmony. The sadness and the hope, the dream and the longing, will haunt us long after the lights are dimmed, the curtain fallen, the playhouse empty, the magic departed. Here we once lived and were illumined and aware. Now there is nothing left but dust and sleep.

In the theater we must handle the delicate fabric of THE TEMPEST with the lightest and most sensitive touch. It is, I think, the play above all others where we cannot hope to match the reader's free imagination; yet this very speech was written to be spoken; there is in it as much music as dream. Here, designer, director, and actors must bring much more than theater competence to the service of the play, for vision alone will transmit vision. The two people who will have the hardest task will be the designer and the actor who plays Ariel. Probably the setting should be, essentially, as simple and as indicative as in Thornton Wilder's OUR TOWN, where the audience was given a signpost to Grovers' Corners, and left to imagine its own niche within "the Earth, the Universe, the Mind of God." The movie of the same play, doing its representational best, never gave us our spiritual money's worth as the almost bare stage did. And Shakespeare's island in "the still-vex'd Bermoothes" wears a different aspect for each man's differing mind.

We are told little of its physical features, though Caliban's material mind gives us something, Gonzalo and his companions a detail or two more. The island is "of a subtle, tender and delicate temperance"; it is ringed with sands on which

> . . . the elves with printless foot
> Do chase the ebbing Neptune and do fly him
> When he once comes back.

We cannot reproduce these yellow sands, nor the cloven pine, nor the spurred cedar. We cannot " 'twixt the green sea and the azur'd vault Set roaring war" at Prospero's command. It will be hard for our musicians, even, to give the elusive island echoes, "Sounds and sweet airs, that give delight and hurt not." Composer, designer, director, actors, most especially Ariel, must try to capture a quality once ascribed to David Garrick, of whose work it was said that "he generally perceives the finest attitude of things." We must free our audience to sail their own seas to their own haven, suggesting only the outline it may take.

Writers who have analyzed THE TEMPEST have seen in it a hundred different allegories. They have been touched to beautiful and perceptive flights of the imagination; they have agreed, almost without exception, that there is much more in this play than is yielded from its surface, and symbolic explanations abound. The over-simple pigeonholing of Caliban for the flesh, Prospero for the mind, and Ariel for the spirit has been elaborated in as many different ways as there have been poets and critics to examine it. There is no question but that the play deals with themes which are of transcendent and timeless importance. The use and abuse of power is one of them; the search for freedom is another, shadowed with the penetrating implication that freedom often turns out to be different from what we had imagined, involving responsibility and not merely license, and that each of us must find his own way to the resolution of the conflict within himself.

Shakespeare is perhaps also suggesting that you cannot educate anyone by keeping him in a state of slavery; that Prospero fails with Caliban for just this reason; and that, however benevolent the despotism may be, it must fail, until the feet of the ignorant are set upon the path which they alone, of their own will and choice, must travel. Finally, the play is filled with the longing for peace and reconciliation; it leads from the old story of wrongs unresolved and violence unrequited to compassion and the promise of "a clear life ensuing." After twelve years of privation and discipline in the mastery of his own powers, Prospero gains his victory and denies himself the easy fruits of it: "The rarer action is in virtue than in vengeance . . . My charms I'll break, their senses I'll restore, And they shall be—themselves."

But Shakespeare is too good a showman to force a sermon down our throats and too experienced a theater man to do less than provide us with entrancing entertainment, leaving us to draw the moral for ourselves. We must be as flexible as the play itself. We must not attempt to trim its wings according to our particular conception of what a wing should look like and how many feathers it should have.

Mark Van Doren has written what is, for me, a definitive conclusion to the arguments about the symbolism and allegorical significance of THE TEMPEST:

Notwithstanding its visionary grace, its tendency toward lyric abstraction, it keeps that life-like surface and humor with which Shakespeare has always protected his meaning if he had one: that impenetrable shield off which the spears of interpretation invariably glance—or return, bent in the shaft and dulled at the point, to the hand of the thrower. It may well be that Shakespeare in THE TEMPEST is telling us for the last time, about the world. But what he is telling us cannot be simple, or we should agree that it is this or that. Perhaps it is this: that the world is not simple. Or, mysteriously enough, that it is what we all take it to be, just as THE TEMPEST is whatever we would take it to be. Any set of symbols, moved close to this play, lights up as in an electric field. Its meaning, in other words, is precisely as rich as the human mind.

In attempting to preserve the "life-like surface and humor" of the play we must pay due attention to Alonzo, Gonzalo, and their companions, who, like the lovers in A MIDSUMMER NIGHT'S DREAM, are often dismissed as bores. Surrounded by Ariel's evanescent grace, Caliban's thick and ominous savagery, and Prospero's probing mind, they may indeed seem ordinary; but this is precisely what they are; just for this reason they, like the lovers in the DREAM, will put all the degrees of strangeness into perspective for us. They must reflect what the ordinary man might feel, shipwrecked on this uncharted island. They perceive, as we might, according to the varying receptivity of their minds, the "quality o' the climate," and feel, as we might, the strange drowsiness in the air. Through them, as clearly as through Ariel the messenger, we too shall sense the awe of powers beyond ourselves, "delaying, not forgetting" in their slow, inexorable wrath. With them we shall make the progress, the pilgrim's progress, through "heart's sorrow" to "a clear life ensuing." They must not be dummies; nor need they be so, for every one is stamped with characteristics of his own, plain enough to the actor with a seeing mind.

The comics, too, must remember the "quality" of the isle. That they are bemused is the essence of their comedy. Stephano and Trinculo get drunk with a difference, befuddled with more than wine. The conventional tricks of a "drunk scene" will not do. This wine is headier stuff; it has in it the power to transmute Caliban to an outburst far from comic, the senseless, raging, ungovernable

'Ban, 'Ban, Ca-caliban
Has a new master, get a new man.
Freedom, hey-day! hey-day, freedom! freedom, hey-day, freedom!

II, 2, 183

Freedom. Caliban yearns for the freedom to destroy; Ariel sees the freedom of "Merrily, merrily shall I live now, Under the blossom that hangs on the bough"; Ferdinand and Miranda discover a freedom of loving, and Gonzalo a profound one, in finding "all of us ourselves, When no man was his own." Prospero is free of an accomplished task, free to say:

> . . . I'll break my staff,
> Bury it certain fathoms in the earth,
> And deeper than did ever plummet sound,
> I'll drown my book.   v, 1, 54

This freeing of the spirit we must give to the last, in some sense the loveliest, of the plays. We receive it, as it were, in trust; and, rendering it back to our audience, may well conclude, as Prospero does: "Let your indulgence set me free."

Conclusion

14. Shakespeare Today

IN REVIEWING thus briefly the potentialities of Shakespeare's plays in our contemporary theater I have not attempted to supply a ready-to-wear solution for any of their problems but simply to point out certain aspects of those problems. In doing so, I am acutely aware of the danger of generalizations. Every producer, designer, director, every company of actors, will bring qualities of mind and spirit to bear on the texts which will illuminate them from a different angle. Every play, self-evidently, requires a particularized treatment. Each separate text presents its own specific difficulties; settings and costumes must be considered in relation to the mood and emotional pattern of each. The musical accompaniment, whether it be indicated or required by the script itself, or added to it as a supplementary factor, must equally be devised to enhance and vivify the essential spirit of each play. So the actors' personal gifts or shortcomings must be welded together into an interpretative whole, not violating the author's intention, but translating it anew into the living language which is shared by actors and audience alike. No part of the theater is machine-made, and no part may be governed by mathematical formulas. Human fallibility being what it is, none of us may be assured of encompassing our vision; all we can do is to try to bring this vision into focus with Shakespeare himself and pursue it with such integrity as we may.

If a modern producer were dealing with an author with thirty-seven plays to his credit, most of them successes and a dozen or so smash hits, he would at least listen with respect to what that author had to say and take some trouble to appreciate the workings of his mind. Shakespeare is still one of Broadway's most successful playwrights. His pay checks, if he still received them, would top the lists of Dramatists' Guild members. Every year or two a major motion-picture company acquires one or another of his scripts and his name appears regularly on TV credit titles though what happens on the screen thereafter may not always do him credit. His royalties from amateur rights alone would be worth a fortune. Surely so durable a dramatist rates a little investigation, perhaps even a trifle of respect, from those who exploit his works.

There is a German play in which Goethe, reincarnating himself as a college student about to take an examination on Goethe, fails hopelessly to answer the questions put to him. Either he does not remember at all incidents which the examiners seem to consider of supreme importance, or his replies run directly counter to the textbooks of accepted criticism. It is probable that we should be appalled by Shakespeare's inability to satisfy some of our burning inquiries and that he would be at a loss to understand why we should get so exercised over seeming trifles.

But it is unlikely that we should ever find him without an explanation of the purpose of his stagecraft, or a reason for his dramatic intention. I think we are justified in assuming that he would readily suggest modifications to suit our revivals; he would probably understand our audiences as well as or better than we do. We are perhaps too ready to accept current shibboleths as to what an audience will or will not like. He probably would find no difficulty in adapting the practice of his theater to the usage of ours; and, if he found it unnecessary to make all the changes we at first demanded, we might well discover in the end that he was right. However, because we cannot claim his aid, we must do our best to think with his mind and bring his standards into harmony with our own.

The principles on which a director must base his approach to a Shakespearean play are, after all, no different from those which govern his approach to any other play. Methods will vary, because the technique of directing is itself subject to every degree of personal idiosyncrasy. But I believe that every director should determine first the mood of the play, its material and spiritual atmosphere, its structural pattern, the wholeness of its effect. What kind of world is this of Arden or Elsinore, Illyria or Verona? What forces are at work in it? What values or what standards hold good within its confines? Shakespeare will have employed certain dramatic devices whose origin and purpose we must learn to recognize through a knowledge of the material, human or inanimate, which he employed. But what was the intention behind these theater devices? Knowing his method, we may guess at his mind; perceiving the familiar, we may divine the transcendental. With the former, the director must sometimes take liberties of adaptation; the latter he may not violate, except at his own peril.

It is, of course, essential that we should interpret Shakespeare to our audiences through the medium of our common experience and our common humanity. And these channels of communication are precisely what the director must use to reach the heart of the plays themselves. He must learn to know the human beings who people them, all of them, from King Lear to the Third Citizen. Who are they? What are they like? They have a certain background, sometimes of historical fact, sometimes of tale or legend; they have an Elizabethan background in Shakespeare's Elizabethan mind. These we shall want to understand, for they will bring light into shadowed places. But, above all, what qualities in their minds and hearts do we share? What is their kinship with us? What is it in their blood which we also feel to be in our own?

The tangible things by which they are surrounded, the hats and cloaks they wear, the weapons they use, their food and drink, may belong almost exclusively to Shakespeare's England. Even the conventions of love and honor, hate and merriment, may differ from our own. But we can still lay our hands upon the pulse of each one of them; Shylock's speech may still stand for the universality of man, annihilating the gap of time as easily as the division of race. We too have "organs, dimensions, senses; affections, passions." We are "subject to the same diseases, healed by the same means, warmed and cooled by the same winter and summer . . . If you prick us do we not bleed? if you tickle us do we not laugh? if you poison us do we not die? and if you wrong us, shall we not revenge?" It is always a sense of closeness at which the director should aim, rather than an emphasis of separation.

But he should not underrate either the author or the audience. There is no need to assume that they can be brought into accord only by such devices as dressing Hotspur in Air Force uniform or translating Ancient Rome into terms of South Side Chicago. Many directors and designers are rightly anxious that their theater should be "contemporary" in its approach. But Shakespeare is not merely local, and the attempt to make him so can become precious and pretentious unless it is used with discretion. The timeliness of the plays is more than costume deep; their truth is universal, and the analogies of external circumstance no more than a fortuitous, though sometimes poignant, reminder that the returning paths of history have been trodden by many feet.

With Shakespeare, as with any classic playwright, the importance of the settings is not exactly what it might be in the case of a new play in a contemporary idiom. The designer, like the director, has an interpretative function. But he will not be able to start from scratch, as with an original script; he will have to face precedents and comparisons. Neither director nor designer should let this trap him into mistaking novelty for penetration nor eccentricity for vitality. It is the truth of the vision which matters.

But the designer has, I think, a greater contribution to make than the convinced Globolators allow. We must transport our audiences into a world of illusion and we must appeal to their eyes as well as their ears. It is part of the theater's legitimate business to draw the eye with visual beauty. Shakespeare's men knew this. Although they had few scenic resources and no opportunity for lighting effects, they made up the decorative deficiency by lavish expenditure on "props" and costume.

We are well equipped to satisfy the eyes of our audience; but we must do it by going a little deeper than "something pretty to look at." Sets and costumes are a part of the interpretative vision and they can translate it by the simplest of means. But even if we decide to strip our stages of all redundant decoration, we should still preserve a rhythm and harmony of composition. Our settings do not have to be harsh or ugly because they are economical and austere. A man may carry away a picture in his mind even when the words have faded. It may be the impression of a background, a flight of steps, a shaft of light, a crimson curtain; it may be a group, a massing of people in action or repose. We must see to it that all these things have significance; there is drama in the pictorial composition on which the curtain rises, in a combination of color or of light and shadow. Equally, there is drama in the tension of an actor's body, as he listens, as he waits, as he stands in thought or as he unleashes action; in a gesture, an attitude or a piece of business silently executed. For the actor, too, must interpret to the eye and must be given a costume which will most vividly help him to do so.

It is instructive to find that all through theater history the writers whose comments are preserved for us have cherished most keenly the things their eyes remembered. Kean, as Richard, stooped and "drew in the dust with the point of his sword"; Sothern, as Romeo, reeled right across the stage as he cried "O! I am fortune's fool!" Charles Laughton as Angelo, in my own recollection, stood crouching over Isabella, his arms outstretched like a black bird of prey. These things sound trivial in print, because the emotion with which they were informed defies recapture. But they can illuminate the very essence of a character or of a play.

The vigor and liveliness of a production, the extent to which it remains memorable in the eyes and minds of those who see it depends, ultimately, on the fierceness and intensity of its drive for truth in the interpretation of human beings. To this the director and designer enormously contribute; but its final expression lies with the actors, not with the textual arrangement, the music, the costumes, the sets, or the kind of theater building in which it is played. The actors are the author's instruments, on whom he must at last depend. It is probable that, if you could put Edwin Booth onto a bare Elizabethan stage, John Barrymore among some eighteenth-century perspective "wings," Richard Burbage into a production of the Belasco school, or Edwin Forrest upon some architectural formation evolved by Norman Bel Geddes, in each case the actor would stare for a few moments and presently get back into the skin of Hamlet. The lines that have echoed through three hundred years would begin to exercise their old power. The audience would concentrate upon the actor and forget all about his background. Dramatic truth has many faces, many voices; it is more important than any arrangements of canvas and lumber and paint.

But the actor's ability to bring the real Shakespeare to life depends, in its turn, on one thing above all others—not on his looks, charm, or "box office appeal," but on his ability to speak the written text. Shakespeare, above all dramatists who have written in English, has given us the magic means to enchant the ears of our audience, whether with a grace and delicacy which is Mozart in speech, or with the sweeping orchestration of sound which lifts LEAR and OTHELLO to a dimension beyond the mind.

We need actors who can imprint thought and passion upon the human voice. They must have minds and lungs and vocal cords trained to this use of language. They must not use Shakespeare's verse, or prose, as if it were a barrier between themselves and the clear expression of their meaning but as a rich inheritance that they know how to spend richly. Present-day reformers might do well to concentrate on demanding a standard of fine speech from the actors and to bother less about the type of stage from which they are to speak.

Fine speaking is of the most crucial importance to the interpretation of Shakespeare in the theater. A sense of style is almost equally essential. It has become the fashion to belittle the need for this much misinterpreted quality. "Style" is supposed to consist of a lot of outworn flourishes and mannerisms indicative of some dead and forgotten period when men wore long, curled hair and women encased their digestive apparatus in steel and whalebone. It is regarded as a superficial affectation, far removed from actuality, which had better be discarded along with the other "vestigial remains" that the scholars so frequently discuss.

This is a misconception. Style, to begin with, is much more than a harmonious visual effect. You can learn how to drape a cloak or wear a sword or put on a wig, a ruff, or a farthingale by studying pictures and prints—though, in point of fact, very few actors ever bother to look at such things. But style in the wearing of costume is not merely an arbitrary imitation; it is a functional necessity. You wear your sword so because otherwise the scabbard will get between your legs and you will fall over it; you take the weight of your cloak over the elbow and fling it thus around your shoulder because in this way it will keep you warm without tying you up in a cocoon; you swing your farthingale like this because otherwise, when you sit down, it will bounce up in front of you. You hold your shoulders back because they must carry the weight of armor; you keep your knees straight because, in tights, you would look knock-kneed if you didn't.

If you do not take the trouble to find out these things, the appurtenances of costume will seem like awkward excrescences. But rightly used they will acquire rhythm and dignity. More than that, they will begin to belong to you and you will gain a feeling of reality. They will cease to be "costume" and become clothes. That is, they will become an intrinsic part of the character you are playing; and it is the style proper to this person which the actor must seek, in outward appearance as in inner thought. You cannot put his hands in your pockets, because he had none. Neither can you put your thoughts in his head. You cannot claim that this or that feels false or unreal to you because you yourself would feel it or say it differently. There is style in thought as there is in speech or dress, a kind of inner breeding, and acting is the perfect fusion of these things. If you are playing King Richard II you must wear his crown as of right and your mind must put on the habit of authority; if you are playing Olivia your very fingers must be fastidious, touching delicately the ring you take from your hand or the veil you throw over your hair.

Shakespeare's characters, the major ones, are likely to be bigger in mental stature than the average modern actor, more perceptive in imagination, bolder and freer in action, sharper in wit, swifter in words. You must not drag the agonized self-searching of Hamlet down to the level of a college debate nor reduce Beatrice's glancing and ironic humor to the sour wise-cracks of a cocktail party. You must translate yourself into the character, probe to its depths, rise to its heights; and you must look like what you are.

We have plenty of acting talent in America today. There are thousands of young actors or would-be actors with intelligence, imagination, and a good physique. But they completely lack practice in their craft. They do not know, because they have never seen, stature and "manner" in acting Shakespeare; they think of it as something exaggerated and "ham" and believe that the slipshod speech and lazy, commonplace attitudes of the present day are, in some obscure way, more "real." They have almost no opportunity either to see or play Shakespeare except at the amateur level.

In the old days, repertory companies playing Shakespeare abounded both in England and the United States. Not all of them were very good. But they went at the plays whole-heart-edly and they met with a similar response. Also, they afforded the actor one enormous advantage. Under the repertory system, he could alternate the playing of great parts with lesser ones; he did not have to wreck his larynx and his soul by attempting to beat out a Hamlet or an Othello eight times a week, which is a physical and spiritual impossibility. We like to flatter our-selves that we have improved greatly on standards of Shake-spearean production since "the old days." But, in fact, almost no Shakespeare is now to be seen in the commercial theater; and we have, of course, no endowed or permanent company on the lines of the Comédie Française or the Old Vic. Eva Le Gallienne's Civic Repertory Theatre of the late Twenties and early Thirties was the last attempt to establish such a theater, except for the short-lived American Repertory Theatre of 1947–1948. Without such theaters, standards and traditions of classic playing must necessarily vanish; and at the present time the professional playing of Shakespeare seems in danger of vanishing altogether.

Why is this? Does it mean that there is no longer any audience for Shakespeare in the United States? The answer to this is a categorical negative. I could adduce a great deal of personal evidence to prove that the response to Shakespeare is as eager and alive as ever. I have experienced it myself, both in giving lectures and Shakespeare readings and in traveling productions of his plays over the length and breadth of America. But there is a vast quantity of clearer and more concrete proof. There is, for instance, the extraordinary number of Shakespearean productions which are done in community and college theaters. Every year, almost every one of the thirty-seven plays, even the most obscure, gets a nonprofessional production of some kind; and the most popular, such as HAMLET, THE MERCHANT OF VENICE, or AS YOU LIKE IT, are usually performed by three or four different groups. The summer Festivals in Antioch, Ohio, and Ashland, Oregon, attract an enthusiastic and faithful following. They are partly professional in character, but were organized and initiated by college groups.

Campus activities are, naturally, closely tied to the demands of the curriculum; but in most cases college drama departments are also dependent on the audiences they can attract to their performances; and their audiences do come to see Shakespeare. Generally they see him done with valor, sincerity of purpose, and a kind of infectious enjoyment. Since the atmosphere is one of general good will, this ought, perhaps, to be enough. "The best in this kind are but shadows," says Theseus of the amateur players, "and the worst are no worse if imagination amend them." But "it must be your imagination then, and not theirs," replies Hippolyta, giving utterance to a sour truth. Sometimes these campus productions are fresh and stimulating; often they are beautifully mounted, since many of our colleges and universities boast revolving stages, electronic switchboards, curved cycloramas, and other enviable equipment, unseen in the professional theater for many a long year. But sometimes the quality of the acting has served only to demonstrate that Shakespeare in the theater is absolutely indestructible. You simply cannot stop him from being entertaining no matter what you do or fail to do.

The work done by the nonprofessional theater has been of inestimable value. Without it, all Shakespeare's minor plays and many of his greater ones would have been lost to the living theater in the United States. But it is, I hope, no disparagement to maintain that he deserves the services of the finest of his professional fellow-craftsmen or that his plays might occasionally be seen in the major theaters of America, as they are, continuously, in all the finest theaters of Europe.

It has been contended, however, that we keep Shakespeare sufficiently alive in photographs, whether on the seventy-foot scale of Cinemascope or the seventeen-inch dimension of television. It is true that on occasion the motion-picture medium can render him extraordinary service. Laurence Olivier's HENRY V was such a case. It was probably as fine an interpretation, or illumination, of this play as has ever been seen, anywhere. It was, moreover, an enormous commercial success and proved that it had "box-office appeal" for a wider cross section of the American public than most of Hollywood's prize-winning products. But it was a rare phenomenon, rarely equalled. For Shakespeare, after all, created his masterpieces for a certain medium—that of the living theater; and you cannot translate them into any other without some distortion, any more than you could paint the Winged Victory of Samothrace or sculpt the Mona Lisa.

To produce Shakespeare adequately on television, at least in its present state of development, is much more difficult and much less satisfactory than the making of a motion picture. It means a reduction in terms of time; the attempt to give a reasonable notion of KING LEAR in seventy-three minutes proved to be absurd, at least when the attempt was governed by the present peculiar orthodoxy of television methods. It means a reduction in terms of space, and often a waste of the little there is available; tiny figures jostle one another indistinguishably in all the general scenes and are usually, for some reason known only to TV directors, edged off the screen by horses, dogs, and other colorful fauna about whom Shakespeare did not write. It is, however, a sobering thought that on the afternoon RICHARD II was shown over an American television network it was probably seen by more people than have ever witnessed the play before in the entire world, since the day it was first given at the Globe.

If the numbers of his audience were an acceptable standard of measurement, we might say that Shakespeare is better served now than he has ever been. But I wonder. It is not the province of this book to examine the case for the living theater as opposed to the mechanical media. But two points which are of particular application to Shakespeare may be pertinent. The first concerns language. This, as I have tried to emphasize, is Shakespeare's supreme and enduring glory. His dramatic poetry was intended to be spoken by the human voice directly to living ears. In it he told his stories and revealed the hearts of his protagonists; through it he touched the heights of passion and of vision.

But to the movie-makers language is officially known as "wordage." The art of the camera is the art of action and the eye; its objective is to find the short cuts which avoid "wordage." Nor is it yet considered possible, at least in the television medium, to hold the viewer with words alone. The visual angle must continually change. You must cut to a listener's reaction, or shift to a long shot, or come back to the speaker with a camera focused down the back of his neck. This, supposedly, achieves variety; it keeps things moving; it obviates the perils of being static and talky. But Shakespeare is never static, for the very reason that he talks so much; it is the talk itself which moves.

Let us hope that TV will rapidly outgrow these self-imposed limitations; yet the problem of the microphone will still remain. Shakespeare wrote his words not only to whisper and caress but to ring and thunder; there are trumpets in his orchestra as well as muted strings. The microphone is a very truthful instrument, faithful, penetrating, and subtle; but amplifiers, by their very nature, distort the ranging vibrance of the human voice. At least, however, every listener will be able to hear every word and every looker-on will see whatever is on the screen. Nobody will be quite as well off as the man in the orchestra seat, but nobody, on the other hand, will suffer the same deprivations as the man at the back of the balcony. If Shakespeare's craftsmanship could be adapted to the usage of these new media, or if they would try honestly to preserve him rather than to substitute their own wonders for his, all might be well—enough; except for one thing: there would still be no human contact, no living union between him and us.

This is the glory of the living theater, and of the living theater alone; it is also the essence of Shakespeare's magic, that the spectators should themselves take part in the process of creation. The actor's art is spontaneous; every performance he gives is unique, never exactly the same as before, never identically repeated afterwards. And the audience participates in it; it is they who either give him wings or tie leaden weights to his feet. There is, in the theater, a communication of the spirit, electric and exultant. The spark which leaps from the stage to the auditorium can set the whole theater ablaze. This is a personal magic; it can open our hearts, dazzle our eyes, lift us into a shared experience beyond ourselves. This is Shakespeare's magic; to its creation his genius was dedicated. You cannot print it in a book or confide it to a microphone. You cannot photograph it at all.

Our theater has all the resources with which to bring to life the masterpieces he left for us; we have audiences eager and hungry to hear them. Why, quoting Hamlet, do we "live to say 'this thing's to do,' sith we have cause and will and strength and means to do't"? It is, very simply, because at the present time costs of production and operation have risen so high in the professional theater that we can no longer afford to stage and run a Shakespearean play without risking very heavy losses. Further, as production costs have risen, the price of tickets has inevitably risen also. The audiences who really want to see Shakespeare can no longer afford the privilege, even when they have the chance. For he has never been a pet of the carriage trade, and he did not write for the benefit of a small handful of scholars and specialists. He wrote to provide entertainment for an assorted crowd of noisy, eager, demanding, and far from affluent citizens. He was, is, and will remain a people's playwright. But theater-going in the United States is no longer a people's habit; the local movie house is far cheaper than the theater, even in those communities where theaters still exist; or you can stay at home by the fire and get your entertainment for nothing, simply by turning a knob. People have forgotten, indeed most of them have never known, that to see Shakespeare in the theater can be a rich and rewarding experience. They are afraid that it will be a dutiful but boring cultural labor. Shakespeare and his audience have lost each other.

The factors which have led to this sad state of affairs are many and various and belong rather to a study of economics than to a study of Shakespeare. We may surmise that if he himself were to take a look at our American theater he might well be a little stunned by the considerations which govern it. He had the imagination of a poet; he was used to inventing non-existent kingdoms and creatures of magic power. Neither the existence of the North American continent nor the mechanical wonders which abound in it would necessarily leave him very greatly at a loss. He could conceive the miracle of expansion; the black magic of spiritual contraction might be harder for him to understand. He was used to a theater where everybody did everything from sheer love of the job and pride in their mastery of it. We wonder what he would make of union regulations which prevent anybody from doing anything without the requisite "card" and limit all activity to a stringently regulated number of hours. Would he not, perhaps, be a little aghast at such phenomena as backers' percentages, real estate interests, advertising methods, or even the long-run formula and the star system? Being a realist, in the theatrical business anyway, he would easily understand how the aggregation of such things had ended by overwhelming the kind of theater he had lived and worked in. He might well think it a pity. So may we.

For living Shakespeare is now almost wholly lost to the average American citizen. In high schools it is very rare for the student to read anything more than HAMLET, MACBETH, or occasionally JULIUS CAESAR, and from these he thankfully shakes himself free the moment the examinations are over. I have found that I had to explain, even to college audiences, just exactly who Falstaff or Othello was; I had to try to persuade them that to laugh with Falstaff is to know a larger dimension of laughter and to suffer with Othello is to gain a deeper insight into human suffering. To many young people poetry has come to be regarded as "sissy," an escapist hobby for the weak and ineffectual, nothing to do with the marvels of modern science or even with the practical everyday business of earning a living.

But if Shakespeare is brought back to them alive, in the

theater where he belongs, faithfully and truthfully interpreted, all these things, the mistrust and reluctance and incomprehension and ignorance, are swept away. The old spell works, as powerfully as ever. I once talked with a group of college students after a performance of HAMLET which had been received with tremendous enthusiasm. I asked them what it was that had appealed to them most. One said it was the sound of the words themselves, another the color and glamour and pictorial drama, a third the excitement of the story itself, the fights and the thrill of action; but the fourth expressed a different point of view. "It's funny," he said, "but while you're there you don't think—you forget about everything. But when you come away, you realize you've been through something—something that's made you different—an experience."

I do not believe that this experience has lost its validity or ever will lose it. It is a part of our inheritance. For three hundred and fifty years Shakespeare has been, for the English-speaking peoples, the voice of hope and love and laughter; he has comforted our griefs and spoken our triumphs with the sound of trumpets. He is beyond the divisions and barriers of contention; for there is singularly little hatred in the plays, and infinite understanding. It would be a barren world which ever felt that it had gone beyond his wisdom and compassion.

Nor shall we outgrow him as long as we have the ears to hear his own magnificent challenge: "What a piece of work is a man! how noble in reason! how infinite in faculties! in form and moving how express and admirable! in action how like an angel, in apprehension how like a god! the beauty of the world! the paragon of animals!" We cannot part company from him unless we abrogate our kinship with the angels.

And Shakespeare in the theater is a source of wealth we cannot afford to lose. Everyone can draw from it—the poet, the philosopher, the businessman, the truck driver, or the college student. Each will take from the plays as much as his mind and heart will carry, just as everyone concerned in producing or acting them will bring to their service all he has, and find it fully absorbed. Shakespeare's stamp and seal of honor has been set on every actor who has won a lasting reputation and on every theater company of enduring accomplishment. Shakespeare is not only the glory of the language which we speak; he is part of the stuff from which our civilization has been forged. It is for the theater to accept the high responsibility of preserving his living work; then only can we claim our rightful share in his immortality.

Index

ABOUT THE AUTHOR

MARGARET WEBSTER, the daughter of Dame May Whitty and Ben Webster, noted English stage and screen actors, was born in New York in 1905. She played her first role on the stage at the age of eight; her professional debut was in 1924. The year following she appeared in her first Shakespearean production, as a member of the cast of John Barrymore's "Hamlet." Wide experience with English repertory companies, including the Ben Greet Shakespearean Company and the Old Vic, playing parts in Shakespeare and Shaw, Ibsen and Barrie, Greek tragedy and a variety of other plays, prepared her for the directing career in which her star was to shine brightest. In 1937 she directed the Maurice Evans "Richard II," a smash hit on Broadway, which she followed with "Henry IV," the uncut "Hamlet," "Twelfth Night," "Macbeth," "Othello," "The Tempest," "Henry VIII," and "Richard III," all of which achieved unusual critical acclaim for their imagination and vitality and brought her general recognition as the foremost interpreter of Shakespeare to modern audiences. Her own Shakespeare on Wheels Company, 1948-1950, traveled over 60,000 miles, playing in 44 states and bringing Shakespeare to hundreds of communities which had never seen his plays professionally acted. Her lecture and recital tours brought her into close touch with college and community theaters from coast to coast and earned her honorary degrees from four distinguished colleges. During the fifties and sixties, she continued her active directing career, and branched out into opera, directing numerous productions at the Metropolitan Opera and the New York City Opera. She also returned to acting, touring in "The Brontes," a one-woman show. She died in 1972.

A CATALOG OF SELECTED
DOVER BOOKS
IN ALL FIELDS OF INTEREST

A CATALOG OF SELECTED DOVER
BOOKS IN ALL FIELDS OF INTEREST

CONCERNING THE SPIRITUAL IN ART, Wassily Kandinsky. Pioneering work by father of abstract art. Thoughts on color theory, nature of art. Analysis of earlier masters. 12 illustrations. 80pp. of text. 5⅜ x 8½. 23411-8 Pa. $4.95

ANIMALS: 1,419 Copyright-Free Illustrations of Mammals, Birds, Fish, Insects, etc., Jim Harter (ed.). Clear wood engravings present, in extremely lifelike poses, over 1,000 species of animals. One of the most extensive pictorial sourcebooks of its kind. Captions. Index. 284pp. 9 x 12. 23766-4 Pa. $14.95

CELTIC ART: The Methods of Construction, George Bain. Simple geometric techniques for making Celtic interlacements, spirals, Kells-type initials, animals, humans, etc. Over 500 illustrations. 160pp. 9 x 12. (USO) 22923-8 Pa. $9.95

AN ATLAS OF ANATOMY FOR ARTISTS, Fritz Schider. Most thorough reference work on art anatomy in the world. Hundreds of illustrations, including selections from works by Vesalius, Leonardo, Goya, Ingres, Michelangelo, others. 593 illustrations. 192pp. 7⅛ x 10¼. 20241-0 Pa. $9.95

CELTIC HAND STROKE-BY-STROKE (Irish Half-Uncial from "The Book of Kells"): An Arthur Baker Calligraphy Manual, Arthur Baker. Complete guide to creating each letter of the alphabet in distinctive Celtic manner. Covers hand position, strokes, pens, inks, paper, more. Illustrated. 48pp. 8¼ x 11. 24336-2 Pa. $3.95

EASY ORIGAMI, John Montroll. Charming collection of 32 projects (hat, cup, pelican, piano, swan, many more) specially designed for the novice origami hobbyist. Clearly illustrated easy-to-follow instructions insure that even beginning papercrafters will achieve successful results. 48pp. 8¼ x 11. 27298-2 Pa. $3.50

THE COMPLETE BOOK OF BIRDHOUSE CONSTRUCTION FOR WOODWORKERS, Scott D. Campbell. Detailed instructions, illustrations, tables. Also data on bird habitat and instinct patterns. Bibliography. 3 tables. 63 illustrations in 15 figures. 48pp. 5¼ x 8½. 24407-5 Pa. $2.50

BLOOMINGDALE'S ILLUSTRATED 1886 CATALOG: Fashions, Dry Goods and Housewares, Bloomingdale Brothers. Famed merchants' extremely rare catalog depicting about 1,700 products: clothing, housewares, firearms, dry goods, jewelry, more. Invaluable for dating, identifying vintage items. Also, copyright-free graphics for artists, designers. Co-published with Henry Ford Museum & Greenfield Village. 160pp. 8¼ x 11. 25780-0 Pa. $10.95

HISTORIC COSTUME IN PICTURES, Braun & Schneider. Over 1,450 costumed figures in clearly detailed engravings–from dawn of civilization to end of 19th century. Captions. Many folk costumes. 256pp. 8⅜ x 11¾. 23150-X Pa. $12.95

STICKLEY CRAFTSMAN FURNITURE CATALOGS, Gustav Stickley and L. & J. G. Stickley. Beautiful, functional furniture in two authentic catalogs from 1910. 594 illustrations, including 277 photos, show settles, rockers, armchairs, reclining chairs, bookcases, desks, tables. 183pp. 6½ x 9¼. 23838-5 Pa. $11.95

AMERICAN LOCOMOTIVES IN HISTORIC PHOTOGRAPHS: 1858 to 1949, Ron Ziel (ed.). A rare collection of 126 meticulously detailed official photographs, called "builder portraits," of American locomotives that majestically chronicle the rise of steam locomotive power in America. Introduction. Detailed captions. xi + 129pp. 9 x 12. 27393-8 Pa. $13.95

AMERICA'S LIGHTHOUSES: An Illustrated History, Francis Ross Holland, Jr. Delightfully written, profusely illustrated fact-filled survey of over 200 American light-houses since 1716. History, anecdotes, technological advances, more. 240pp. 8 x 10¾. 25576-X Pa. $12.95

TOWARDS A NEW ARCHITECTURE, Le Corbusier. Pioneering manifesto by founder of "International School." Technical and aesthetic theories, views of industry, economics, relation of form to function, "mass-production split" and much more. Profusely illustrated. 320pp. 6⅛ x 9¼. (USO) 25023-7 Pa. $9.95

HOW THE OTHER HALF LIVES, Jacob Riis. Famous journalistic record, exposing poverty and degradation of New York slums around 1900, by major social reformer. 100 striking and influential photographs. 233pp. 10 x 7⅞. 22012-5 Pa. $11.95

FRUIT KEY AND TWIG KEY TO TREES AND SHRUBS, William M. Harlow. One of the handiest and most widely used identification aids. Fruit key covers 120 deciduous and evergreen species; twig key 160 deciduous species. Easily used. Over 300 photographs. 126pp. 5⅜ x 8½. 20511-8 Pa. $3.95

COMMON BIRD SONGS, Dr. Donald J. Borror. Songs of 60 most common U.S. birds: robins, sparrows, cardinals, bluejays, finches, more–arranged in order of increasing complexity. Up to 9 variations of songs of each species. Cassette and manual 99911-4 $8.95

ORCHIDS AS HOUSE PLANTS, Rebecca Tyson Northen. Grow cattleyas and many other kinds of orchids–in a window, in a case, or under artificial light. 63 illustrations. 148pp. 5⅜ x 8½. 23261-1 Pa. $5.95

MONSTER MAZES, Dave Phillips. Masterful mazes at four levels of difficulty. Avoid deadly perils and evil creatures to find magical treasures. Solutions for all 32 exciting illustrated puzzles. 48pp. 8¼ x 11. 26005-4 Pa. $2.95

MOZART'S DON GIOVANNI (DOVER OPERA LIBRETTO SERIES), Wolfgang Amadeus Mozart. Introduced and translated by Ellen H. Bleiler. Standard Italian libretto, with complete English translation. Convenient and thoroughly portable–an ideal companion for reading along with a recording or the performance itself. Introduction. List of characters. Plot summary. 121pp. 5¼ x 8½. 24944-1 Pa. $3.95

TECHNICAL MANUAL AND DICTIONARY OF CLASSICAL BALLET, Gail Grant. Defines, explains, comments on steps, movements, poses and concepts. 15-page pictorial section. Basic book for student, viewer. 127pp. 5⅜ x 8½. 21843-0 Pa. $4.95

THE CLARINET AND CLARINET PLAYING, David Pino. Lively, comprehensive work features suggestions about technique, musicianship, and musical interpretation, as well as guidelines for teaching, making your own reeds, and preparing for public performance. Includes an intriguing look at clarinet history. "A godsend," The Clarinet, Journal of the International Clarinet Society. Appendixes. 7 illus. 320pp. 5⅜ x 8½. 40270-3 Pa. $9.95

HOLLYWOOD GLAMOR PORTRAITS, John Kobal (ed.). 145 photos from 1926-49. Harlow, Gable, Bogart, Bacall; 94 stars in all. Full background on photographers, technical aspects. 160pp. 8⅜ x 11¼. 23352-9 Pa. $12.95

THE ANNOTATED CASEY AT THE BAT: A Collection of Ballads about the Mighty Casey/Third, Revised Edition, Martin Gardner (ed.). Amusing sequels and parodies of one of America's best-loved poems: Casey's Revenge, Why Casey Whiffed, Casey's Sister at the Bat, others. 256pp. 5⅜ x 8½. 28598-7 Pa. $8.95

THE RAVEN AND OTHER FAVORITE POEMS, Edgar Allan Poe. Over 40 of the author's most memorable poems: "The Bells," "Ulalume," "Israfel," "To Helen," "The Conqueror Worm," "Eldorado," "Annabel Lee," many more. Alphabetic lists of titles and first lines. 64pp. 5³⁄₁₆ x 8¼. 26685-0 Pa. $1.00

PERSONAL MEMOIRS OF U. S. GRANT, Ulysses Simpson Grant. Intelligent, deeply moving firsthand account of Civil War campaigns, considered by many the finest military memoirs ever written. Includes letters, historic photographs, maps and more. 528pp. 6⅛ x 9¼. 28587-1 Pa. $12.95

ANCIENT EGYPTIAN MATERIALS AND INDUSTRIES, A. Lucas and J. Harris. Fascinating, comprehensive, thoroughly documented text describes this ancient civilization's vast resources and the processes that incorporated them in daily life, including the use of animal products, building materials, cosmetics, perfumes and incense, fibers, glazed ware, glass and its manufacture, materials used in the mummification process, and much more. 544pp. 6⅛ x 9¼. (USO) 40446-3 Pa. $16.95

RUSSIAN STORIES/PYCCKNE PACCKA3bl: A Dual-Language Book, edited by Gleb Struve. Twelve tales by such masters as Chekhov, Tolstoy, Dostoevsky, Pushkin, others. Excellent word-for-word English translations on facing pages, plus teaching and study aids, Russian/English vocabulary, biographical/critical introductions, more. 416pp. 5⅜ x 8½. 26244-8 Pa. $9.95

PHILADELPHIA THEN AND NOW: 60 Sites Photographed in the Past and Present, Kenneth Finkel and Susan Oyama. Rare photographs of City Hall, Logan Square, Independence Hall, Betsy Ross House, other landmarks juxtaposed with contemporary views. Captures changing face of historic city. Introduction. Captions. 128pp. 8¼ x 11. 25790-8 Pa. $9.95

AIA ARCHITECTURAL GUIDE TO NASSAU AND SUFFOLK COUNTIES, LONG ISLAND, The American Institute of Architects, Long Island Chapter, and the Society for the Preservation of Long Island Antiquities. Comprehensive, well-researched and generously illustrated volume brings to life over three centuries of Long Island's great architectural heritage. More than 240 photographs with authoritative, extensively detailed captions. 176pp. 8¼ x 11. 26946-9 Pa. $14.95

NORTH AMERICAN INDIAN LIFE: Customs and Traditions of 23 Tribes, Elsie Clews Parsons (ed.). 27 fictionalized essays by noted anthropologists examine religion, customs, government, additional facets of life among the Winnebago, Crow, Zuni, Eskimo, other tribes. 480pp. 6⅛ x 9¼. 27377-6 Pa. $10.95

FRANK LLOYD WRIGHT'S DANA HOUSE, Donald Hoffmann. Pictorial essay of residential masterpiece with over 160 interior and exterior photos, plans, elevations, sketches and studies. 128pp. 9¼ x 10¾. 29120-0 Pa. $12.95

THE MALE AND FEMALE FIGURE IN MOTION: 60 Classic Photographic Sequences, Eadweard Muybridge. 60 true-action photographs of men and women walking, running, climbing, bending, turning, etc., reproduced from rare 19th-century masterpiece. vi + 121pp. 9 x 12. 24745-7 Pa. $10.95

1001 QUESTIONS ANSWERED ABOUT THE SEASHORE, N. J. Berrill and Jacquelyn Berrill. Queries answered about dolphins, sea snails, sponges, starfish, fishes, shore birds, many others. Covers appearance, breeding, growth, feeding, much more. 305pp. 5¼ x 8¼. 23366-9 Pa. $9.95

ATTRACTING BIRDS TO YOUR YARD, William J. Weber. Easy-to-follow guide offers advice on how to attract the greatest diversity of birds: birdhouses, feeders, water and waterers, much more. 96pp. 5³⁄₁₆ x 8¼. 28927-3 Pa. $2.50

MEDICINAL AND OTHER USES OF NORTH AMERICAN PLANTS: A Historical Survey with Special Reference to the Eastern Indian Tribes, Charlotte Erichsen-Brown. Chronological historical citations document 500 years of usage of plants, trees, shrubs native to eastern Canada, northeastern U.S. Also complete identifying information. 343 illustrations. 544pp. 6½ x 9¼. 25951-X Pa. $12.95

STORYBOOK MAZES, Dave Phillips. 23 stories and mazes on two-page spreads: Wizard of Oz, Treasure Island, Robin Hood, etc. Solutions. 64pp. 8¼ x 11. 23628-5 Pa. $2.95

AMERICAN NEGRO SONGS: 230 Folk Songs and Spirituals, Religious and Secular, John W. Work. This authoritative study traces the African influences of songs sung and played by black Americans at work, in church, and as entertainment. The author discusses the lyric significance of such songs as "Swing Low, Sweet Chariot," "John Henry," and others and offers the words and music for 230 songs. Bibliography. Index of Song Titles. 272pp. 6½ x 9¼. 40271-1 Pa. $9.95

MOVIE-STAR PORTRAITS OF THE FORTIES, John Kobal (ed.). 163 glamor, studio photos of 106 stars of the 1940s: Rita Hayworth, Ava Gardner, Marlon Brando, Clark Gable, many more. 176pp. 8⅜ x 11¼. 23546-7 Pa. $14.95

BENCHLEY LOST AND FOUND, Robert Benchley. Finest humor from early 30s, about pet peeves, child psychologists, post office and others. Mostly unavailable elsewhere. 73 illustrations by Peter Arno and others. 183pp. 5⅜ x 8½. 22410-4 Pa. $6.95

YEKL and THE IMPORTED BRIDEGROOM AND OTHER STORIES OF YIDDISH NEW YORK, Abraham Cahan. Film Hester Street based on Yekl (1896). Novel, other stories among first about Jewish immigrants on N.Y.'s East Side. 240pp. 5⅜ x 8½. 22427-9 Pa. $6.95

SELECTED POEMS, Walt Whitman. Generous sampling from *Leaves of Grass*. Twenty-four poems include "I Hear America Singing," "Song of the Open Road," "I Sing the Body Electric," "When Lilacs Last in the Dooryard Bloom'd," "O Captain! My Captain!"—all reprinted from an authoritative edition. Lists of titles and first lines. 128pp. 5³⁄₁₆ x 8¼. 26878-0 Pa. $1.00

THE BEST TALES OF HOFFMANN, E. T. A. Hoffmann. 10 of Hoffmann's most important stories: "Nutcracker and the King of Mice," "The Golden Flowerpot," etc. 458pp. 5⅜ x 8½. 21793-0 Pa. $9.95

FROM FETISH TO GOD IN ANCIENT EGYPT, E. A. Wallis Budge. Rich detailed survey of Egyptian conception of "God" and gods, magic, cult of animals, Osiris, more. Also, superb English translations of hymns and legends. 240 illustrations. 545pp. 5⅜ x 8½. 25803-3 Pa. $13.95

FRENCH STORIES/CONTES FRANÇAIS: A Dual-Language Book, Wallace Fowlie. Ten stories by French masters, Voltaire to Camus: "Micromegas" by Voltaire; "The Atheist's Mass" by Balzac; "Minuet" by de Maupassant; "The Guest" by Camus, six more. Excellent English translations on facing pages. Also French-English vocabulary list, exercises, more. 352pp. 5⅜ x 8½. 26443-2 Pa. $9.95

CHICAGO AT THE TURN OF THE CENTURY IN PHOTOGRAPHS: 122 Historic Views from the Collections of the Chicago Historical Society, Larry A. Viskochil. Rare large-format prints offer detailed views of City Hall, State Street, the Loop, Hull House, Union Station, many other landmarks, circa 1904-1913. Introduction. Captions. Maps. 144pp. 9⅜ x 12¼. 24656-6 Pa. $12.95

OLD BROOKLYN IN EARLY PHOTOGRAPHS, 1865-1929, William Lee Younger. Luna Park, Gravesend race track, construction of Grand Army Plaza, moving of Hotel Brighton, etc. 157 previously unpublished photographs. 165pp. 8⅞ x 11¾. 23587-4 Pa. $13.95

THE MYTHS OF THE NORTH AMERICAN INDIANS, Lewis Spence. Rich anthology of the myths and legends of the Algonquins, Iroquois, Pawnees and Sioux, prefaced by an extensive historical and ethnological commentary. 36 illustrations. 480pp. 5⅜ x 8½. 25967-6 Pa. $10.95

AN ENCYCLOPEDIA OF BATTLES: Accounts of Over 1,560 Battles from 1479 B.C. to the Present, David Eggenberger. Essential details of every major battle in recorded history from the first battle of Megiddo in 1479 B.C. to Grenada in 1984. List of Battle Maps. New Appendix covering the years 1967-1984. Index. 99 illustrations. 544pp. 6½ x 9¼. 24913-1 Pa. $16.95

SAILING ALONE AROUND THE WORLD, Captain Joshua Slocum. First man to sail around the world, alone, in small boat. One of great feats of seamanship told in delightful manner. 67 illustrations. 294pp. 5⅜ x 8½. 20326-3 Pa. $6.95

ANARCHISM AND OTHER ESSAYS, Emma Goldman. Powerful, penetrating, prophetic essays on direct action, role of minorities, prison reform, puritan hypocrisy, violence, etc. 271pp. 5⅜ x 8½. 22484-8 Pa. $7.95

MYTHS OF THE HINDUS AND BUDDHISTS, Ananda K. Coomaraswamy and Sister Nivedita. Great stories of the epics; deeds of Krishna, Shiva, taken from puranas, Vedas, folk tales; etc. 32 illustrations. 400pp. 5⅜ x 8½. 21759-0 Pa. $12.95

THE TRAUMA OF BIRTH, Otto Rank. Rank's controversial thesis that anxiety neurosis is caused by profound psychological trauma which occurs at birth. 256pp. 5⅜ x 8½. 27974-X Pa. $7.95

A THEOLOGICO-POLITICAL TREATISE, Benedict Spinoza. Also contains unfinished Political Treatise. Great classic on religious liberty, theory of government on common consent. R. Elwes translation. Total of 421pp. 5⅜ x 8½. 20249-6 Pa. $9.95

MY BONDAGE AND MY FREEDOM, Frederick Douglass. Born a slave, Douglass became outspoken force in antislavery movement. The best of Douglass' autobiographies. Graphic description of slave life. 464pp. 5⅜ x 8½. 22457-0 Pa. $8.95

FOLLOWING THE EQUATOR: A Journey Around the World, Mark Twain. Fascinating humorous account of 1897 voyage to Hawaii, Australia, India, New Zealand, etc. Ironic, bemused reports on peoples, customs, climate, flora and fauna, politics, much more. 197 illustrations. 720pp. 5⅜ x 8½. 26113-1 Pa. $15.95

THE PEOPLE CALLED SHAKERS, Edward D. Andrews. Definitive study of Shakers: origins, beliefs, practices, dances, social organization, furniture and crafts, etc. 33 illustrations. 351pp. 5⅜ x 8½. 21081-2 Pa. $8.95

THE MYTHS OF GREECE AND ROME, H. A. Guerber. A classic of mythology, generously illustrated, long prized for its simple, graphic, accurate retelling of the principal myths of Greece and Rome, and for its commentary on their origins and significance. With 64 illustrations by Michelangelo, Raphael, Titian, Rubens, Canova, Bernini and others. 480pp. 5⅜ x 8½. 27584-1 Pa. $9.95

PSYCHOLOGY OF MUSIC, Carl E. Seashore. Classic work discusses music as a medium from psychological viewpoint. Clear treatment of physical acoustics, auditory apparatus, sound perception, development of musical skills, nature of musical feeling, host of other topics. 88 figures. 408pp. 5⅜ x 8½. 21851-1 Pa. $11.95

THE PHILOSOPHY OF HISTORY, Georg W. Hegel. Great classic of Western thought develops concept that history is not chance but rational process, the evolution of freedom. 457pp. 5⅜ x 8½. 20112-0 Pa. $9.95

THE BOOK OF TEA, Kakuzo Okakura. Minor classic of the Orient: entertaining, charming explanation, interpretation of traditional Japanese culture in terms of tea ceremony. 94pp. 5⅜ x 8½. 20070-1 Pa. $3.95

LIFE IN ANCIENT EGYPT, Adolf Erman. Fullest, most thorough, detailed older account with much not in more recent books, domestic life, religion, magic, medicine, commerce, much more. Many illustrations reproduce tomb paintings, carvings, hieroglyphs, etc. 597pp. 5⅜ x 8½. 22632-8 Pa. $12.95

SUNDIALS, Their Theory and Construction, Albert Waugh. Far and away the best, most thorough coverage of ideas, mathematics concerned, types, construction, adjusting anywhere. Simple, nontechnical treatment allows even children to build several of these dials. Over 100 illustrations. 230pp. 5⅜ x 8½. 22947-5 Pa. $8.95

THEORETICAL HYDRODYNAMICS, L. M. Milne-Thomson. Classic exposition of the mathematical theory of fluid motion, applicable to both hydrodynamics and aerodynamics. Over 600 exercises. 768pp. 6⅛ x 9¼. 68970-0 Pa. $20.95

SONGS OF EXPERIENCE: Facsimile Reproduction with 26 Plates in Full Color, William Blake. 26 full-color plates from a rare 1826 edition. Includes "TheTyger," "London," "Holy Thursday," and other poems. Printed text of poems. 48pp. 5¼ x 7. 24636-1 Pa. $4.95

OLD-TIME VIGNETTES IN FULL COLOR, Carol Belanger Grafton (ed.). Over 390 charming, often sentimental illustrations, selected from archives of Victorian graphics—pretty women posing, children playing, food, flowers, kittens and puppies, smiling cherubs, birds and butterflies, much more. All copyright-free. 48pp. 9¼ x 12¼. 27269-9 Pa. $7.95

PERSPECTIVE FOR ARTISTS, Rex Vicat Cole. Depth, perspective of sky and sea, shadows, much more, not usually covered. 391 diagrams, 81 reproductions of drawings and paintings. 279pp. 5⅜ x 8½. 22487-2 Pa. $7.95

DRAWING THE LIVING FIGURE, Joseph Sheppard. Innovative approach to artistic anatomy focuses on specifics of surface anatomy, rather than muscles and bones. Over 170 drawings of live models in front, back and side views, and in widely varying poses. Accompanying diagrams. 177 illustrations. Introduction. Index. 144pp. 8⅜ x11¼. 26723-7 Pa. $8.95

GOTHIC AND OLD ENGLISH ALPHABETS: 100 Complete Fonts, Dan X. Solo. Add power, elegance to posters, signs, other graphics with 100 stunning copyright-free alphabets: Blackstone, Dolbey, Germania, 97 more–including many lower-case, numerals, punctuation marks. 104pp. 8⅛ x 11. 24695-7 Pa. $8.95

HOW TO DO BEADWORK, Mary White. Fundamental book on craft from simple projects to five-bead chains and woven works. 106 illustrations. 142pp. 5⅜ x 8. 20697-1 Pa. $5.95

THE BOOK OF WOOD CARVING, Charles Marshall Sayers. Finest book for beginners discusses fundamentals and offers 34 designs. "Absolutely first rate . . . well thought out and well executed."–E. J. Tangerman. 118pp. 7¾ x 10⅝. 23654-4 Pa. $7.95

ILLUSTRATED CATALOG OF CIVIL WAR MILITARY GOODS: Union Army Weapons, Insignia, Uniform Accessories, and Other Equipment, Schuyler, Hartley, and Graham. Rare, profusely illustrated 1846 catalog includes Union Army uniform and dress regulations, arms and ammunition, coats, insignia, flags, swords, rifles, etc. 226 illustrations. 160pp. 9 x 12. 24939-5 Pa. $10.95

WOMEN'S FASHIONS OF THE EARLY 1900s: An Unabridged Republication of "New York Fashions, 1909," National Cloak & Suit Co. Rare catalog of mail-order fashions documents women's and children's clothing styles shortly after the turn of the century. Captions offer full descriptions, prices. Invaluable resource for fashion, costume historians. Approximately 725 illustrations. 128pp. 8⅜ x 11¼. 27276-1 Pa. $11.95

THE 1912 AND 1915 GUSTAV STICKLEY FURNITURE CATALOGS, Gustav Stickley. With over 200 detailed illustrations and descriptions, these two catalogs are essential reading and reference materials and identification guides for Stickley furniture. Captions cite materials, dimensions and prices. 112pp. 6½ x 9¼. 26676-1 Pa. $9.95

EARLY AMERICAN LOCOMOTIVES, John H. White, Jr. Finest locomotive engravings from early 19th century: historical (1804–74), main-line (after 1870), special, foreign, etc. 147 plates. 142pp. 11⅜ x 8¼. 22772-3 Pa. $10.95

THE TALL SHIPS OF TODAY IN PHOTOGRAPHS, Frank O. Braynard. Lavishly illustrated tribute to nearly 100 majestic contemporary sailing vessels: Amerigo Vespucci, Clearwater, Constitution, Eagle, Mayflower, Sea Cloud, Victory, many more. Authoritative captions provide statistics, background on each ship. 190 black-and-white photographs and illustrations. Introduction. 128pp. 8⅞ x 11¾. 27163-3 Pa. $14.95

LITTLE BOOK OF EARLY AMERICAN CRAFTS AND TRADES, Peter Stockham (ed.). 1807 children's book explains crafts and trades: baker, hatter, cooper, potter, and many others. 23 copperplate illustrations. 140pp. 4⅝ x 6.
23336-7 Pa. $4.95

VICTORIAN FASHIONS AND COSTUMES FROM HARPER'S BAZAR, 1867–1898, Stella Blum (ed.). Day costumes, evening wear, sports clothes, shoes, hats, other accessories in over 1,000 detailed engravings. 320pp. 9⅜ x 12¼.
22990-4 Pa. $15.95

GUSTAV STICKLEY, THE CRAFTSMAN, Mary Ann Smith. Superb study surveys broad scope of Stickley's achievement, especially in architecture. Design philosophy, rise and fall of the Craftsman empire, descriptions and floor plans for many Craftsman houses, more. 86 black-and-white halftones. 31 line illustrations. Introduction 208pp. 6½ x 9¼.
27210-9 Pa. $9.95

THE LONG ISLAND RAIL ROAD IN EARLY PHOTOGRAPHS, Ron Ziel. Over 220 rare photos, informative text document origin (1844) and development of rail service on Long Island. Vintage views of early trains, locomotives, stations, passengers, crews, much more. Captions. 8⅞ x 11¾.
26301-0 Pa. $13.95

VOYAGE OF THE LIBERDADE, Joshua Slocum. Great 19th-century mariner's thrilling, first-hand account of the wreck of his ship off South America, the 35-foot boat he built from the wreckage, and its remarkable voyage home. 128pp. 5⅜ x 8½.
40022-0 Pa. $4.95

TEN BOOKS ON ARCHITECTURE, Vitruvius. The most important book ever written on architecture. Early Roman aesthetics, technology, classical orders, site selection, all other aspects. Morgan translation. 331pp. 5⅜ x 8½.   20645-9 Pa. $8.95

THE HUMAN FIGURE IN MOTION, Eadweard Muybridge. More than 4,500 stopped-action photos, in action series, showing undraped men, women, children jumping, lying down, throwing, sitting, wrestling, carrying, etc. 390pp. 7⅞ x 10⅝.
20204-6 Clothbd. $27.95

TREES OF THE EASTERN AND CENTRAL UNITED STATES AND CANADA, William M. Harlow. Best one-volume guide to 140 trees. Full descriptions, woodlore, range, etc. Over 600 illustrations. Handy size. 288pp. 4½ x 6⅜.
20395-6 Pa. $6.95

SONGS OF WESTERN BIRDS, Dr. Donald J. Borror. Complete song and call repertoire of 60 western species, including flycatchers, juncoes, cactus wrens, many more—includes fully illustrated booklet.   Cassette and manual 99913-0 $8.95

GROWING AND USING HERBS AND SPICES, Milo Miloradovich. Versatile handbook provides all the information needed for cultivation and use of all the herbs and spices available in North America. 4 illustrations. Index. Glossary. 236pp. 5⅜ x 8½.
25058-X Pa. $7.95

BIG BOOK OF MAZES AND LABYRINTIIS, Walter Shepherd. 50 mazes and labyrinths in all—classical, solid, ripple, and more—in one great volume. Perfect inexpensive puzzler for clever youngsters. Full solutions. 112pp. 8⅛ x 11.
22951-3 Pa. $5.95

CATALOG OF DOVER BOOKS

PIANO TUNING, J. Cree Fischer. Clearest, best book for beginner, amateur. Simple repairs, raising dropped notes, tuning by easy method of flattened fifths. No previous skills needed. 4 illustrations. 201pp. 5⅜ x 8½. 23267-0 Pa. $6.95

HINTS TO SINGERS, Lillian Nordica. Selecting the right teacher, developing confidence, overcoming stage fright, and many other important skills receive thoughtful discussion in this indispensible guide, written by a world-famous diva of four decades' experience. 96pp. 5³/₈ x 8½. 40094-8 Pa. $4.95

THE COMPLETE NONSENSE OF EDWARD LEAR, Edward Lear. All nonsense limericks, zany alphabets, Owl and Pussycat, songs, nonsense botany, etc., illustrated by Lear. Total of 320pp. 5⅜ x 8½. (USO) 20167-8 Pa. $7.95

VICTORIAN PARLOUR POETRY: An Annotated Anthology, Michael R. Turner. 117 gems by Longfellow, Tennyson, Browning, many lesser-known poets. "The Village Blacksmith," "Curfew Must Not Ring Tonight," "Only a Baby Small," dozens more, often difficult to find elsewhere. Index of poets, titles, first lines. xxiii + 325pp. 5⅜ x 8¼. 27044-0 Pa. $8.95

DUBLINERS, James Joyce. Fifteen stories offer vivid, tightly focused observations of the lives of Dublin's poorer classes. At least one, "The Dead," is considered a masterpiece. Reprinted complete and unabridged from standard edition. 160pp. 5³/₁₆ x 8¼. 26870-5 Pa. $1.00

GREAT WEIRD TALES: 14 Stories by Lovecraft, Blackwood, Machen and Others, S. T. Joshi (ed.). 14 spellbinding tales, including "The Sin Eater," by Fiona McLeod, "The Eye Above the Mantel," by Frank Belknap Long, as well as renowned works by R. H. Barlow, Lord Dunsany, Arthur Machen, W. C. Morrow and eight other masters of the genre. 256pp. 5⅜ x 8½. (USO) 40436-6 Pa. $8.95

THE BOOK OF THE SACRED MAGIC OF ABRAMELIN THE MAGE, translated by S. MacGregor Mathers. Medieval manuscript of ceremonial magic. Basic document in Aleister Crowley, Golden Dawn groups. 268pp. 5⅜ x 8½. 23211-5 Pa. $9.95

NEW RUSSIAN-ENGLISH AND ENGLISH-RUSSIAN DICTIONARY, M. A. O'Brien. This is a remarkably handy Russian dictionary, containing a surprising amount of information, including over 70,000 entries. 366pp. 4½ x 6¼. 20208-9 Pa. $10.95

HISTORIC HOMES OF THE AMERICAN PRESIDENTS, Second, Revised Edition, Irvin Haas. A traveler's guide to American Presidential homes, most open to the public, depicting and describing homes occupied by every American President from George Washington to George Bush. With visiting hours, admission charges, travel routes. 175 photographs. Index. 160pp. 8¼ x 11. 26751-2 Pa. $11.95

NEW YORK IN THE FORTIES, Andreas Feininger. 162 brilliant photographs by the well-known photographer, formerly with *Life* magazine. Commuters, shoppers, Times Square at night, much else from city at its peak. Captions by John von Hartz. 181pp. 9¼ x 10¾. 23585-8 Pa. $13.95

INDIAN SIGN LANGUAGE, William Tomkins. Over 525 signs developed by Sioux and other tribes. Written instructions and diagrams. Also 290 pictographs. 111pp. 6⅛ x 9¼. 22029-X Pa. $3.95

ANATOMY: A Complete Guide for Artists, Joseph Sheppard. A master of figure drawing shows artists how to render human anatomy convincingly. Over 460 illustrations. 224pp. 8⅜ x 11¼. 27279-6 Pa. $11.95

MEDIEVAL CALLIGRAPHY: Its History and Technique, Marc Drogin. Spirited history, comprehensive instruction manual covers 13 styles (ca. 4th century thru 15th). Excellent photographs; directions for duplicating medieval techniques with modern tools. 224pp. 8⅜ x 11¼. 26142-5 Pa. $12.95

DRIED FLOWERS: How to Prepare Them, Sarah Whitlock and Martha Rankin. Complete instructions on how to use silica gel, meal and borax, perlite aggregate, sand and borax, glycerine and water to create attractive permanent flower arrangements. 12 illustrations. 32pp. 5⅜ x 8½. 21802-3 Pa. $1.00

EASY-TO-MAKE BIRD FEEDERS FOR WOODWORKERS, Scott D. Campbell. Detailed, simple-to-use guide for designing, constructing, caring for and using feeders. Text, illustrations for 12 classic and contemporary designs. 96pp. 5⅜ x 8½. 25847-5 Pa. $3.95

SCOTTISH WONDER TALES FROM MYTH AND LEGEND, Donald A. Mackenzie. 16 lively tales tell of giants rumbling down mountainsides, of a magic wand that turns stone pillars into warriors, of gods and goddesses, evil hags, powerful forces and more. 240pp. 5⅜ x 8½. 29677-6 Pa. $6.95

THE HISTORY OF UNDERCLOTHES, C. Willett Cunnington and Phyllis Cunnington. Fascinating, well-documented survey covering six centuries of English undergarments, enhanced with over 100 illustrations: 12th-century laced-up bodice, footed long drawers (1795), 19th-century bustles, 19th-century corsets for men, Victorian "bust improvers," much more. 272pp. 5⅜ x 8¼. 27124-2 Pa. $9.95

ARTS AND CRAFTS FURNITURE: The Complete Brooks Catalog of 1912, Brooks Manufacturing Co. Photos and detailed descriptions of more than 150 now very collectible furniture designs from the Arts and Crafts movement depict davenports, settees, buffets, desks, tables, chairs, bedsteads, dressers and more, all built of solid, quarter-sawed oak. Invaluable for students and enthusiasts of antiques, Americana and the decorative arts. 80pp. 6½ x 9¼. 27471-3 Pa. $8.95

WILBUR AND ORVILLE: A Biography of the Wright Brothers, Fred Howard. Definitive, crisply written study tells the full story of the brothers' lives and work. A vividly written biography, unparalleled in scope and color, that also captures the spirit of an extraordinary era. 560pp. 6⅛ x 9¼. 40297-5 Pa. $17.95

THE ARTS OF THE SAILOR: Knotting, Splicing and Ropework, Hervey Garrett Smith. Indispensable shipboard reference covers tools, basic knots and useful hitches; handsewing and canvas work, more. Over 100 illustrations. Delightful reading for sea lovers. 256pp. 5⅜ x 8½. 26440-8 Pa. $8.95

FRANK LLOYD WRIGHT'S FALLINGWATER: The House and Its History, Second, Revised Edition, Donald Hoffmann. A total revision–both in text and illustrations–of the standard document on Fallingwater, the boldest, most personal architectural statement of Wright's mature years, updated with valuable new material from the recently opened Frank Lloyd Wright Archives. "Fascinating"–*The New York Times*. 116 illustrations. 128pp. 9¼ x 10¾. 27430-6 Pa. $12.95

PHOTOGRAPHIC SKETCHBOOK OF THE CIVIL WAR, Alexander Gardner. 100 photos taken on field during the Civil War. Famous shots of Manassas Harper's Ferry, Lincoln, Richmond, slave pens, etc. 244pp. 10⅝ x 8¼.   22731-6 Pa. $10.95

FIVE ACRES AND INDEPENDENCE, Maurice G. Kains. Great back-to-the-land classic explains basics of self-sufficient farming. The one book to get. 95 illustrations. 397pp. 5⅜ x 8½.   20974-1 Pa. $7.95

SONGS OF EASTERN BIRDS, Dr. Donald J. Borror. Songs and calls of 60 species most common to eastern U.S.: warblers, woodpeckers, flycatchers, thrushes, larks, many more in high-quality recording.   Cassette and manual 99912-2 $9.95

A MODERN HERBAL, Margaret Grieve. Much the fullest, most exact, most useful compilation of herbal material. Gigantic alphabetical encyclopedia, from aconite to zedoary, gives botanical information, medical properties, folklore, economic uses, much else. Indispensable to serious reader. 161 illustrations. 888pp. 6½ x 9¼. 2-vol. set. (USO)   Vol. I: 22798-7 Pa. $9.95
Vol. II: 22799-5 Pa. $9.95

HIDDEN TREASURE MAZE BOOK, Dave Phillips. Solve 34 challenging mazes accompanied by heroic tales of adventure. Evil dragons, people-eating plants, blood-thirsty giants, many more dangerous adversaries lurk at every twist and turn. 34 mazes, stories, solutions. 48pp. 8¼ x 11.   24566-7 Pa. $2.95

LETTERS OF W. A. MOZART, Wolfgang A. Mozart. Remarkable letters show bawdy wit, humor, imagination, musical insights, contemporary musical world; includes some letters from Leopold Mozart. 276pp. 5⅜ x 8½.   22859-2 Pa. $7.95

BASIC PRINCIPLES OF CLASSICAL BALLET, Agrippina Vaganova. Great Russian theoretician, teacher explains methods for teaching classical ballet. 118 illustrations. 175pp. 5⅜ x 8½.   22036-2 Pa. $5.95

THE JUMPING FROG, Mark Twain. Revenge edition. The original story of The Celebrated Jumping Frog of Calaveras County, a hapless French translation, and Twain's hilarious "retranslation" from the French. 12 illustrations. 66pp. 5⅜ x 8½.   22686-7 Pa. $3.95

BEST REMEMBERED POEMS, Martin Gardner (ed.). The 126 poems in this superb collection of 19th- and 20th-century British and American verse range from Shelley's "To a Skylark" to the impassioned "Renascence" of Edna St. Vincent Millay and to Edward Lear's whimsical "The Owl and the Pussycat." 224pp. 5⅜ x 8½.   27165-X Pa. $5.95

COMPLETE SONNETS, William Shakespeare. Over 150 exquisite poems deal with love, friendship, the tyranny of time, beauty's evanescence, death and other themes in language of remarkable power, precision and beauty. Glossary of archaic terms. 80pp. 5³⁄₁₆ x 8¼.   26686-9 Pa. $1.00

BODIES IN A BOOKSHOP, R. T. Campbell. Challenging mystery of blackmail and murder with ingenious plot and superbly drawn characters. In the best tradition of British suspense fiction. 192pp. 5⅜ x 8½.   24720-1 Pa. $6.95

THE WIT AND HUMOR OF OSCAR WILDE, Alvin Redman (ed.). More than 1,000 ripostes, paradoxes, wisecracks: Work is the curse of the drinking classes; I can resist everything except temptation; etc. 258pp. 5⅜ x 8½.   20602-5 Pa. $6.95

SHAKESPEARE LEXICON AND QUOTATION DICTIONARY, Alexander Schmidt. Full definitions, locations, shades of meaning in every word in plays and poems. More than 50,000 exact quotations. 1,485pp. 6½ x 9¼. 2-vol. set.
Vol. 1: 22726-X Pa. $17.95
Vol. 2: 22727-8 Pa. $17.95

SELECTED POEMS, Emily Dickinson. Over 100 best-known, best-loved poems by one of America's foremost poets, reprinted from authoritative early editions. No comparable edition at this price. Index of first lines. 64pp. 5³⁄₁₆ x 8¼.
26466-1 Pa. $1.00

THE INSIDIOUS DR. FU-MANCHU, Sax Rohmer. The first of the popular mystery series introduces a pair of English detectives to their archnemesis, the diabolical Dr. Fu-Manchu. Flavorful atmosphere, fast-paced action, and colorful characters enliven this classic of the genre. 208pp. 5³⁄₁₆ x 8¼.   29898-1 Pa. $2.00

THE MALLEUS MALEFICARUM OF KRAMER AND SPRENGER, translated by Montague Summers. Full text of most important witchhunter's "bible," used by both Catholics and Protestants. 278pp. 6⅝ x 10.   22802-9 Pa. $12.95

SPANISH STORIES/CUENTOS ESPAÑOLES: A Dual-Language Book, Angel Flores (ed.). Unique format offers 13 great stories in Spanish by Cervantes, Borges, others. Faithful English translations on facing pages. 352pp. 5⅜ x 8½.
25399-6 Pa. $8.95

GARDEN CITY, LONG ISLAND, IN EARLY PHOTOGRAPHS, 1869–1919, Mildred H. Smith. Handsome treasury of 118 vintage pictures, accompanied by carefully researched captions, document the Garden City Hotel fire (1899), the Vanderbilt Cup Race (1908), the first airmail flight departing from the Nassau Boulevard Aerodrome (1911), and much more. 96pp. 8⅞ x 11¾.   40669-5 Pa. $12.95

OLD QUEENS, N.Y., IN EARLY PHOTOGRAPHS, Vincent F. Seyfried and William Asadorian. Over 160 rare photographs of Maspeth, Jamaica, Jackson Heights, and other areas. Vintage views of DeWitt Clinton mansion, 1939 World's Fair and more. Captions. 192pp. 8⅞ x 11.   26358-4 Pa. $12.95

CAPTURED BY THE INDIANS: 15 Firsthand Accounts, 1750-1870, Frederick Drimmer. Astounding true historical accounts of grisly torture, bloody conflicts, relentless pursuits, miraculous escapes and more, by people who lived to tell the tale. 384pp. 5⅜ x 8½.   24901-8 Pa. $8.95

THE WORLD'S GREAT SPEECHES (Fourth Enlarged Edition), Lewis Copeland, Lawrence W. Lamm, and Stephen J. McKenna. Nearly 300 speeches provide public speakers with a wealth of updated quotes and inspiration–from Pericles' funeral oration and William Jennings Bryan's "Cross of Gold Speech" to Malcolm X's powerful words on the Black Revolution and Earl of Spenser's tribute to his sister, Diana, Princess of Wales. 944pp. 5⅜ x 8⅜.   40903-1 Pa. $15.95

THE BOOK OF THE SWORD, Sir Richard F. Burton. Great Victorian scholar/adventurer's eloquent, erudite history of the "queen of weapons"–from prehistory to early Roman Empire. Evolution and development of early swords, variations (sabre, broadsword, cutlass, scimitar, etc.), much more. 336pp. 6⅛ x 9¼.
25434-8 Pa. $9.95

AUTOBIOGRAPHY: The Story of My Experiments with Truth, Mohandas K. Gandhi. Boyhood, legal studies, purification, the growth of the Satyagraha (nonviolent protest) movement. Critical, inspiring work of the man responsible for the freedom of India. 480pp. 5⅜ x 8½. (USO)   24593-4 Pa. $8.95

CELTIC MYTHS AND LEGENDS, T. W. Rolleston. Masterful retelling of Irish and Welsh stories and tales. Cuchulain, King Arthur, Deirdre, the Grail, many more. First paperback edition. 58 full-page illustrations. 512pp. 5⅜ x 8½.   26507-2 Pa. $9.95

THE PRINCIPLES OF PSYCHOLOGY, William James. Famous long course complete, unabridged. Stream of thought, time perception, memory, experimental methods; great work decades ahead of its time. 94 figures. 1,391pp. 5⅜ x 8½. 2-vol. set.
Vol. I: 20381-6 Pa. $13.95
Vol. II: 20382-4 Pa. $14.95

THE WORLD AS WILL AND REPRESENTATION, Arthur Schopenhauer. Definitive English translation of Schopenhauer's life work, correcting more than 1,000 errors, omissions in earlier translations. Translated by E. F. J. Payne. Total of 1,269pp. 5⅜ x 8½. 2-vol. set.
Vol. 1: 21761-2 Pa. $12.95
Vol. 2: 21762-0 Pa. $12.95

MAGIC AND MYSTERY IN TIBET, Madame Alexandra David-Neel. Experiences among lamas, magicians, sages, sorcerers, Bonpa wizards. A true psychic discovery. 32 illustrations. 321pp. 5⅜ x 8½. (USO)   22682-4 Pa. $9.95

THE EGYPTIAN BOOK OF THE DEAD, E. A. Wallis Budge. Complete reproduction of Ani's papyrus, finest ever found. Full hieroglyphic text, interlinear transliteration, word-for-word translation, smooth translation. 533pp. 6½ x 9¼.
21866-X Pa. $11.95

MATHEMATICS FOR THE NONMATHEMATICIAN, Morris Kline. Detailed, college-level treatment of mathematics in cultural and historical context, with numerous exercises. Recommended Reading Lists. Tables. Numerous figures. 641pp. 5⅜ x 8½.
24823-2 Pa. $11.95

PROBABILISTIC METHODS IN THE THEORY OF STRUCTURES, Isaac Elishakoff. Well-written introduction covers the elements of the theory of probability from two or more random variables, the reliability of such multivariable structures, the theory of random function, Monte Carlo methods of treating problems incapable of exact solution, and more. Examples. 502pp. 5³/₈ x 8¹/₂.   40691-1 Pa. $16.95

THE RIME OF THE ANCIENT MARINER, Gustave Doré, S. T. Coleridge. Doré's finest work; 34 plates capture moods, subtleties of poem. Flawless full-size reproductions printed on facing pages with authoritative text of poem. "Beautiful. Simply beautiful."–*Publisher's Weekly.* 77pp. 9¼ x 12.   22305-1 Pa. $7.95

NORTH AMERICAN INDIAN DESIGNS FOR ARTISTS AND CRAFTSPEOPLE, Eva Wilson. Over 360 authentic copyright-free designs adapted from Navajo blankets, Hopi pottery, Sioux buffalo hides, more. Geometrics, symbolic figures, plant and animal motifs, etc. 128pp. 8⅜ x 11. (EUK)   25341-4 Pa. $8.95

SCULPTURE: Principles and Practice, Louis Slobodkin. Step-by-step approach to clay, plaster, metals, stone; classical and modern. 253 drawings, photos. 255pp. 8⅛ x 11.
22960-2 Pa. $11.95

THE INFLUENCE OF SEA POWER UPON HISTORY, 1660–1783, A. T. Mahan. Influential classic of naval history and tactics still used as text in war colleges. First paperback edition. 4 maps. 24 battle plans. 640pp. 5⅜ x 8½.   25509-3 Pa. $14.95

THE STORY OF THE TITANIC AS TOLD BY ITS SURVIVORS, Jack Winocour (ed.). What it was really like. Panic, despair, shocking inefficiency, and a little heroism. More thrilling than any fictional account. 26 illustrations. 320pp. 5⅜ x 8½.
20610-6 Pa. $8.95

FAIRY AND FOLK TALES OF THE IRISH PEASANTRY, William Butler Yeats (ed.). Treasury of 64 tales from the twilight world of Celtic myth and legend: "The Soul Cages," "The Kildare Pooka," "King O'Toole and his Goose," many more. Introduction and Notes by W. B. Yeats. 352pp. 5⅜ x 8½.   26941-8 Pa. $8.95

BUDDHIST MAHAYANA TEXTS, E. B. Cowell and Others (eds.). Superb, accurate translations of basic documents in Mahayana Buddhism, highly important in history of religions. The Buddha-karita of Asvaghosha, Larger Sukhavativyuha, more. 448pp. 5⅜ x 8½.   25552-2 Pa. $12.95

ONE TWO THREE . . . INFINITY: Facts and Speculations of Science, George Gamow. Great physicist's fascinating, readable overview of contemporary science: number theory, relativity, fourth dimension, entropy, genes, atomic structure, much more. 128 illustrations. Index. 352pp. 5⅜ x 8½.   25664-2 Pa. $8.95

EXPERIMENTATION AND MEASUREMENT, W. J. Youden. Introductory manual explains laws of measurement in simple terms and offers tips for achieving accuracy and minimizing errors. Mathematics of measurement, use of instruments, experimenting with machines. 1994 edition. Foreword. Preface. Introduction. Epilogue. Selected Readings. Glossary. Index. Tables and figures. 128pp. $5^3/8$ x $8^1/2$.
40451-X Pa. $6.95

DALÍ ON MODERN ART: The Cuckolds of Antiquated Modern Art, Salvador Dalí. Influential painter skewers modern art and its practitioners. Outrageous evaluations of Picasso, Cézanne, Turner, more. 15 renderings of paintings discussed. 44 calligraphic decorations by Dalí. 96pp. 5⅜ x 8½. (USO)   29220-7 Pa. $5.95

ANTIQUE PLAYING CARDS: A Pictorial History, Henry René D'Allemagne. Over 900 elaborate, decorative images from rare playing cards (14th–20th centuries): Bacchus, death, dancing dogs, hunting scenes, royal coats of arms, players cheating, much more. 96pp. 9¼ x 12¼.   29265-7 Pa. $12.95

MAKING FURNITURE MASTERPIECES: 30 Projects with Measured Drawings, Franklin H. Gottshall. Step-by-step instructions, illustrations for constructing handsome, useful pieces, among them a Sheraton desk, Chippendale chair, Spanish desk, Queen Anne table and a William and Mary dressing mirror. 224pp. 8⅛ x 11¼.
29338-6 Pa. $13.95

THE FOSSIL BOOK: A Record of Prehistoric Life, Patricia V. Rich et al. Profusely illustrated definitive guide covers everything from single-celled organisms and dinosaurs to birds and mammals and the interplay between climate and man. Over 1,500 illustrations. 760pp. 7½ x 10⅛.   29371-8 Pa. $29.95

Prices subject to change without notice.

Available at your book dealer or write for free catalog to Dept. GI, Dover Publications, Inc., 31 East 2nd St., Mineola, N.Y. 11501. Dover publishes more than 500 books each year on science, elementary and advanced mathematics, biology, music, art, literary history, social sciences and other areas.